SORROW BUILT A BRIDGE

"Sorrow built a bridge for me into the infinite. It often does . . . One has to accept sorrow for it to be a healing power, and that is the most difficult thing in the world." From *Darby and Joan,* by MAURICE BARING

"Sorrow, my friend, when shall you come again,
 When shall you come again ?
 The wind is slow, and the bent willows send
 Their silvery motions wearily down the plain.
 The bird is dead
 That sang this morning through the summer rain.

"Sorrow, my friend,
 I owe my soul to you,
 And if my life with any glory end
 Of tenderness for others, and the words are true
 Said, honoring, when I'm dead,
 Sorrow, to you the mellow praise, the funeral wreath
   are due."

ROSE HAWTHORNE LATHROP

Rose Hawthorne Lathrop.

SORROW BUILT A BRIDGE

A Daughter of Hawthorne

BY

KATHERINE BURTON

Copy 2

LONGMANS, GREEN AND CO.

LONDON · NEW YORK · TORONTO

1942

LONGMANS, GREEN AND CO.
55 FIFTH AVENUE, NEW YORK
221 EAST 20TH STREET, CHICAGO

LONGMANS, GREEN AND CO. LTD.
39 PATERNOSTER ROW, LONDON, E.C. 4
CHITTARANJAN AVENUE, CALCUTTA
NICOL ROAD, BOMBAY
36A MOUNT ROAD, MADRAS

LONGMANS, GREEN AND CO.
215 VICTORIA STREET, TORONTO

BURTON
SORROW BUILT A BRIDGE

First Edition October 1937
Reprinted twice December 1937
January 1938, April 1938
July 1938, September 1938
November 1938, January 1939
November 1939, May 1940
March 1942

PRINTED IN THE UNITED STATES OF AMERICA

To

THE RIGHT REVEREND JOSEPH H. MCMAHON,
PH.D., LL.D.,

WITH GRATITUDE AND AFFECTION

ACKNOWLEDGMENT

For help in putting together this book I wish to thank : Brother Julian of the Christian Brothers, for letters and numbers of the Reports and of *Christ's Poor ;* Mother M. Rose Huber, O.S.D., for additional numbers of *Christ's Poor ;* the Right Reverend Joseph H. McMahon, Ph.D., for his constant suggestions and recommendations ; Reverend Clement Thuente, O.S.D., for his generous assistance ; Reverend John O'Hara, President of Notre Dame University, for the letters of Mother Alphonsa to Brother Dutton ; Miss Margaret Lothrop for her kindness in allowing me to be a guest at The Wayside and for her introductions ; James J. Walsh, M.D., Ph.D., for numbers of *Christ's Poor ;* Miss Annie McManus, for the letters of her aunt.

I wish to thank also Mr. Walter How for allowing me to use a photograph of Rose Hawthorne.

PART I

1

The Hawthorne family was peacefully listening to Mr. Hawthorne reading from *David Copperfield,* when their friend Herman Melville made one of his dramatic arrivals at the little house at Lenox.   They were glad to see him, and Mr. Hawthorne went out into the kitchen to prepare a champagne foam for him, since the day was chilly and the ride from Pittsfield a cold one.

"Not a thing I care for much," said Mr. Melville, "hearing people read aloud at me."

Mrs. Hawthorne was quick in her defense.   "But Mr. Hawthorne reads so wonderfully, it is not just mere reading.   He makes each person so distinct and I think in his breast is Gabriel's harp.   I like it better than any acting I ever saw."   She stopped suddenly before she remembered that her husband was out in the kitchen putting together beaten eggs and sugar and champagne for the guest.   He did not like to be praised before a third person, so she turned to showing Mr. Melville the engraved heads of Hawthorne which Mr. Ticknor, his publisher, had just sent up from Boston.

He scarcely had time to admire them before he felt little Julian tugging at his coat.   "Over at Luther's farm . . . it's about the horse.   When Luther grinds oats, the horse is in a treadmill and he can't get out.   Not even if he wants to," he added indignantly.

3

Una, his elder sister, just seven that day, looked at the visitor with her gray eyes and shook her aureole of red gold curls. "Not even if he wants to," she said disapprovingly.

Mr. Melville sympathized with the unfortunate animal and was given more detailed information until the host returned with his warming drink. Then Mr. Melville announced the reason for the visit. He wanted them all to come over and pay him a visit at Pittsfield for a few days. He had been working very hard at his new book, a sea tale about a white whale, and he needed a little respite from it. He thought that perhaps Hawthorne, too, would do well to get away from his pen for a little while.

It was finally decided that Una and her father were to go, leaving five-year-old Julian at home to take care of his mother, so said his father. Mrs. Hawthorne, who was expecting another baby very soon, felt that the trip might be too much for her, partly perhaps because Mr. Melville was a very strenuous companion for one who loved peace and quiet as much as Sophia Hawthorne did.

In her diary of the next day, while the travelers were still away, she wrote : "Now that he has gone away I have put his picture up before me, so that I can see it every time I lift my eyes. Was ever one so loved ?" She looked up from her writing to see Julian examining the engravings which were intended by Mr. Ticknor for *Twice Told Tales*. The pictures were really Hawthorne, even though they were black and white and so did not show the deep gray eyes and the brown of the mass of hair that waved away from his forehead.

She rocked away, watching Julian play, hoping Una was warm enough, glad to know that her hard-working Nathaniel was enjoying a brief vacation. He went away seldom, since he was not overly fond of visiting, or being visited, though he was the soul of hospitality when anyone came. She remembered how Mr. Emerson, coming to the Manse one day, said his way was regal like a prince even when he handed the bread. Mrs. Hawthorne had liked the compliment, but she told her mother later that as a matter of fact he had no chance to talk : Mr. Emerson did all the talking. "Mr. Hawthorne, though, looks the answers."

4

She really liked the little house they had rented here in the Berkshires. It stood a half mile out of Stockbridge on the road to Lenox, a small story and a half frame house. It was some distance from the pretentious homes of the town, and the Hawthornes preferred this, not because it was so much cheaper and they had little money, but because it was quiet, on a hillside and in the very middle of an orchard. And then, too, it had been something of a relief to get away for a while from the too much history of Salem and Concord to this atmosphere of sky and land. Hawthorne had made but one complaint about it when he first settled there : it was difficult for him to write in the presence of so much of the grandeur of God.

The children liked living like this on a small farm. Julian grew brown until his mother said he looked like a real chestnut. Una sat on the doorstep for hours making wreaths of mountain laurel for everyone. And twice a day they went with their mother to feed the hens, Julian's favorite pastime. Una loved best to repeat their names aloud : Snowdrop, Fawn, Crown Imperial, Queenie. For Una, always a temperamental child, this place was ideal. Julian, of sturdier emotional mold, got along anywhere, but Una needed quiet.

During those intervals when there was no servant, Mr. Hawthorne always insisted on helping with the housework, and Mrs. Hawthorne missed him now. Down in Salem was Tall Anne who used to work for them, and she had been trying to get her to come here to them, but Anne felt she had to have her church services and her communions and would not come even though Mrs. Hawthorne wrote to her invitingly that she would find it with them as quiet as heaven. But while Mr. Hawthorne was away on this visit Mrs. Peterson came to them, a dignified Negress, who seemed a forbidding sort of person. Apparently the color line had been drawn against her too closely somewhere, but Mrs. Hawthorne's gentleness melted her, and she was soon at home in the tiny kitchen.

Hawthorne's literary work in the Lenox house proved happy too. For here he wrote *The House of the Seven Gables* and the

5

Wonder Book for Boys and Girls. The latter book he had planned to finish in six weeks — and actually did. It was begun in June and finished in the middle of July, written at his favorite desk, on the little drawers of which he had painted tiny faces of elves and imps to amuse the children.

He worked well here. He could forget in this quiet spot the political calumny which had been the partial cause for their leaving Salem. And there was all about him a literary and artistic colony — a thing Hawthorne liked, if only he did not have to mingle with them too much. Fanny Kemble lived at Lenox. Over in Pittsfield Oliver Wendell Holmes had a summer home. The children preferred him to the other guests because he always brought his huge Newfoundland dog with him when he came to call. Miss Catherine Sedgewick, who had written many novels of a slightly realistic trend — an unusual thing for those days when everyone else was writing historical or mythological ones — lived at Lenox, and ran a school ; one of her pupils was Harriet Hosmer, whom the Hawthornes were to meet again in Rome, busily sculpting. But Mrs. Hawthorne grew lonesome sometimes for her own gay family. She tried to lure her mother into coming to them for a while, promising her "peace and rest and quiet walks in stately woods." Mrs. Peabody was unable to come, but Dr. Peabody came when, shortly after, his daughter was in need of his professional services.

The house where Rose Hawthorne was born on a sunny day in May looked quite large on the outside, but inside it was very different. "It is," said Sophia Hawthorne, "the littlest reddest thing."

The gate was a crooked affair, but past it there was a gravel walk thickly bordered with peonies and tiger lilies and syringa. On entering the low front door the visitor's eye was caught first by the porcelain figure of a lion and a lamb on the mantel, and a copy of the Madonna del Pesces above it. Opposite these hung a copy of Crawford's sculptured Glory to God in the Highest ;

and Correggio's Madonna of the Chair smiled at the children as they sat in their small chairs listening to their father, in a big shabby one, reading to them.

The house was always flower-filled from the moment they began to bloom in early spring : pink lobelia from the woods ; pale columbines which grew close to the lake in rocky corners ; red wild geraniums, almost too delicate to pick unless they were hurried to the house and put in water immediately.   And blue violets in a wide flat bowl.

Only the day before the new baby was born, Sophia was writing to her mother, one of her frequent voluminous letters : "After a winter and a spring such as I haved passed of tranquil and complete joy with mountain air to live on I do not see how this new Hawthorne bud can have aught but a lovely and glad existence."

She was feeling the deep content of an evening spent gathered round the astral lamp, while Hawthorne read for them his manuscripts of *Tanglewood Tales* and the *Wonder Book*, and the dog slept peacefully at their feet.   *Tanglewood Tales* derived its title from a particularly lovely bit of meadow and woods where they often picnicked, and where many of the stories had, in their earliest form, been told to the children.

The day after Rose was born Hawthorne wrote to his sister, "You have another niece.   She made her appearance at three o'clock and is a very promising child, kicking valiantly and crying obstreperously.   Her hair is very much the color of Una's." And in July he wrote again, "The baby is flourishing and seems to be the brightest and strongest baby we have.   Her hair is more red than Una's."

At about this time he began to speak of moving from the red house.   "It is really, my dear, an incovenient and wretched little hovel."

"But the milk," objected his wife, "is only three cents a quart, the butter fourteen and the beef only nine here — and a very good quality."

"And the view," admitted her husband, "is the most beautiful in the Berkshires." So for the time being they stayed.

But Hawthorne never cared to stay long in one place, no matter how beautiful it was. So in November they moved to a house in West Newton, which belonged to Mrs. Hawthorne's sister and brother-in-law, the Horace Manns, now living in Washington.

The children were filled with gloom because the five cats could not go along. Even the baby stirred and fussed in her mother's arms, as if sensing that something was wrong. Una and Julian were even gloomier when the cats, who had followed until it was apparent even to them that they were not wanted, sat in a dismal row outlined against the sky on the hilltop.

It was a miserable day, cold and rainy ; the woods looked black and everything else was gray and dingy brown. As they passed Luther's farm, they heard the creaking of the cider press and knew the old horse was patiently going round his track.

"The poor beast — making the liquor he can never enjoy," mused Hawthorne, then stole a look at Julian, whose indignation about the horse had waxed rather than waned during the summer.

They took the train at Pittsfield and were at West Newton that evening.

To Hawthorne this town was never more than a stopping place, but he was working hard at the *Blithesdale Romance,* which he had begun at Lenox, and it was very quiet at West Newton. He had meant, instead of coming here, to rent Mrs. Fanny Kemble's summer home at Stockbridge, but the inland heat of the summer had not agreed with him at all. What he really wanted to do was to settle again in Concord, and he wrote to Ellery Channing to ask him about finding a house for him there.

A typically Channing letter came back. "Emerson is gone and no one here to bore you. The skating is dam good. Come and see for yourself." But a few days later he felt less kindly about Concord. "It is bitter cold here," he wrote, "how about a villa in the Augean Hills ?"

8

After discussion and many letters Hawthorne made arrangements to buy the Alcott house in Concord. It had twenty acres of land and the soil, much of it, the owner assured them, was excellent for gardening. In June they left West Newton and moved to the house on the Lexington highway.

It looked much better than they had remembered it, for Alcott had put on a wing and a porch and had done away with much of its former box-like appearance. It was a very old house, for the main part of it had been built before 1700. When the British tramped past it was already old. Alcott had bought it in 1845 and named it the Hillside. He and his family now moved to the house next on the right, called Orchard House. The neighbor on the left was Mr. Bull, busy then and for years after in perfecting the grape later named for the town.

The house stood close to the road but there was plenty of privacy at the back where a hill sloped gently to a flat rise where Hawthorne could walk, safe from intrusion, plotting his work, and looking out at Wachusett, pale blue in the distance against the gleaming river and the sumachs, green when he came, but soon to flame rust red.

One reason Hawthorne was interested in the place was that Emerson had told him, while he was still at the Manse, that Alcott's old Hillside had once been inhabited by a man who firmly believed he would never die. Unfortunately he had moved away and no one had ever checked up on his future, but it was one of those odd legends that caught Hawthorne's fancy.

Mrs. Hawthorne and Una went down to the village on their first day back in Concord and on the highway met Mr. Emerson and Mr. Thoreau on their way to welcome old neighbors back again. They went on to greet Hawthorne while Una and her mother hurried to buy tacks and shelf paper. Even the aesthetic Una was willing to help nail down brown paper to go under the floor rugs — the handsome green and gold Brussels for the dining-room and the lapis blue one for the study. Everything was newly painted and gleamed with cleanliness. The pictures went up that very first day, and Endymion and Apollo in marble

9

watched over the study. In addition to her Madonnas Mrs. Hawthorne put up a fine copy of the Transfiguration which Emerson had given the family as a welcome home gift.

The children lived here in simplicity and health. Their mother, having been so overdosed in her youth by strong medicine that it made of her for years an invalid with a terrible migraine, hated medicines, and saw that the children were kept well and that they were given only simple remedies when they felt ill. But there was no undue sympathy for ailments in that household. "I never thought it any trial to bear my own pain," said Mrs. Hawthorne, after she had listened to a complaining visitor wail her troubles at great length. "I could arrange that in the grand economy of events. After using all human means to be in the best health, I am content if they utterly fail. I am happy because my heart and daily more and more my reason, assure me there is a God." On this simple Christian philosophy she built her family's attitude to health and sickness. Her own suffering, her son Julian said long years later, instead of concentrating her thoughts on herself, turned them toward others.

Rose was a little more than a year old when her mother wrote to Grandmother Peabody, "Rose is our best plaything here. Her sister and brother regard her in the light of a special providence. Our Rosebud is a comfort and joy from morning to night and has rosy cheeks and clear blue eyes that are pleasant to see. She takes jokes with perfect understanding, looking up from beneath her hair with the drollest expression. Her hair curls up behind and will be waving curls like Una's. She has vivid perceptions and sees things picturesquely. She has an air of command that is very funny."

When they wrote Grandmother Peabody that Rose was now able to take wavering steps on the lawn, that alarmed woman wrote back to her daughter cautioning her always to put a rug around the baby when she was outdoors. But Sophia wrote back in amusement at the suggestion. "I should as soon think of keeping an untamed bird on a rug as baby. Since she has had the use of her feet she does not pause in the race of life."

To her husband she said, "She is a real Pe-Boadie."

"A what ?" demanded Julian. "It sounds like Grandmother's name but not quite. Will you spell it for me ?"

Mrs. Hawthorne obligingly spelled it for them on a piece of paper. "And Rose is especially a Pe-Boadie. You see they were the children and grandchildren of Boadicea, Queen of Britain, and after her death they fled into the woods to escape doom and later they emigrated in many directions. They say her hair was red too — like Una's and Rose's."

Hawthorne sold his tall grass for thirty dollars that fall and hugely enjoyed wandering through his own woods cutting his own bean poles. And he was very happy when he had finally finished the *Tanglewood Tales*.

Then their peace was broken by two deaths. First the tragedy of Louisa Hawthorne, Nathaniel's sister, drowned when she leaped from a burning excursion ship. It made both him and his wife realize how glad they were that they both believed in a future life. "For," wrote Sophia to her mother, "God has never knit my soul with my husband's for such a paltry moment as this human life."

Then came the death of this mother. When they asked her if she wanted them to send for her daughter she, unselfish as ever, said, "Oh, no, don't let her come and leave that poor baby." But her daughter came to West Newton and was with her till the end.

By the time she was two Rose was a very busy person whose favorite spot was the kitchen — a fascinating place for which she hurried whenever she could. She chattered a good bit now and had a way of laughing, of being much amused as with some private matter, of having superior insight into things, said her mother. She loved to get her small hands on the very heaviest tools and garden busily, hating to come in the house even to drink her milk. And when Mr. Bull from next door came to bring her an English rose tree she helped delightedly with the planting.

11

But when Mary the maid found a snake while she was cleaning the Wayside garret, Rose clung to her mother as her father carried the ugly dangling thing down.

"Rather like a fiend haunting the house," he commented to his wife.

Sophia too shivered at sight of it and would not look again. But Una remained an interested observer. "It is really very lovely," she reported, "all plaided in lemon and black."

Rose would not look closely enough to see what Una so admired. It made her shiver for some time after it had been taken away, and her mother was relieved when, by evening, she had forgotten it.

2

Politics — that visitor so incongruous for such a household — entered it again but much more importantly than in the Salem days. Franklin Pierce, who had been a close friend of Hawthorne at Bowdoin College, and who was now running for President of the United States on the Democratic ticket, asked Hawthorne to write his biography which was to be used as campaign material.

It was not the sort of work that Hawthorne cared to undertake, and he felt some qualms about doing so, but he had so high a regard for Pierce that he finally consented to write it. His fear was that his friend had risen so high politically and might well rise even higher in the near future, that he might be accused of an ulterior motive in writing it. But, having once made up his mind, he began the work with his usual serene indifference to public opinion.

As he had guessed and feared, the comment was extremely acrid when later he accepted a post in the consular service in England which President Pierce offered him. It was at Liverpool, then the prize plum among diplomatic posts. As a matter of simple fact, the offer was a godsend to the always impecunious Hawthorne. He was making some money now with his writing but it was far from regular and not much at any time. Here he would be sure of a definite salary for some years to come and he

13

hoped to save a good bit of it and then come home and write at his leisure. He was certain he would do no writing while he was away. In this surmise he was correct : for six years he wrote only consular dispatches and his diaries. He took little materials with him to work on, feeling he would have no time and having decided on this trip with one object : to make enough money so that later he need do nothing but write.

He burned many of his letters before they left Concord. "What should we do without Fire and Death ?" he asked Thoreau, who had come in for a last chat.

Before leaving America, Hawthorne found it was necessary to go to Washington and consort with politicians. He was very glad when that trip was over, when he was again in his unpolitical family circle, where Julian greeted him with a rousing shout, and where Rose was brought from her crib to shake hands ceremoniously with him and then got into his lap and went to sleep again.

Mr. Alcott ran over to hear the news and wish the travelers well. But Thoreau had not done that ; he had kept shaking his head at this nonsense of leaving Concord for such a silly reason.

In June of 1854 they sailed from Boston for Liverpool on the Cunarder *Niagara,* with the firm intention of coming home from time to time. But they made no return trip until in 1860 when they came home to stay and to find a very different Concord from the one they had left. Now the two elder Hawthornes were looking forward eagerly to seeing all the glories of art and architecture about which they had read for so long. None of them was afraid of the Atlantic ; in fact, Mrs. Hawthorne wrote back home that the ship was as "safe as a parlor." Julian and Una enjoyed it as much as their elders, and Rose was gay with their gaiety. The vessel had a cow on board and a flock of hens. When the children saw these they were unwilling to take a last look at America, though their father scolded them for being so unsentimental about their native land.

The *Niagara* was Sam Cunard's prize ship. She was two hundred feet long and when the children were in the bow they could hear the hens clucking in the stern. The salon was in crimson

14

plush, and did duty as sitting-room and dining-room. On a shelf was a library — twelve volumes in red cloth — a meagre assortment for the Hawthorne contingent. The staterooms were, said Julian, exactly the size of packing boxes for pianos.

Captain Leitch was a small active man who had very bright eyes and black whiskers, and wore the heaviest of gold watches on the broadest of gold chains. Hawthorne, who knew that much of his time in the consulate would be spent in dealing with seamen, had long talks with him in order to get his opinion on many possible contingencies.

The fog was gray and heavy when the *Niagara* went past the little town of Birkenhead and dropped anchor in the muddy Mersey. The children were amazed to see their baggage so roughly handled and even opened on the gray granite wharf. The cab they took tossed them as, said Hawthorne, the Atlantic had not done. The gray stones, the fog, the darkly dressed people made no appeal to the children as they rumbled in the cab to the Waterloo Hotel.

This proved to be a dark place that held little of interest to the inquisitive children except three great turtles in tubs in the cellar. The little Concord turtles that skittered across the dusty road were mere insects compared to these awesome creatures. Rose held tight to Julian's right hand and to Una's left while she eyed the terrible things, their flat feet paddling around the tubs.

Next day they found a better place : Mrs. Blodgett's boarding house in Duke Street, a house where they were so content that they went back to it later whenever they could, and Julian spoke of it years after as the most comfortable and most hospitable boarding house that ever existed. The food was good, too, and Mrs. Blodgett had bright cheeks and brown curls clustered on each side of her face and a very black dress and a dazzlingly white cap.

At least twenty people sat at the long table in the dining-room at dinner, Mrs. Blodgett at one end because it was near the kitchen, and Hawthorne at the other because he was the consul. The rest were all American sea captains and their wives, this being the only variety of guests Mrs. Blodgett would take.

15

The children liked the strange breakfasts — finnan haddie or mackerel, crumpets and marmalade. As for the dinners, they were so huge that Mrs. Hawthorne was dismayed. "Where can be her profit ?" she wondered.

One exciting day — it was Christmas Eve — the children saw Miss Maria, Mrs. Blodgett's niece and helper, being roundly kissed by a husky sea captain. They also saw Mrs. Blodgett boxing the sea captain's ears in reprisal. But best of all were the smile and the blush of shy little Miss Maria.

Here they stayed until friends found for them a little villa of their own at Rockferry, only a few minutes from Liverpool by ferry. Here life was better in every way. This was more like home, more like the lamented Wayside. The children had a lawn to race over, and bushes in which to play hide and seek. Rose liked best the tiny English robins. The linnets and the thrushes came too "when they heard the news about the free crumbs," said Julian.

Julian had a six-foot-square garden of his own and some goose-berry bushes that were his especial property. Una had a small flower garden. Rose merely picked the tops off things and let gardening go. The one thing none of them liked was the sight of the strange disfigured fruit trees that were flattened against the walls instead of growing round and free as a tree should. They were very sure that Mr. Thoreau and Mr. Alcott would have hated them too.

The first American who came to their English home was Mr. Ticknor, who was received with great joy. He brought the most extravagant gifts to them all, but the big wax doll he gave Rose proved something of a trial for weeks because Rose felt the doll must be suffering from the chill of the English air, and at every opportunity put her close to the fire to get warm.

To Mr. Ticknor they admitted that they had been much dis-appointed in England at first — its fogs, its rains. "Some-times," said Sophia, "we think of the dear Wayside with despair."

They told him too of Harriet Martineau who, hearing that Concord writers were in Liverpool, dropped in on them with a

16

brilliant idea she had with which she wanted Hawthorne's help. She sat with her ear trumpet in her lap.

"I want to open a shop in London for infidel literature," she announced, "so that the world may receive the unbiased truth."

"To what unbiased truth do you refer ?" asked Hawthorne cautiously.

"To the fact that there is nothing at all in this religious nonsense. We must educate the people to know that and rely on themselves."

But the Hawthornes had not been receptive. When Sophia was telling about it to Mr. Ticknor, she added, "I have read that Mr. Clough said 'There is no God and Harriet is his prophet' is Miss Martineau's motto. I see now what he meant. Imagine no God and no future life !"

Hawthorne, no churchgoer at any time, had nevertheless been shocked too, for he had a very definite belief in a Deity.

But Sophia suddenly laughed aloud. "The worst of it was," she said ruefully, "she has the advantage of us : she can put her ear trumpet down whenever she wants to, and not hear replies."

There had been another who came their way, talking transcendentalism, thinking of course that at Concord there was no other philosophy. "He talked so much about it," said the exasperated Mrs. Hawthorne, "that I was tempted to fling him to the fishes to baptize him in realities."

But there were others whom it was a joy to welcome at Rockferry. Henry Bright used to come and read poetry to them at tea time. Rose sat on his knee listening very quietly to her favorite

> "For men may come and men may go
> But I go on forever."

Bright had spread the fame of Hawthorne's books in England, and even Mrs. Hawthorne was quite satisfied by his unqualified appreciation of her husband. Bright wore a monocle, which fascinated Rose almost as much as the brook that went on forever, and it was he who had suggested their settling at Rockferry. In

17

Rose's mind he was always associated with a Chinese junk anchored at the harbor which she was sure he had provided especially for her. This craft had come all the way from Hong Kong and now for tuppence one could go over it, watch its crew of slant-eyed sailors and sniff the delightful flavor of incense that hung over it.

Francis Bennoch, merchant and friend to half of England, became an intimate of the family, and it was from him that Hawthorne learned much of English ways. He taught them how to poke up an English fire until it blazed as well as a New England one.

Lord Milne was another friend, who had a pleasant habit of inviting people to breakfasts that went on from noon until evening. About him, who had so many possessions, Mrs. Hawthorne used to wonder, because he carried always so sad an air. James Buchanan came to the Rockferry villa too, and talked and talked. Even then he was hinting that perhaps Hawthorne might like his present post — at the Court of St. James's — when he gave it up. But a short year had taught them that they wanted no more diplomatic appointments after this one was over.

In the streets of Liverpool Hawthorne one day met Charlotte Cushman, whom he had known slightly in America and liked. He asked Sophia to invite her for dinner and to stay the night. Rose greatly admired the treasures that hung from her watch chain and was allowed to play with them as long as she pleased : a cross of the Legion of Honor, a tragic and a comic mask of ivory, a tiny opera glass, a gold poodle, and a dozen other fascinating trifles. Miss Cushman sang Spanish ballads for them after dinner and proved a charming guest.

Sometimes Mr. William Jerdan, from London, came up to call. He knew, it was said, every important literary man of the past fifty years. On his first visit Rose who happened to be in the room came at his invitation to sit in his lap. There she sat and stared with unwinking earnest eyes straight in his face. "I have never known such a look," he said amused, "except Talleyrand. He had this habit to a disconcerting degree."

Rose was unmoved by his smile or his talk. She merely stared on.

"What a judge you would make," he said. "I should not like to be the fellow to take sentence from you in your black cap."

There was no response from Rose for some minutes more, then suddenly her face widened in a smile. She beamed at him. "Ah, now I know," he said complacently ; "you see, she knows now that she loves me."

Mrs. Hawthorne decided quite suddenly one Sunday to take the children to church. Not one of them had ever been inside such an edifice and she felt that for a first visit she would take them to a cathedral, so that, as she put it, their first impression of social worship would be commensurate with its real sublimity. But it was not an entirely successful trip.

There was not enough music and far too much sermon. Una wrote home to her aunt about it later and said, "It was very tiresome — it was about the skin that Adam and Eve wore. It was tegeuse." In the stillness, with the voice droning far in front of them, Julian suddenly gave a mighty and audible yawn, which so startled his father that he ejaculated, quite loudly, "Good God," which hardly helped matters.

But Mrs. Hawthorne had made up her mind to go to church oftener, despite the effect of the sermon. "I have scarcely been since Una was born," she said to her husband. She went quite regularly after that. But after some months she said to her husband, "Something is wrong. The churches are so beautiful, but the English Church seems to me cold and timid."

He laughed at her earnestness. "It is true," she insisted. "No wonder some strong souls with warm hearts and the fire of genius in them should go back to Romanism from its icy presence."

Since Hawthorne occupied so important a position, there was of necessity a certain unavoidable amount of entertaining and being entertained — ambassadors, governors, mayors. Herman Melville stopped in on his way to Africa. Delia Bacon came, sent by Elizabeth Peabody, with her theory that Shakespere's works were in cipher and written by Bacon besides. To her Hawthorne was very kind and even wrote a preface for her rambling book, although he had little faith in her theory. Lord Houghton . . . the Brights. . . A Mrs. H. is recorded only by her initials ; she shocked Hawthorne by telling him that she preferred chickens to children. Miss Martineau again, as infidel as ever, to Sophia's increasing annoyance. "She must be either a fool or mad who says there is no God," she said with unusual severity for her.

She cared for the entertaining no more than he, but she did get a vast amount of satisfaction in watching her husband. She thought he fitted so well the lofty apartments, that he always looked as if he were born for a palace. There were many functions where full dress was required, and he hated that most of all. Meeting nobility and officialdom was bad enough, but the white muslin cravat which the times demanded for gentlemen's full dress irked him most. His family, however, thought him very distinguished in black with the white about his throat, and the children always watched him with awe when he departed for some state affair.

Mrs. Hawthorne too, who really loved to dress, would give her children great satisfaction when she was ready to join her husband at dinner or reception. Rose was usually asleep long before that, but one evening Mrs. Hawthorne came into her room adorned with a head-dress of pearls, in white silk with a long gleaming scarf, to find Rose still awake in her crib. She took one look at this strange regal person and burst into tears, so startled was she to see her gentle little mother in all this magnificence.

Then, of course, the Hawthornes had to entertain in turn, and Rose told, when she was grown, of peeking into the dining-room to see the splendid silver covers "trooping down the damask." But no more was spent for banquet and dress than was absolutely necessary. The Hawthornes were too busy saving for their children's education and their future to spend much on themselves.

20

And of course there was charity : there Hawthorne would give more than he could afford.   One of the first things Rose remembered hearing him say was, "Home duties are not so necessary or loving as duty toward the homeless."

The consular income was fairly high, but the expenses were equally so.   Hawthorne was determined to put aside all he could for them to live on when they went home again.   Mrs. Hawthorne complained in her letters of the cost of living in England : "Meat never below fourteen cents and potatoes thirty cents a peck.   No good fruit — how can there be with a sun crying its eye out every day ?"

They had a jewel of a nurse in the person of Fanny Wrigley. She came, that is, as nurse, but she was everything.   An English country woman, tall and big, with soft brown hair in a careless mass on her head, they all loved her.   She believed, said Mrs. Hawthorne, in so many different things that it was a delight : the Thirty-nine Articles, boiling eggs a certain way, making tea by a definite ritual and letting children do as they liked.

Una and Julian were growing fast, and were well ahead in their studies under the tutelage of their father and mother and of Miss Ada Shepard who had been added to the family as governess at the warm recommendation of the Horace Manns.   She was the first woman graduate of Antioch College, a girl of great charm and extraordinary mentality, who proved of value in their travels when even Mrs. Hawthorne's deep erudition failed.   She joined them in 1857 and remained with them in the triple capacity of governess, friend, and guide about Europe.

Rose too was growing rapidly out of babyhood.   "You would rejoice to see," wrote Una to Aunt Elizabeth in America, "our Rosebud now.   She is sitting on Mama's knee at this moment watching Julian dancing round her under the idea that it will make him cooler.   Her round rosy face and her waving hair make her look so pretty.   She is very sharp and has a great deal of fun in her.   She says the *Cuckoo* and *Hark Hark the Lark* and *Where the Bee Sucks There Suck I*.   She has a sweet way of saying them."

Hawthorne was a splendid playfellow and a good companion to his children. He took Rose to see her favorite "Tom Thump" more than once and averred hers was the much superior pronunciation. And he called her Rose Thump, because he said she did so much of it. On rainy Sunday afternoons, and there were plenty of them, he played blind man's buff with the three and Rose remembered years later with what awe she had tied the handkerchief around the fine crispness of his hair. He was a different man when he romped with them from the serious man he was at work, and this fact sometimes overwhelmed his younger daughter when she watched him playing about the parlor. "I looked at him," she wrote years afterward, "as a traveler who had caught the Sphinx humming would certainly be inclined to sit down and watch for her to do it again." And she added, "But even when he was gay he was never far removed from his companion, like Virgil. And his companion was a knowledge of the sin and tragedy of the world."

Often on rainy holidays they gathered around the fire as they had done in Concord. But there was no gracious Madonna here to smile at them. Instead there was a portrait in oils of a Mr. Campbell who had once owned the house and who must have been a rather depressing person. "He looks," said Mrs. Hawthorne, gazing at it with disfavor, "as if he would put his own mother on a short allowance."

When Rose was four they all spent a happy two weeks on the Isle of Man where they found a staid youth to row them over to Saint Mary's Rock of an afternoon. The whole fortnight was sunny, which they were told was very unusual. The donkeys and the donkey boys fascinated Rose and so did the gray cats with no sign of a tail.

Christmases followed a certain pattern no matter where the Hawthornes happened to be. In the parlor was a series of covered tables and upon each the gifts for one member of the family. Rose remembered best of her English Christmases the one when her doll Pompey received a little watch, and Mrs. O'Sullivan

22

from Lisbon sent her a lovely thing in a dainty box : porcelain beads of soft colors which her mother told her people called a rosary. That was the same Christmas that Mrs. Hawthorne found a Milton among her gifts and could read from a new volume the poem they read aloud each year — *"The Hymn on the Nativity."*

Gifts were always simple. The little extra money they had to spend had to help with various charities. There was never enough of that for Mrs. Hawthorne. "Oh," she exclaimed one year when making out her lists, "having money to give away must be like a foretaste of Heaven." The children never really learned to save money, for their parents could do that only badly, but they did learn to go without the luxuries that money can procure. "Thus," said Rose long afterwards, "we learned to toughen the sinews of endurance."

It was usually Fanny who gave them their most elaborate presents. What they gave away they often made themselves, and Rose said her own gifts as a child were usually "long and Penelope-like in preparation."

During the week there was no time for Hawthorne to play with the children. And there was no time for Hawthorne to write. From nine to five he was in his office and there were demands on his time at other hours. There were the shipwrecked sailors by the dozen for whom he had to provide. Some of them were impostors and then the carefully saved money which he had loaned them was lost, since he could not in honor ask the government to pay it back to him. Sophia said it was by no means all drudgery, but it was imprisonment and in harness, which was a hard thing for him. Then to make it worse, certain fees were eliminated altogether, so that now he had only his expenses and no chance to save what he had hoped to. When Congress passed a law reducing the amount all consuls received so that every chance of saving for the future was lost, Hawthorne grew restless. Besides, the new administration at Washington was hinting its wish to put in a consul of its own choosing at Liverpool.

While he was debating this an invitation came for Sophia and the children to visit the O'Sullivans at Lisbon where Mr. O'Sullivan was consul. They were old friends of the Hawthornes from Salem days, and Hawthorne, who was worried about a persistent cough that the damp climate had given his wife, insisted on her going and taking the girls, while he kept Julian with him.

The American visitors had an enjoyable time. Mrs. Hawthorne met the King, to the excitement of her daughters, who danced around her and admired her, arrayed in white satin with white feathers in her hair, a jet bracelet on her arm, in her white gloved hands an Indian fan. It was a very democratic little Court at Portugal, and the Hawthornes had entrée there at any time. Mrs. Hawthorne helped one of the princes with his drawing and felt very proud of the advance in art he made under her tutelage.

Rose liked this Court atmosphere very much, and she liked playing the rôle of princess, even at five. Once running into the palace, she tried to make an attaché understand what she was telling him and failed utterly. Suddenly, to the embarrassment of Una, coming up behind, and the amusement of the prince who was with her, she stamped her foot and demanded, with regal annoyance, "Understandy ? Don't you understandy ?"

They went to Madeira and enjoyed the sunshine, even though they were missing the ones at home. Julian too was evidently feeling the loss and was besides a bit nervous about the good conduct of Rose, for he wrote his mother, "Tell Rosebud I love her very much and wrote her a letter a litel while ago. She is the best litel girl in the world, is she not ? Does she ever get out of humor ? I wish to know if she behaves prettily always as a young lady should. Is she kind to nurse ?"

In June they went back home again, happy at being re-united. During that summer they went on various short trips. To Southport where the tea was so weak that Hawthorne said the landlady put soda in it to make it any color ; to Manchester where Hawthorne caught a glimpse of Tennyson in an art gallery and brought all the children into the salon where he was so that they might hear his deep shy voice. In the March following Hawthorne

24

suddenly decided it was time to take a real trip somewhere, so they decided on the Lake country and Yorkshire.

The Devonshire Arms at Skipton to which they had been recommended, proved a good inn and they asked the landlady where they ought to go first for sight-seeing. She shook the cherry ribbons in her cap. "Well, Skipton Wood is very pleasant and not too far for the children." So to Skipton Wood they went and before long came upon a castle. They wondered if it were open to the public. Hearing behind them a creaking noise, and finding it came from a pram pushed by a sturdy Britisher, they asked him.

"I think ye can," he said after due deliberation, "it being Good Friday and so a holiday. The lady that used to live there was a good 'un. She married a Pembroke and a Dorset and a Montgomery, and ye can see a picture of her in there with all three around her."

They saw the castle and the picture of the haughty lady and her three noble husbands. There was also a picture of a small boy with an apple in his hand which fascinated Julian. The housekeeper who was showing them around sighed when she saw his interest. "His young Lordship choked to death on that piece of apple. He was not very wise." Then apparently feeling this was too weak an estimate, she added, "He was a fool."

On the way back Julian picked a piece of yew from the batlements eight hundred years old, and they carried it like a prize back to the hotel where in their sitting-room they found excellent books in a case. Pickering's edition of Spenser, all of Scott's poems, some of the *Wide Wide World*. They settled down to hear their father read aloud.

Bolton Abbey made Sophia Hawthorne sigh with satisfaction. "How well those old abbots and priors knew how to crystallize their ideas of repose and worship into stone," she said. "Thomas à Kempis might have written his divine sentences here — that are so like a drop that sings and shines and falls. So everything seems here."

"Do you know," said Hawthorne, "since I have visited as

guest or merely as tourist so many of the great houses of England that once belonged to monks, I have often thought of this — somewhere between a fantasy and a belief — this feeling that to those who were given that property a curse went along with the houses and lands."

It grieved his wife to think that so many great ideals had been lost now that many of the priories lay in ruins. When she learned that this Bolton Abbey had been founded by young Egremont's mother after his drowning, she quoted to the children the lines :

> "For never more was young Romilly seen
> Till he rose a lifeless Corse."

Through dirty ugly Leeds they traveled to York and stopped at the Black Swan. In the guest book they found many familiar names : Nortons from Cambridge, Quincys, Frank Peabody of Salem. It made them feel close to home.

Manchester, which his mother called an "emporium of soot and mire," found Julian suddenly complaining of homesickness. "Twice," he added gloomily.

"Twice what ?" asked his puzzled sister.

"Twice homesick. Once for home and once for my anemones."

At the Cathedral it was found difficult to get Mrs. Hawthorne out of the Lady Chapel. She went back "just once" several times. She showed the children a deep place in the pavement worn by the knees of those who had come there to pray. And she showed them the empty shrine.

"The place where the Virgin of Virgins stood so long is empty," she whispered to them. "Her worship has almost passed from the land but see, here is the deep print of their homage left."

The travelers were interested to see Boston in Lincolnshire, that first Boston called Saint Botoph's town, for which their own Boston was named. When they arrived they found the hotel — the best one — poor enough. The waiter in the grimy parlor

26

was a grim looking personage who looked to the New England-ers like a genuine Puritan. Hawthorne thought thankfully of how totally different was that other Boston, with its Long Wharf, its Faneuil Hall, its State House.

Rambling through the English Boston, Hawthorne found a queer old book shop and asked if he might bring his wife to see some of the treasures the old bookseller owned. The latter was so happy in their pleasure that he said he would show them his chief treasure. He had shown them so many things that they wondered what this could possibly be. They had seen pen and pencil studies by Raphael and Rembrandt and Cellini, and Mrs. Hawthorne had been particularly taken with one Rembrandt head in brown ink with a hat over one eye. They had also been shown a Book of Secrets which once belonged to Queen Elizabeth. Haw-thorne opened it at random and Mrs. Hawthorne, looking over his shoulder, gasped at what she read. "How to kill a fellow quick." But her husband laughed and reassured her : she had not read it correctly. The word was "fellon."

The bookseller brought them his treasure, a quilt of fine white silk embroidered all over with bird patterns and arabesques. "Mary Stuart made it while she was a prisoner at Fotheringay Castle," he told them. "See, here is her cipher. M.S. And here again."

Mrs. Hawthorne drew off her glove and let her hand rest for a moment on the yellowed silk. "What weary thoughts she must have had as she sat over it. This stain — perhaps it was her tear that stained the silk. Poor ill-fated queen."

By June they were in Scotland, a land blooming with gorse and honeysuckle, the latter Rose's favorite flower, though her name for it was beesuckle. Having seen so many of the cathe-drals of England, they felt they must also visit a Scottish kirk, but they emerged much the worse for wear in disposition and temper. The service had been four hours long and most of it had been preaching. "The last hour and a half were against my will and capability," commented the exhausted Hawthorne.

27

But it was the architecture that had especially appalled Mrs. Hawthorne. "That barnlike house to give the Lord when there are near at hand such splendid houses for men. Why don't they render their best homage in art and architecture to our Supreme Father as well as their best devotion ?"

"You mean their longest devotion," said her husband.

But Mrs. Hawthorne admitted that the singing had been very beautiful. "It made me think of Concord when the sun rises over closed lilies and the chalices open and give out their incense."

At Glasgow even the music was denied her by the stern Scots. When she asked where the organ was the verger said disapprovingly, "We have no kist of whistles here."

The children, and the grownups as well, enjoyed the coaches in which they often rode. One variety especially enthralled Mrs. Hawthorne. "It has a small body or calyx," she wrote to Elizabeth Peabody, "and a wide spreading corolla. We were in the calyx and innumerable people were perched on the corolla like so many bees." They liked Ben Ledi too, standing alone. "Like a monarch !" exclaimed Mrs. Hawthorne. "A Saul among his brethren and taller than any."

At Castle Douglas they went into the gun room and were permitted to handle the sword of William Wallace, but they were all glad to get out into the sunshine again. They looked with interest at the courtyard where cannon balls were laid out in geometric designs on the green lawns.

"It makes one feel that war is a myth and a phantom, as if it had never been and never would be a fact," sighed Mrs. Hawthorne.

"It may be," said her husband, "that one day they will all learn to live by the love of Christ."

From Inverness the parents had gone on to a hotel at Loch Katrine for dinner, and when they returned Mrs. Hawthorne commented on the homeliness of all the men in the dining-room. "In fact there was only one handsome man there."

"You know who that was," said Una.

"Papa," said Rose confidently.

28

Of course it was true that his own family thought Hawthorne the best looking man on earth, but he must really have been very well favored.   Bayard Taylor said that his eyes were the only ones he ever saw that really flashed fire.   Charles Reade said he had never seen such eyes in a human head, and in London many compared him to Byron and Burns.   Horatio Bridge told of an old gypsy woman who said to him one day at Bowdoin, "Are you man or angel ?"

"What sort of little boy were you ?" asked Julian at Loch Katrine, but before he could answer Mrs. Hawthorne interposed.   "A dear old lady in Salem told me he was a pleasant child with golden curls and quite handsome — at one week."

But Hawthorne turned aside these compliments with a recollection of a newspaper printed by him at the age of ten, and selling for twelve cents a year.   "Your Aunt Ebie showed me a copy just before we left America.   My main story that month had been this item : 'The lady of Mrs. Winthrop has a son and heir.   Mrs. Hawthorne's cat, seven kittens.   We hear that the above ladies are in a state of convalescence.' "

Late in July they returned to Rockferry, weary but full of history and loving England and its reality even more than ever.

"What a country it is," said Hawthorne ; "one cannot look abroad but a thousand illustrious shades spring up before him."

Rose was six now and beginning to use her senses in new ways.   At night, when she could not go to sleep promptly, she would imagine she heard wonderful music.   Through her ears would sweep a whole orchestra which fiddled and blew and beat all for her.   They had invented the music for her too. They dedicated it to her, the unknown musician.   And she was sole audience.   Sometimes she used her eyes instead of her ears and saw suddenly a great bazaar full of toys of every sort.   And every toy of course in the whole store was for her, the sole purchaser.   It took great will power to evoke this music and these toys, for it was to her not imagination but reality.   The sound and the vision would not last long, usually only a few minutes, but they possessed reality while they did and had a marvelous distinctness and color.

Later she began to practice imagining people in the same way. This was much harder for it meant using her will power on two senses at once. And she instinctively never tried to extend the time ; a few minutes of seeing them, of hearing them talk, and then she let them drift from her consciousness and she, herself, fell asleep.

Years later when she mentioned this feat at a dinner table, she was amazed to find the guests surprised at her story. She had thought it a very ordinary thing which everyone did if one could not get to sleep.

And then of course if these imagined people did not respond, nor the scene, either, or if she grew tired of them, there was always her favorite reality to meditate on — her father. Fanny, the nurse, said once that even before the lights were lit, the room was bright with his face if he were there, and so he lighted up the dreamy world for his child. In the thought of his affection and joy she would fall asleep.

The trip over England had served only to make Hawthorne more restless to be away from the consulship, which grew more and more tedious. He felt too that it was high time for him to get back to his real work again and to inform the government at Washington of his intention. The family were all deep in French and Italian language books now, for they were going on the Continent for a time when they left England.

But hearts were broken all round when it was found that Fanny was not going along. Three years of her had made her one of the family. But it was clear that she belonged in England and could be happy only there, so they parted, with bitter tears from Fanny and laments from the children.

3

In 1858 Hawthorne sent in his resignation, and not long after they left England for Paris. Paris was cold and rainy and they did not tarry long. They were bitterly cold in Genoa, and when they reached the Rome of their dreams and hopes it was so chilly and wet that they did not get really warm for a month.

They reached Rome at midnight of January 24th and went to Spillman's, the only hotel where they could find rooms. Later they went to the Palazzo Larazan near the Villa Malta, where Hawthorne sat in front of the fireplace with his great coat on over his other coats, sighing for the logs of England to feed the fires instead of the small fagots lost in the cavernous hearth. The marble floors chilled their feet. Rose looked out in amazement to see the fountains frozen in the *piazza,* and the Roman children sliding about on the ice. It was too cold for even Mrs. Hawthorne's fingers to write letters home.

By the middle of February Hawthorne ventured out to pay a call on the Storys at Palazzo Barberini, but he refused to accept an invitation to their fancy dress ball — it was much too cold for fancy dress ! But he and the family began to leave the fireplaces and venture out into Rome to see the Forum and the Arch of Septimus and the Appian Way and Saint Peter's — all those places they had so eagerly read about in Salem and Concord.

By the time it had grown really warm the Hawthornes realized that they had fallen deeply in love with Rome. Even Hawthorne, the coldest of them all, left his fireplace and some of his shawls and went to the Carnival where he shook confetti off his black suit to his own annoyance and the delight of his children. This mixing of religion and play as Rome did it — this celebrating saints' days with riots of food and flowers — at first disturbed the Puritan in him who remembered the dark, still Sundays of his youth, the fear of not having learned his Scripture lesson well, the remorse for dreaming fairy dreams during the long sermons.

The clowns and harlequins, the Papal Dragoons in steel helmets and white cloaks — all the pageantry of a Roman holiday was before them. And already, slowly but definitely, there was forming in the mind of Hawthorne a new novel, a novel of Rome.

And freed from cold as now were the icy fountains of the city, so Mrs. Hawthorne's pen flowed again as her fingers grew warmer. "I am in Rome, Rome, Rome," she wrote her sister. "Years ago Sarah Clarke said that my children would one day play in the Temple of Peace, and now they shall. And I have been to the Pantheon, once consecrated to the immortal gods and now to the Immortal God. I have been to Saint Peter's — there alone in Rome is perpetual summer. It shut the world out when I went in and I was folded down as if the angels had wrapped their wings about me."

From one trip she came home greatly annoyed. "Why do Popes keep putting their names on everything?" she wondered. "It was Gregory or Benedict ten or seven or eight who did this or that. Can't they illuminate and restore without putting their cognomens all over?"

The family began now in earnest to visit the treasures of Rome, seldom in need of a guide book, for Mrs. Hawthorne had read and studied so much that her comments were better than a book to her children. She showed them the martyrdom of Saint Sebastian, Domenichino's great picture.

"See, children," she said, "he has made the triumph over pain complete and he seems willing the sacrifice though aware of the pain. Though it is a dreadful sight I can't feel the horror I usu-

32

ally do over such themes, but rather the peace that passes understanding."

And the children, gazing, felt they understood. They had
always been treated as human beings with sense and understanding by their parents, and it was only natural that they should
respond at least in some degree. Dimly they knew what their
mother meant, and it stayed back in their minds, even though it
was not until years later that they understood it.

She showed them Saint Peter's for the first time and bade them
stand on the very spot in the Mamertine Prison where Saint
Peter had been imprisoned. "He was chained here hand and
foot like a criminal, and now he rules Christendom from the most
magnificent cathedral in the world. You see, he was in black
darkness, but he died for his Lord Jesus Christ, and now he has
light enough, for he transformed his life and he can never lose
it again."

When Una's birthday came in March, they hired a big ba-
rouche for a trip on the Appian Way. As they clattered along,
Hawthorne stared down at the pavement. "Think what horses
and chariots have passed this way on these very stones. Really
the very stones, for the old Appian Way has very recently been
laid bare by order of the Pope. And how strange to think that
this way went Horace and all the poets."

"And Zenobia," chimed in Julian, proud of his learning.

Mrs. Hawthorne waved a hand in the direction of the Dome.
"I thank the Pope," she said.

They looked at some of the tombs, the Columbaria, which
Mrs. Hawthorne declared an odd name when you stopped to
think how undovelike were many of those interred there. In the
tomb of the Scipios a weird old man took them down winding
ways among the graves. The rest clung to the ropes, but Rose
felt safer hanging tight to her mother's hand with one hand and
clutching her dress with the other. *Moculli* — small tapers —
were all that relieved the blackness. Rose thought the tomb
contents pretty tawdry — silly little urns and rusty bric-a-brac
and tear bottles left here for a thousand years. It was like their

visit to the Catacombs ; she was not exactly afraid, but there was nothing reassuring about things either.

While Hawthorne took frequent walks by himself, pondering now over the story that was beginning to shape itself in his thoughts, Mrs. Hawthorne took Julian and the girls to various places of interest. One day during Lent they all went to Saint Peter's to see Pio Nono at his prayers, as he came there to pray every Friday during the Lenten season. It would be, she thought, a good quiet time to see his face.

The pageantry held the children absorbed and quiet. First the attendants in old-fashioned cloaks and three-cornered hats. "They look like old long ago kings," whispered Julian. Then the Swiss Guards with their full trousers and bright striped tunics. "And they look like tulips," whispered his mother to him.

The floor near the gate was covered with crimson velvet and gold, and over this was set a *prie-dieu,* likewise covered. There was silence and a stir. Cardinals in violet robes preceded and followed the Pope, in white silk with red shoes and red mantle and a white cap, looking grave and yet kingly, thought Mrs. Hawthorne. He blessed the crowd with a gracious majestic gesture. Everyone knelt ; even the Concord Hawthornes dropped to their knees as if it had been an accustomed gesture. The silence was deep about them. The children saw the lips of the people all around them moving.

When they came out of the Cathedral, Mrs. Hawthorne looked troubled. She had been more moved than she wanted to admit. Later to her husband she said, after they had all told him about the sight they had just seen, "How even more impressive it would have been, if we could have believed him saint and virtually head of the Church."

They attended Tenebrae for the first time. The children were awed by the lights extinguished one by one until the last was carried behind the altar, and the great building was dark and silent. Then one voice rose in the night, clear and high and sad. "Miserere, miserere," it wept. And when they went out into the Roman night, Una's eyes were full of tears, to her father's dismay.

"It was the violet colors and the music," she explained ; "it was so lovely and so sad." Above the Plaza Mrs. Hawthorne called their attention to one single star in the clear sky. When she voiced what it had reminded her of, she found the rest had had the same thought : of the Star that had stood over the place where Christ lay.

But the next day, still stirred by the scene she had witnessed, Mrs. Hawthorne, leaving the children with Ada, decided to go back alone to Saint Peter's and sketch a bit, and it was a less successful spiritual adventure. A stately priest in purple and lace was kneeling near her at prayer, and she began to put him down in her little sketch book. Suddenly he took out his snuff box and took a good pinch, and Mrs. Hawthorne abruptly stopped drawing and went home.

"Making himself jolly with snuff," she said indignantly, "when I thought he was wrapped in devotion. What a religion !"

"Did you go right away, Mama ?" asked sympathetic Una.

But it appeared Mrs. Hawthorne on her way out had been caught by a procession of nuns. "And I was feeling quite happy again, for they were really intent on their faith and not on snuff, when some officious stranger came along and suggested a better place for me to stand. So I came away. I'll take some of you with me next time I go there."

Rose was too young to have remembered about her first few years back in the United States, though she often spoke with great importance of "When I was in Morica," but she had been old enough in England to know that Rome had a very different culture from the Anglican. Life here was like a play. Brown monks trotted through the streets past their windows. She sometimes had a private feeling that they were demons lurking to destroy her, so she often left the window when they went by or shrank against Ada or her mother on the street. She liked much

35

better the Penitents, in their neat clothing, their hooded faces that were like church steeples, and the two holes out of which their eyes glistened. They did not disturb her as did the good brown monks. Perhaps it was that she had heard her mother say she thought they were freer of superstition because they were cleaner.

She watched the procession bearing the dead to burial and heard the chanted prayers — foolish praying to her practical Yankee mind, yet fascinating. In later years she was greatly astonished to learn that those chants had been nothing more than honest praying right out of the Bible.

She preferred it inside the churches ; it seemed more real. She used to feel waves of peace going through her when she stepped softly past the kneeling people, and sometimes felt in herself a wish that all her family did this too. But at home she felt less spiritual and amused them all with imitations of the chants, the low grumbling tones of the priests, the shrill notes of the choristers.

During the Lent booths were set up directly under their windows ; cakes were fried in oil and spooned directly from the kettles to the buying public. Julian and Una found them fairly good, but Rose did not like these delicacies. Their pretty tints made her expect them to be much more delicious than they turned out, and they were tasteless in the extreme. Had the cakes been better, she told amused friends years later, she would have been much earlier interested in Catholicism, but this tastelessness convinced her that "the Italians lacked mental grace and salvation."

With all the family she was stirred at sight of the Holy Father during Holy Week coming out on his balcony to give the assembled people his blessing. Mrs. Hawthorne reported this incident fully to her sister. "The heart of Rome is Saint Peter's and its pulse is the Pope. He looked most kingly as he stood there, but not like other kings. The white he wore was not whiter than his pallor."

On the way home she and her husband were speaking of the

36

deep sincerity in the Pope's face, and were surprised to hear their younger daughter say suddenly as she trotted along beside them, "He is honest."

Only a few weeks after this, when Rose and her mother were taking a walk through the Vatican Gardens, and Rose as usual was dashing about peering at first one flower and then another, she bumped suddenly into someone walking toward her. To her surprise and alarm she saw that the person she had hit was the Holy Father himself, strolling about his small domain. Mrs. Hawthorne looked up at her daughter's explosive "Oh!" and came forward to apologize, but Pio Nono only smiled at her and the little girl. He put his thin white hand on the tumbled red curls and gave her his blessing.

Rose could talk of nothing else all the way home. Next day her mother bought her a little medal of the Holy Father and a gold *scudo* that bore his likeness, and they were put away in Rose's box of chief treasures.

She quite forgot the Pope, however, in the excitement of having her portrait painted. Mr. Thompson had just finished one of Mr. Hawthorne, and Rose went with him to see it. On the way home she acknowledged on his questioning that she thought it a very good picture of her father.

"Do you like his work?" he asked gravely.

"Yes," she answered as gravely. "It is not as good as Raphael, but his angels are very nice. They are so clean and pretty."

She went back the next day for her first sitting. The artist had liked the eager little face with its tawny hair, and Rose had felt very important about her sittings. But she grew very bored, with none of her own family around to talk to her, and she soon had a vague feeling that she was being punished instead of painted. And she did not at all like the way Mr. Thompson looked her up and down in such a patronizing way. She hated his pictures too by the time hers was finished, but felt rather guilty about that and did her hating in private since her father and mother greatly admired this artist's work. Anyway she much preferred Mr. Story's studio and the statues, even though the

37

angels were a gloomy lot.   She decided that of all the statues in Rome she liked best the Apollo in the Vatican : he looked so proud.   That was the way to feel — very proud always.

It was on Sunday during the late afternoons that Rose had her best time of the week.   That was when she and her father took a walk to the Pincian Hill.   Sometimes they played a game with stones on the gray benches, and she would glow with the joy of having him as her opponent.   Crowds strolled by, but they played on peacefully, seeing no one.   This was the time of day when he smoked the one cigar he allowed himself.   He would take out the bronze match-box with the little Greek figures on it that Una had given him, and they would first admire it together.   Then she held it while he struck a match, lighted the cigar, and puffed at it deliberately, while the enchanting aroma stole out on the air and the blue smoke floated between their faces.

When it began to grow dark, they usually stood for a few moments before they went home looking at the west, the sunset outlining what he in the *Marble Faun* was to call the "grandest edifice ever built by man painted against man's loveliest sky."

Besides being the center of so much religious activity, Rome was a gay and social place.   The Hawthornes had come at an interesting time ; the American colony was made up of many real artists and writers and many English and American personalities met there.   There were, too, those who played at art, bored with their native land, and were living here in Bohemian fashion. Hawthorne was astonished at first at sight of them strolling among the ruins, singing American patriotic songs in the Coliseum, playing about Rome as if the place had been built with the one object of making them happy.

Hawthorne enjoyed walks along the Tiber with John Motley, the historian.   General Pierce stopped there on a continental tour.   Mrs. Browning came to call.   Mrs. Story invited the Hawthornes to dine at the Barberini Palace, which was a meeting place of celebrities, so much so, in fact, that people used to point

38

to a stone lion at the foot of the staircase and say it was the only lion that had not gone up Mrs. Story's staircase. Mr. Browning would be met on walks, darting about "like a glowing cordial," said Mrs. Hawthorne. Miss Maria Mitchell, who had bought Rose warm gingerbread in chilly Paris was here, too, and, having a passion like Mrs. Hawthorne's for seeing every building and monument in the Eternal City, they went about together after the others were weary of sight-seeing. Miss Elizabeth Hoar of Concord was living here too.

One day Una was taken for a drive in the Corso, and she came home proudly bearing a bouquet which the Prince of Wales had tossed directly in her lap from a balcony.

Hawthorne could now, being thoroughly warm, sometimes be lured into the Barberini Palace, but it is feared that it was rather because he loved the place than because he wanted to talk to the people. He would wander through the great mansion with its queer shaped rooms, its odd little staircases, its views from quaint windows. He made use of many of these in the *Marble Faun,* the plot which was forming more and more in his mind. The Roman background he had, and many of the characters. When one day Mr. Story and he went to the Capitol, Hawthorne lingered long before the Faun of Praxiteles in the sculpture gallery. That night he wrote in his notebook, "It seems to me a story might be contrived on the idea of their having intermingled with the human race."

When the really malarial weather came, the Hawthornes decided to spend a month or two in Florence and to go there by carriage. The *vetturino* — the man who drove and was to take care of things for them — promised them the trip for one hundred dollars including everything but tips along the way. His name was Gaetano, and he looked not too Italian, but rather like a nice New England farmer.

Inside the carriage there was room for four people. In front of that space there was a sort of wide coupé that held two more, and in front of that was the box where sat the *vetturino.* Baggage was tucked in the back and on the top, and it was a full load that clattered out on the Flaminian Way at eight of a hot June morning.

Hawthorne looked back. "I am glad it is not a final departure," he said. "What a deep hold this city of the soul can have on the mind."

The sight of soldiers — a whole regiment of them — made them pretend they were Roman legions returning from victory, although the dust they raised was less pleasant than the dream. Tomb after crumbling tomb they passed, but Gaetano could answer none of their eager queries about these, and the Hawthornes had to be satisfied with enjoying the view of the rolling Campagna and the sight of Saint Peter's, which became smaller and smaller in the distance and finally disappeared altogether.

Gaetano took care of all their meals, too, and, when the first stop brought them a beefsteak, omelette, bread, cheese and wine, they decided he was a very good provider and jolted on in contentment. This content with life, however, lasted only until they passed a *carragio* which had no windows at all but only little holes in the ceiling. This time Gaetano was able to enlighten them: it was a *carcellaria*, full of prisoners.

The occupants of the carriage were depressed all the way to Siena. It took the town of Foligno to cheer them again — Hawthorne called it by its proper name of Fulginium — and the vale of Clitumnis of which Virgil sang. At Assisi, Gaetano permitted them to stop and look around, since this was one of the places mentioned in his contract with them. A Franciscan took them around to show them the paintings and they all deplored the dimness of some of the lovely masterpieces. "I don't like to see these miracles vanishing," mourned Mrs. Hawthorne.

It was when they neared Perugia that they were for the first time a bit startled and apprehensive, wondering how Gaetano could accomplish the task of getting them up the steep height before them. But Gaetano the trusty showed them how it was done. He uttered a loud resounding cry as if he were really preparing to storm heaven. A voice as loud and as strong as his own answered him, and suddenly they drove up to a farmhouse where stood a man with two white steers. These were promptly harnessed to the carriage and up it went. They all got out and walked to ease the toiling animals' burden, except Mrs. Hawthorne, who reclined at her ease in the carriage, where she was presently joined by Rose, who had managed to climb her breathless way with the rest until almost the top.

At Perugino Gaetano escorted them to the Church of Saint Dominic and left them while he dealt with the steers and their owner. They wandered about until they came to Perugino's Saint Columba. Their father translated for them the verse from the Canticles written under it : "Show me thy face, my dove, my beloved, at the threshold of the door."

In her white Dominican habit she stood there, a dove on her hand, a wreath of white daisies about her head. Over the white garments a black veil lay in heavy folds about her. The painter had caught her innocence, and her face seemed to have the silver tints of a dove.

The others moved away but Rose lingered before Saint Columba in fascinated interest. "I like her," she greeted her returning mother, "because the birds like her and she likes the daisies."

Mrs. Hawthorne looked at her Rose, so different from the painted girl before them. In this picture Una would have found the spiritual loveliness of the young saint. But to Rose it was the life in the picture that appealed : the birds, the flowers, the natural things. This rosy, impetuous, vigorous child had an energy neither she nor her husband had, a heartiness that went straight out to meet life. She felt she would make her way in the world better than would Una or Julian ; but her impetuous demands were offset by her deep affections ; in fact, there was no doubt where the danger lay for the future in that stormy affectionateness.

They forgot until they were back in their carriage again that they had meant to go to the Staffa Gallery. Miss Elizabeth Hoar had urged them to go to see the beautiful Saint Rose there, "especially since she is little Rose's patron saint." By the sixth day they were at Lake Thrasymene where Julian found new shells for his collection and Rose hunted for flowers, finding a spike of purple bells such as none of them had ever seen ; the "botanist," her father called her.

In Arezza they visited Petrarch's house, and Rose called their attention to a dove perched on the upper step of the house, so tame that it never stirred at their approach. "Perhaps," suggested Ada, "it is Laura haunting the spot."

A day later, having had no accidents whatever, they were in Florence. "There is," declared Mrs. Hawthorne, "no thorn on the rose of our success."

4

In Florence they had rented for the remainder of June and all of July a house there called Casa Bello.   The back of the house opened on a great terrace that led into a garden of roses and jessamine and a grove of lemon and orange trees and, its branches shading everything, a great willow tree.   There were thirteen living-rooms, with space enough for every one to be alone and remote if he wanted to.   The study was hung with crimson curtains and had two couches, stuffed easy chairs and a deep carpet.

"At last," said Mrs. Hawthorne, "the artist of the beautiful has what up till now he ought to have had and had not."   A servant was there, too, who went with the place ; her name was Stella, but, they soon admitted ruefully, she was not nearly so bright as her name.

On her first morning in Florence, Mrs. Hawthorne sat writing busily to her sister.   Julian was in his own little study drawing Pericles.   Una, looking very romantic in white muslin, was reading Tennyson, and Rose was playing with Stella.   Hawthorne was out luxuriating in the garden, and his wife sat feeling the stillness of the air — "only two contending butterflies were stirring it if it stirred at all."   She liked the green Arno after the muddy Tiber, and when she went out in the streets she rejoiced to find them smoothly paved.

By next day they were ready for churches and museums, at

least the indefatigable Mrs. Hawthorne was and one or more of the children usually trooped along. The Duomo was near at hand ; so were the Pitti and the Uffizi.

The day they went to see the Madonna della Seglio their father went along, for he thought it the most beautiful picture in the world, and could not visit it enough. The Perugino Deposition was another painting to which they went often. From this picture Hawthorne came away one day with the solemnest face Rose had ever seen him wear. "It is that boundless love in her face. Her grief communicates itself to all who see it, for it is a real and not a painted grief." The open arcades at each side of the streets and the statues in the niches at the corners, were greatly appreciated by the Hawthornes. They felt they were in a sort of fairy place.

Everyone felt so, that is, excepting the youngest member of the family. Rose did not like Casa Bello, and did not feel happy there. She liked sitting in one after another of the fifteen armchairs the house afforded, but that grew tiresome after a while. The garden she thought very damp and the willow most depressing ; and worst of all, Julian had caught a bird which had been somehow lamed, and had put it in a box to nurse it until it got well. Instead it died, and then the willow hung over everything more drearily than ever. The rest of the family enjoyed eating the purple figs, but Rose, though reveling in apricots and cherries, could not share their liking for this foreign looking fruit.

She got so depressed finally that she experimented with chewing up the seeds in the apricot stones because she had heard they could cause death. But nothing happened. Even the big studio of Mr. Powers opposite their Casa had long dismal galleries full of long dismal statues. The only one among his collection she really felt drawn toward was Angelo's seated figure of Lorenzo de' Medici. He looked as bored as she felt, and it was quite clear that he, too, disapproved of Casa Bello opposite.

Late in June came a reviving bit of excitement. Rose's father and mother had called on the Brownings at Casa Guidi and came home full of their visit.

"Mrs. Browning looks like a spirit," declared Mrs. Hawthorne. "The smallest amount of substance encloses her soul, and every bit is infused with heart and intellect. She tucked the pink roses you sent her into her velvet dress and they looked lovely," she said to Rose.

Ada Shepard who was still with the family had been invited to go with them, and her white muslin with blue ribbons was still vibrating with the excitement of the visit. But most thrilling of all, Mr. Browning had insisted that Una must be brought to call on Mrs. Browning, and had added, "Do bring the little Rose too, that dearest little thing."

She did not go with the others to the Pitti the next morning. She stayed at home to rest up for the great occasion. Mrs. Browning did not usually receive people until after eight in the evening, but that would have been Rose's bedtime, so by special arrangement they were invited for tea.

They rang the bell at Casa Guidi at the appointed time, and rang and rang. No one came in answer. They were just departing in disappointment when a servant came to the door.

"You can't see Mrs. Browning now," she said in surprise, but at last they convinced her they were invited guests, and were admitted. Mrs. Browning was in her drawing-room, pale and ill looking as always, and as always, dynamic. She took Rose in her lap and sat looking almost hungrily at her and Una.

"Oh, how rich and happy you must be to have two daughters and a son and such a husband. My boy is not here. I am so sorry he could not meet your girls, but he has gone to take his music lesson."

"Is he fond of music ?" asked Una.

Mrs. Browning shook an amused head. "No, he applies himself no more than a butterfly. To get his attention I take him in my lap and hold his hands and feet. Like this," and she caught Rose by her hands and feet gently, but firmly.

Rose was enchanted with the soft voice, the deep smile, so much so that she did not struggle to get away as her mother was apprehensive she might. She sat perfectly still while the two women talked.   But after a while she began playing with her little fan, waving it up and down and back and forth.   Mrs. Hawthorne saw that it was distressing Mrs. Browning who was trying to pretend not to notice it, so after a brief interchange of talk, she took the children away.

"But how," she said on the way back to Casa Bello, "how can she ever live long ?   It seems as if her delicate earthly vesture must soon be burnt up and destroyed by her soul of pure fire."

"Did you enjoy your visit ?" asked her father as Rose sat in the garden as far as possible away from the willow tree.   Rose said yes, but she did not tell him how disappointed she had been about one thing.   She had asked her hostess if Galileo was there and Mrs. Browning, not understanding her, said that Galileo had never lived in their house.   Rose had fully expected to see him. She had formed an idea somehow that he belonged to the Browning family, and she thought he sat in a high tower all his own and looked down on the sun which he was holding prisoner in his back yard.   But she got no opportunity to see him at the Brownings'. Her hostess had kindly told her some of Galileo's real story, but Rose knew all that already.   She wanted to see him in person.

For years and years after they left Italy, the Brownings, she so lovely and ghostlike and haunting, he so robust and gay, were mingled in her memories of this Italian period in her life.   A Vatican Diana, a Madonna of Raphael, a statue of Perseus, Beatrice Cenci, the bright wild flowers of the countryside, Power's model of his tiny daughter's hand — and among all these bits of remembered charm, the Brownings came always to her mind's eye.

The Boboli Gardens was a favorite spot for Rose and her mother on mornings when Ada was busy with lessons for Una and Julian, and Stella and her helper were hard at work in the thirteen living-rooms.   When the grounds were open, they would go there together, Rose with her rope and her doll Daisy and her little chair and her fan.   Mrs. Hawthorne was equipped with a book, and bread for the swans, which were usually found in a state

46

of high displeasure with life and beating their snowy wings and uttering ugly groans. Rose would first toss them green leaves which brought them up close, and then bits of bread which they ate haughtily, and then sailed off with no thanks at all.

Rose jumped rope and picked wild flowers and tied them into huge bouquets for the family, while Daisy sat at her ease in her chair, holding her little mother's fan and the steadily increasing pile of nosegays. They usually stayed until Rose found a stone or a dead butterfly that had to be taken to Julian immediately. "It is as if we had a whole rustling blossoming Eden to ourselves," wrote Mrs. Hawthorne to her mother. "The Boboli Gardens and we seem alone on a new earth."

They went one afternoon to San Marco to see the house of Fra Angelico. They walked solemnly up and down the cloister walks where, their mother told them, Fra Angelico himself had walked, "meditating angels and virgins and saints. He must have consecrated the very stones."

Their staid New Englandism, quite lulled to sleep by this time, was jarred awake by a painted wooden group of the Nativity in the church. The Virgin wore white silk and was bedecked with gold strings of beads and pearls ; her bodice was bejeweled, and her fingers were every one hung with gold rings and her wrists with bracelets. The Babe was as ornate as his Mother and lay on cloth of gold.

"So gaudy," murmured Mrs. Hawthorne, "and so unlike the manger and the unadorned young mother."

"And so unlike Fra Angelico," added her husband. "But these people love it, my dear. It is their way of honoring the Virgin."

"Yes," she said impatiently, "and they hear so much about the Queen of Angels and Mother of God and so on, and not reading the Bible they perhaps know nothing of her humble environment." She shook her head and drew her children away from this glitter to the sweet simplicity of the Fra Angelico paintings.

Later at the Academy of Arts she found something that proved her point. That was the Perugino Pieta. Even little Rose

47

saw how much greater was this than the other gaudy group. This was real.

"See," she said to the children, "she is no longer looking to see if he is dead. She knows it all too well now. See how she is still and hopeless with a settled misery. She knows she must bear the fact now. She makes one remember sadly that Mary in the Pitti, you know, the one with her hands folded over her Baby."

At the beginning of August came good news, especially good to Rose who had never really reconciled herself to the gloomy garden of Casa Bello. The Brownings told them of a villa for rent in the hills, one which the owner had never leased before, Montaulto by name. Its Duke was renting it now for a month to desirable tenants.

Over the dusty road to the hills the carriage jolted the Hawthorne ladies on their way to their new home. Julian and his father went on ahead and were waiting to meet them at their destination, full of the glories of Montaulto. Mrs. Hawthorne after one glance pronounced the house large enough to quarter a regiment. Mr. Hawthorne reported with satisfaction that it was said to have a ghost — an old monk.

Here was a place for Hawthorne to revel in. It was shabby and time worn. It had gray walls and stairs, and, said Una after close examination, "almost a hundred rooms of all shapes and sizes." And best of all it had a tower, broken and dusty in some places, and a rather perilous place to climb to. But climb they did, with their father content to caution them not to fall through the holes. And at the top they came out to yellow moss on gray stones, to the golden sun of Florence. There lay the Arno. Fiesole and San Miniato were both visible. The villa of the Brownings was near the end of their estate. They could come up here and see sunsets, too ; they had been afraid to venture out down in the low town.

There was also Galileo's tower, and the lovely hills along the horizon were full of castles and villas. Sometimes there was a great rainbow and rain at once, for as Mrs. Hawthorne put it, "the view is so wide that there are often many little private showers going on round the heights while the sun is shining."

Una had a fascinating room full of madonnas and pyxes. At first they had thought it the chapel, only to discover a real one later. The children were especially taken with a "very undraped little wax boy holding up a heart that looked like a bit of sealing wax," wrote their mother to America. The artificial flowers and the waxen angels were all dark with the dust of years. Hawthorne had a whole suite to himself to work in — "miles away," said Rose.

Rose found it a great joy not to have to go to Florence for a while. The roads were always hot and the only pleasant sight was the sturdy little peasants girls working away knitting socks before their doors. But there was much poverty and beggary along the road. The child felt the misery of it all : the beggars with their maimed children, the something selfish about the crowds that hurried past them. Whether it was in her own heart or something she had heard her father say, she always felt she ought to do something for the crippled children, and always she knew there was nothing she could do. It was better then to stay away, she decided. Later when she read the pages of the *Marble Faun,* she saw how her father had put the pain they both felt into the pages of his most loved book.

The Hawthornes said so little to their children directly, and talked so much indirectly about it, that it was no wonder Rose felt as she did at so young an age. Her father called the sunshine of Italy the "smile of God," and her mother looking over their hills one day said, "How much God has done for man and how much God has done for this lovely land," and Rose could, in her child's way, understand what they meant. But as she saw the joy that they saw, so she felt in her child's heart the sadness too. She had already grasped a little of the truth that where there is beauty and peace on earth, there is also the "herald of the other country — the dark one."

At San Spirito she had seen the burial of a child. Over the coffin lay a white satin pall ; the priest was robed in white and

49

gold and the altar was bright with candles.　Two boys carried long candles in carved sockets.　The organ pealed and everything wore a joyous air.　For years when Rose heard death mentioned, or saw its black pageantry, she remembered this triumphant little burial with its music as if "the angels were welcoming the young child to Paradise."　It drew her gradually to the Catholic ideal as the great paintings and the mighty ceremonies at Saint Peter's had not.

She had often heard her parents discussing the Catholic Church, and she had somehow got the idea that perhaps it was Catholicism that caused the shadows in this happy land.　Her parents felt this faith of Italy should be more perfect than it was and they sought a reason.　Once when they were watching monks in procession at Santo Spirito, Mrs. Hawthorne said indignantly, as if someone was arguing with her, "But this beauty and art are dubious.　God's Providence makes us fear what looks so fair.　And any way only angels are fit to live as monks pretend to."

She had intended talking it over with her friend Mrs. Ward, who had been lately received into the Church at Rome, but she did not.　Had she done so, and made the same remark, Mrs. Ward might have pointed out to her that in those three sentences, Mrs. Hawthorne had managed to crowd three of the greatest errors professed against the Church by those who do not know her.　The truth was that neither Sophia nor her husband liked to admit what a deep hold Italy had upon them ; and if Italy, then, of course, too, the faith of Italy.　They both felt the true weight of Catholicism.　They guessed its true value.　But they were Puritans, from Concord, and that weight, too, was heavy in their minds.

Stella had come with them to Montaulto.　She and Mrs. Browning were together deep admirers of the snowy curtains that hung against the gray walls, and the comfort of a place that did not look at all comfortable.　Stella loved to take care of Rose.　She fed her melon seeds and while the child munched them, she would stare fascinatedly at the dark skin, brown like

50

an autumn leaf, of her companion.   Her own, despite the sun of Italy, remained white.

Stella slept with Rose in a big room, and the latter would, on awakening, often see her on her knees before a big black crucifix. To Rose it seemed quite crazy to pray so much and with no one at all watching.

On the household staff was a very young maid who also used to be found in front of the crucifix, but only when Stella had driven her there.   Rose teased her to get up and run off before Stella came back, but when Stella discovered this, she did not scold the abashed Rose.   Instead she brought the little heathen a wax Bambino, fast asleep, with flowers around him, over him a convex glass for protection.   Rose loved it and put it carefully on her dresser, where it seemed to her the small face was forgiving her for laughing at Stella's praying and for teasing Anna to stop hers.   And the thought came to her that Christ loves us even when He is sleeping.

She remembered that thought because it was on that same day that her father had come in from a walk and said to her mother at luncheon, "I have seen today an old ugly picture of Christ sinking beneath the weight of His cross, and a sense of the fearful wrong mankind did, and does, its Redeemer came into my heart.   It seems to me a pity Protestantism has so entirely laid aside this mode of appealing to religious sentiment."

5

In October, with many regrets, they left Montaulto and started back to Rome, taking the train as far as Siena, a brief three hours' trip. The Storys called on them at their hotel, drove them about the city, and found for them an apartment, for they had suddenly decided to stay for a few days. They wanted to make it a month when they found the city so full of priceless treasure. It was here that Mrs. Hawthorne found the one picture for which she said she could forget all she had seen before. It was the Sodoma fresco of Christ bound to a pillar. She brought the children to see it.

"Look how there is love in His eyes past torture and time," she told them. "He is so often represented as merely beautiful, without force and manliness. But here He is beautiful, yes, but princely and strong as He really was."

When on Sunday they went to the Cathedral, the music held them all enthralled. Even the busy Rose was silent. As the rising harmonies went soaring and swelling, Rose kept asking, "What does it say, Mama?" And Mrs. Hawthorne bent over the little questioner. "It praises the Lord, darling," she whispered. They stayed until everyone had gone and, when they, too, came out, they felt the silence of the great empty space had been as wonderful as the music when it was crowded with worshippers.

"Oh, I love a cathedral," said Mrs. Hawthorne, her arm on her husband's. "It sings, even when there is no sound ; and it prays, too, with pointed arches for folded hands."

On the thirteenth day of their stay they tore themselves away from Siena. They said farewell to the Storys and continued their journey. This time, as on the trip to Florence, they went by carriage ; their *vetturino* was a tall, gorgeous person named by Hawthorne the moment he saw him, the Emperor. This time they had in addition a postillion who could crack his whip so that it sounded like popping muskets.

On top of the carriage was an extra large receptacle for bags and *piccola-roba,* and back of that was a suspended tray for a possible dog, which commodity was supplied by the Emperor whose terrier lay snugly bedded there. The *vetturino,* as on the other trip, was to find for them apartments all along the way and order the meals. This was a more elegant one, however, than Gaetano had been and much better informed. He was not only coachman, but major domo and steward, and they had nothing to do but enjoy themselves.

The steep way made it necessary to use as many as seven horses for part of the journey. At Buonovento, their first stop, they were told it was the place where Henry the Seventh was supposedly poisoned by the Host given him by a monk.

Back in the carriage again Mrs. Hawthorne sniffed. She thought her family, and especially the Emperor, had been impressed by the story. "Since the Host is believed to be the Body of Christ — the real Body — to poison the Body of Christ for the purpose of poisoning the body of a man — why it is too monstrous a thing to be believed." And she raised her voice so that the Emperor would surely hear her.

By the time an old man came up with a tray of medals, she had recovered sufficiently to buy some. With true Concord aplomb, she invested in two — one of the Pope and one of Venus. But it was the former which held her attention. "It is a perfect likeness of his sweet benign face," she said.

The towns along the way were too dirty to suit the fastidious

Hawthornes. Some of them Mrs. Hawthorne despaired of ever seeing washed, and once she wished that all the water they saw pouring off the precipice could be poured through the streets so that they might at least wash themselves, since the inhabitants wouldn't. At Bolsena both eyes and noses revolted, but at Viterbo it was much better, so much so that they all took to sketching at the Palace a great vase in the courtyard. Rose drew it too, and Julian gave the Emperor a pencil and a pad, and he tried his hand, very solemnly, his face dark against the sunset, his dog dashing around him. They all became so absorbed that they nearly forgot to hurry to their hotel out of this dangerous malarial twilight.

The Emperor was very good to the children and gave Ada and Mrs. Hawthorne contented time to themselves. He would wrap Rose in shawls and then put his own cloak behind her and Julian so that they could lean comfortably. Then with odd noises to his horses, he went clattering down the valleys and up the hills of Italy. When they walked the hills to ease the horses, Rose, of her own insistence, walked beside him, though her weight would not have strained a pony, and they trudged along, her small white hand in his great brown paw, she staring up at him adoringly. When once during the trip she gave him a beautiful present of two grapes in a cup made of a chestnut shell, he seemed more appreciative of this offering than even of the prized cigars which Mr. Hawthorne presented to him.

On the second of October they saw the Dome rising before them. The Emperor took off his cap and turned round with a deep smile of joy on his face. "Rome," he said. And Julian gave a shout. "Look how the horses know they are going to Rome."

Hawthorne smiled and looked quizzically at his wife. "I must own I have a comfortable feeling as if after my wandering I were drawing near home. Now that I have known it, Rome certainly draws my heart as not London or little Concord or Salem ever did or will."

Into the Porto del Populo they swept and on to the new apartment in the Piazza Poli which Mrs. Thompson had found for them. But they parted sadly from the Emperor. The rest managed to control their emotions, but Rose wept openly and the Emperor shook the tears out of his own eyes as he went away.

The new apartment was very fine. It even had a stair carpet, a most unusual comfort for Rome. But everything seemed narrow after the vast spaces of Montaulto Villa.

"Oh, well," comforted Hawthorne as they tried to adjust themselves, "it will put us in training for the snugness of our Concord cottage."

Now Rose went to sleep again with a fountain — the Fountain of Triev, splashing her a soft lullaby. The Carnival came again. The sky was blue over them all day. Friends came and went and the Hawthornes were very busy. In the evenings they usually played cards together. Everyone was well and happy. Hawthorne himself, though past his fifty-fourth birthday, looked much younger and he rejoiced in the well-being of his family.

Ada was relieved to know that the Brownings would not return for some time. It was not that she did not still think them wonderful and Mrs. Browning especially so, but during the stay at Montaulto Mrs. Browning, who was then dipping deep into the awesome pleasures of spiritualism, had found Ada to be a marvelous "writing medium," and used to come over to have her perform, or send for her to come to Casa Guidi.

Ada remained a sceptic about it all. She got nothing out of the séances except a bad headache and the knowledge that Mr. Browning, watching them in action, disliked it as much as she did, though she never dared tell him so. The messages would roll out from her helpless hands with Mrs. Browning hovering to see what was being written, and Mr. Browning glowering at them both, no doubt planning destructive verse to appeal to her higher mind. It was a great relief to Ada then to be back here in Rome with no automatic writing to do for at least a while.

Then suddenly, in all this peaceful time, a blow fell that proved almost a fatal one. Ada and Una, forgetful that though the evenings were so warm and pleasant they were yet malaria laden,

55

stayed too long outdoors, and Una was taken ill with the dreaded fever. Plentiful dosing of quinine did not halt it.

The household went on outwardly as usual. Mrs. Hawthorne nursed her daughter with no other help. For thirty days and nights she never once went to bed, sleeping at odd moments in a chair while Ada held watch. Carriages kept drifting up to make inquiries about the invalid. Mrs. de Vere came and Mrs. Story and General Pierce. The American Minister called often. Mrs. Browning, back in Rome, who scarcely ever went anywhere, came herself, and it was her voice, low and sad as if with fear, that frightened Rose about her sister. Most of them came laden with gifts for the invalid.

"Whose broth is this ?" asked the exasperated doctor.

"Mrs. Browning brought it."

"Tell her to write her poetry and not meddle with my orders."

"Whose jelly is this ?"

"Mrs. Story's."

"I wish Mrs. Story would help her husband with his statues and not try to feed Miss Una."

On the night when the parents knew the crisis was at hand, the family gathered to play cards as usual. But Julian was restless, and even Rose's young eyes saw something very wrong with her father. His hand kept making nervous motions until suddenly he got up abruptly. "We play no more," he said, a break in his voice. From the beginning of the illness he had felt that Una would not recover.

Mrs. Hawthorne came down to the room to tell them good night. Upstairs the doctor had just said as he stood by the door with her, "I've done all I can. If she survives, it will be your doing."

She took Rose to her own room to put her to bed. Rose stared up at her solemnly after she was tucked in. "Is Una going to die ?"

Her mother looked at her. A few minutes ago at Una's door she had felt a sudden rebellion at what she feared was going to happen. "I cannot bear it," she said to herself. It was her first rebellion against her faith and reliance in God. "I cannot bear it," and the worst of her suffering was for her husband, knowing what this loss would mean to him.

Suddenly as she looked at Rose, she felt some change in herself. Her heart that had been beating in fear, was quiet, and she smiled an unworried quiet smile at the child. "Just go to sleep and don't worry." Back in the sickroom she felt in herself a sense of surprise in her at this strange remark. Then the hot unhappy rage left her as quickly as it had come. She found herself saying strange words. "If God in His goodness takes her I can give her to Him. I will not fight Him any more."

She went over to the sick bed and found that Una's pulse was slow and regular, her forehead moist, her sleep natural. And she went back downstairs again where Hawthorne had dropped into his chair, the tumbled cards still on the table before him, broken with fear at the dreaded loss of this, his eldest, his dearest child. She touched his hand gently.

"She will live," she said.

This near tragedy determined in Hawthorne's mind what he had been thinking about a great deal during the last few months : that he ought to take his family home again. There is no doubt that had he been the only one to be considered, he would have spent some more years in Italy, but he was very anxious that his daughters should grow up in their own country and that Julian should have an American education. If they stayed too long in Italy, the children might lose their native characteristics and become those saddest of mortals — people who feel themselves exiles from the land of their birth. The years, he felt, had a kind of emptiness when too many of them were spent on a foreign shore.

And he grew lonely sometimes for his own land, and he realized that he would do little writing in this climate. Perhaps an English fog or a New England east wind would get him to work. He needed to get away from Rome to clarify his ideas. He had come up for the first time against disturbing things here ; for one thing, the mighty fact of the Catholic Church. The artist loved her beauty, the New England Puritan hated her rigidity, her force. But he had changed his ideas about many things during the past two years, his attitude being amusingly shown by the fact that he no longer objected to nude sculpture so strongly since he had found out that the Venus of Medici had a dimple in her chin.

They left Rome at the end of May. On the last day Hawthorne walked with Rose to their favorite Pincian Hill for a farewell to Saint Peter's. There it lay, the city about it, with Soracte on the horizon. They both said a long solemn goodbye to their favorite Sunday strolling place, and went back mournfully to Mrs. Hawthorne and the trunks.

"Somehow," he said to his wife, "I feel I know this city better than my birthplace and have known it longer. In fact I might," he hesitated a moment, then went on, "I might fairly own I have a love for it."

Before they reached London, Hawthorne had changed his mind again. He would not go home immediately. Perhaps another few months in England would give him a better chance to finish the book he was engaged on than if he went straight back to the old familiar life. So he found them a place on the seashore, a little town named Redcar, where work on the *Marble Faun* went forward rapidly.

Rose did not care much for the lodgings they took because her father stayed in them all the time and worked so hard he had no time for her. She wanted him out with her on the great sands, watching the long waves, but it was rarely that he stirred out. The rest of the family spent hours hunting for shells for Julian's collection, or for seaweed, or simply sat resting and listening to their mother read aloud. To Rose then and later shells meant happy quiet hours close to her mother, while near them lay Una, regaining her lost strength in this healing air, and Julian sat shading his eyes while their mother read *Oliver Twist* and *Romany Rye* and *Lives of the Last Four Popes,* surely mixed reading. There were the papers, too, where Mrs. Hawthorne always looked anxiously at the foreign news for reports of Pio Nono's illness.

When Rose grew weary of listening to *Oliver Twist* or the

Popes, or finding new sorts of seaweed for Julian's extensive col-lection, there was always Hannah ready to play with her. Han-nah was a young native of the town and Rose was very fond of her though she detested her expremely plain name. The one game they played continually was grocer's shop, for which pebbles and sand and old newspapers served as instruments.

When her father, taking one of his infrequent walks, strayed along, he stopped to watch the game. He said nothing, but it was made quite clear to Rose that he thought it a pretty silly foot-less thing and a frittering waste of time, and for that day at least she said farewell to Hannah, and as she put it later, "devoted her-self to loftier thoughts than those of the counter" for the rest of the day.

When Hawthorne grew restless at Redcar, they went on to Leamington to stay, and there the *Marble Faun* was at last fin-ished. He wanted to wait until it was published before setting out for home, so that he might know what the reception would be of this work which held the stored-up impressions of fourteen months in Rome. But he was in haste now, for the weather had been cold and got foggy, and it was as dark in the morning as in the evening. He began to talk with much longing about the "serenity of a New England winter."

All that Rose remembered of this Leamington interval was that one day they all went to Warwick, and there was a market where little pigs were sold and the town square held an odd mu-seum which contained as its chief treasure a bit of the red beard of Edward the Fourth. And she could recall walking with Jul-ian through lanes of hawthorn. Her mother, coming to the door to meet them, thought it a picture worthy of any painter — the bright hair, the rosy little face smiling through the masses of pink blossoms she had gathered.

The reception with which the *Marble Faun* met was a very mixed one. So far Hawthorne had not had among criticisms of his work that of having readers not understand what he was trying to say. But with this book some who read it felt it meant one thing, some another. Henry Bright wrote that though he did not understand it, there were some "bits of Catholicism and love and sin that were marvellously thought out and gloriously written."

The *Saturday Review* mentioned with some disapproval the way in which he had apparently been moved by Catholicism and added, "It is the priests and the Papal government that seem to have scared Mr. Hawthorne from the Romish church." There was one bitter reference to his "conscienceless Catholicism."

But John Motley wrote that he had "clothed with an air of unreality familiar scenes without making them less familiar. If the tone of my letter is one of undue exhilaration, I can only say that you gave me the wine." Such a sentence made up to the author for many of the criticisms of people who claimed he was merely vague and unreal.

Perhaps the most discerning remark of all was made many years later by Moncure Conway. "Hawthorne," he said, "summoned into life the hard cruel Puritanism of persecution just long enough to unburden its soul and make its confession."

In June they set out for Liverpool, where it was very necessary that they spend a night. They could never go back home without eating a meal with Mrs. Blodgett, who welcomed them in her usual shining black dress and snowy cap, but professed herself utterly unable to believe that this great girl was really her baby Rose.

On embarking for Boston, they found that, though the ship was different, the same black-haired Captain Leitch who had years ago commanded the *Niagara,* was in charge here. This time the trip was stormier, but the Hawthornes were more used to travel now and bore it better, though Rose and her mother made fewer appearances than the others on board or in the dining-room. This set the others, when the laggards did appear, to devising for them remedies for seasickness.

"A few rocs' eggs beaten up by a mermaid on a dolphin's back," suggested Julian.

"Or a dose of salts distilled from Niobe's tears," his father contributed. "We might suggest some menus for not getting sick

60

at all. I think potted owl with Minerva sauce would be very nice."

"Chicken pies made of fowls raised by Mother Carey," said Julian.

"I'll have purple grapes raised by Bacchus," put in Una.

Mrs. Hawthorne raised a head that still ached. "And if we are cold, which I am, we could wear sable clouds with a silver lining."

"You might, my dear, perhaps be warmer in a good shirt made by Nessus and Company," said her husband.

A stray passenger, who had paused to join in the talk, walked on wondering what odd folk these were, but the Hawthornes were too busy laughing to have noticed him.

6

June lay warm over Concord when the Hawthornes came home again. Benjie, Uncle Horace Mann's youngest, had come to the station to meet them. The Hawthorne children were amazed at his accent and his strange use of the word "guess." They drove in the station wagon past the little white houses with their white blinds, past the little red houses, past Mr. Emerson's stately home with the rocking horse still on the lawn, and finally came to their own little buff brown house.

The first thing which Hawthorne noted was that the trees he had sent over from England to be planted on the hill in place of the Alcott apple trees, were flourishing. The first thing Mrs. Hawthorne noted was the excellent order of the inside of the house. The Horace Manns had lived there for part of the time and kept it in fine condition. The greatest change that the village found in the Hawthornes was the sizes of the children — and Mr. Hawthorne's Italian mustache.

First of all now came the matter of the children's education. Julian of course would go to Mr. Sanborn's school, where most of the boys of Concord got their secondary education. Mr. Sanford's position was much changed now. He could talk openly since the war was becoming a certainty, but there had been a time a few years back when the United States senate had wanted to try him for treason for his espousal of the cause of John Brown, and

62

when he lay hidden a night in the Wayside before he fled to Canada. He had incorporated in his school many of Alcott's ideas : there was plenty of play mixed with the work.

Up to this time none of the children had been at any school, for Hawthorne and his wife and Miss Shepard had all taught them. Julian was found to be ahead of his work for his age. His father was a wise and patient teacher and Julian said of him later, "If all instructors were like him, the world would soon be wise."

Una, still delicate from her illness and from the great amount of quinine she had been given, stayed at home studying music and taking lessons in art. She had a Sunday School class too, to whom she gave little books of verse if they learned their Scripture lessons well. Rose was still considered too young for any school, but all the young Hawthornes mixed socially in the life of the town — school picnics, dances, teas. Concord in 1860 was a very pleasant place to be young in.

Mrs. Hawthorne thought that the town was very irreligious, whatever its social capabilities. "The way Concordians observe a fast," she said on their first Good Friday at home, "is by loafing about the streets, dawdling up and down, or driving around. No one seems to mourn his or his country's sins. Such behaviour must disturb our Puritan fathers even on the other side of the Jordan."

Ellery Channing's new book, *Conversations in Rome,* she found very interesting, for it dealt with dialogues between a Catholic and a Unitarian. Channing was the Catholic ; though he was not in the Church, he had come very close to it, but even his arguments to himself evidently did not quite persuade him. What bothered Concord was that while in Rome he had learned to mutter prayers in a foreign fashion instead of standing up and addressing God clearly and distinctly.

She as well as her husband were content to be in Concord again. It was not like the English society, but it had a sturdy intelligence, an outspoken forcefulness, a simplicity that was invigorating. It was pleasant to be back buying groceries at Walcott and Holden's and to go to Jonas Hastings' dark little shop to order shoes or have them repaired.   And there was Mr. Stacy's general store where they bought anything and everything, and since he was the postmaster his store at certain hours of the day became a general club for the whole town.

Dr. Bartlett was fine for small aches and Mr. Sanborn was an excellent teacher.   On the platform of Town Hall stood many well known men who came to lecture, and there were many right in the town who could lecture as well (and often did) as the outlanders could.

Hawthorne fell back quickly into his rôle as a citizen of Concord.   In an old coat and a pair of shoes made by Mr. Jonas, he would wander over the town and its environs, sometimes as far as Walden Pond or out the road that led past the Manse and the bridge where the Minute Men began to fire, or up the twisting street toward Sleepy Hollow Cemetery.   He was busy, too, with his fruit trees and his beans and corn, as befitted a true householder.   And he walked daily the path on the hill that went from Mr. Alcott's log fence to Mr. Bull's wooden pickets.

As at Casa Bello it took time for Rose to adapt herself to the town.   She had after all been very young when they went away, so young that she scarcely could remember Concord at all.   When the wagon brought them from the station, she had been impressed with the very un-Englishness of the landscape.   To her it looked ugly and she hated the funny little cottage they were to live in.   In England they did not have sand in the flower beds, and the one servant here was nothing like the remembered Italian and English ones.

Of course she was a very much traveled child for nine years old, much more so than the children around her ; she had been in England, Italy, Portugal, France, had seen the old world culture, the old world faith.   This little village was not like anything she had seen there and grown accustomed to.   Even the spiders were not like the Italian ones.   When one day she found a huge specimen on the path she felt happy even though she shrank from it, it was so like the terrible ones at Montaulto.   She called Una to see it,

64

but the spider had bustled off. She was disgusted. "At Montaulto they really swaggered," she said to Una, "and they didn't ever get out of your way like this scary American one."

Sometimes she felt a definite homesickness for the little green lizards in the Forum; she had been better than any of the rest at discovering them. She used to go to Mr. Longfellow's house just for his orange tree in the window. She could smell all Italy when she walked by it. She wrote a letter to Hannah of Redcar. "Happy are you," ran her threnody, "who keep warm all the time in England. The frost has made thick leaves on our windows everywhere. I went outdoors to have a good time — a very good time indeed, for there was nothing but frozen ground."

Aunt Ebie, her father's sister, was a trial too. Rose came in the house one day to find her ensconced in the library knitting blue socks for the soldiers. After greetings of a very formal character, she offered to teach Rose to knit. Rose was too much in awe of her to dare refuse, so she sat down in a small chair with alarming needles spiking her in unexpected places as she got more and more involved in this unpleasant undertaking. When some one years later complimented her on her beautiful knitting, she said she had learned it under difficulties, "rounding Hatteras in a swirl of contradictory impressions."

She stole a look at Aunt Ebie now and then, sitting there so upright in her stiff mohair. Rose felt she could have borne it all better if only she had been in soft silk with a fan before her lips. Later outdoors she found her an excellent companion. Aunt Ebie loved ferns and mosses as some people love souls, and Rose's grown-up comment on her was that she "chose the least dangerous objects of affection," but even then Rose preferred the souls her father loved and would try to save if he could, to a "whole forest of vines" of her Aunt Ebie's delight. Rose's other Aunt Elizabeth, her mother's sister, was of quite a different stamp. She much preferred children to vines, and was busy helping Alcott with his educational experiments.

Finally, in her boredom, Rose, who had been watching how this business of writing kept her father absorbed, thought it would

65

relieve the weary days if she, too, were to write some stories out of her own head. Feeling that such a lofty ambition should make her an object of interest to the young people of Concord, most of whose fathers were writing too, she confided her idea to Abby Alcott. "I have one almost done," she announced, proudly ; "and then I shall do another one, and another, and send them to Boston to Mr. Field."

Unfortunately her father happened to be sitting at his study window directly over their heads and heard this dramatic announcement. When the visitor, interested in this sight of genius in the making, had departed, he called Rose up to him. His eyes were flashing and he was really angry.

"Rose, let me never hear of your writing stories," he ordered. "Never, never. I forbid you to write them."

But his admonition was vain, for it merely added attraction to this apparently hazardous profession of writing ; it must be a more difficult thing than she had thought to bring scenes and sounds out of your head. Her notebooks were scribbled full for at least a week. Then came an opportunity to go to Boston with her mother to visit the Fields. The social opportunities of the visit made her quite forget that she was to be in the house of her potential publisher.

The house on Charles Street proved an oasis for one who was weary of Concord. The rich plum cake and the sherry which were served in the library as soon as they arrived made her content, and the library itself, a cool green woods of a place, was splendid to write letters in, to tell Hannah and Concord how grown up she was.

Next day Mrs. Fields insisted they all go to church, but on the way home Mr. Fields confidentially told Rose that he had been as bored as he imagined she had been.

"It is very different in Rome," said Rose sedately. "They don't do it so plain. They have pictures, too, and statues, and lovely clothes to wear."

"Well," said Mr. Fields, "that must be very nice. But I really

66

think what bores me most and makes me sleepy in church are the deacons."

But tea time more than made up for church. The Charles River lay silver in the soft gray afternoon beyond the wall of the garden. A few clouds were tipped with the rose of sunset.

Mrs. Hawthorne, with her passion for relics and remembrances of dead writers and artists, was fascinated by the lock of Keats's hair under glass, which Severn himself had given to Mrs. Fields. But Rose preferred living loveliness to dead poets' curls. She stared with all her eyes at Mrs. Fields who had put on a wonderful red velvet gown and a tiara on her beautiful hair. Mr. Fields said she looked like Moses in the burning bush, but Rose thought that a very unfair comparison. She looked like a beautiful queen of some far and fair country.

They talked of Rome, and Mrs. Fields asked if they had ever met the Brownings' little boy over there.

"No," said Mrs. Hawthorne, "he was away at school most of the time, I believe."

Mrs. Fields smiled reminiscently. "Ah, yes. Well, I saw him once looking very bored because, he said, he was so tired of riding in the Pincio. I suggested the Compagna for a change, but he shook his curls at me reproachfully and said, 'I can't, Mrs. Fields ; I have to ride on the Pincio because, you see, I am one of the sights of Rome.' "

As the months went on, Rose, too, sank happily into the life of Concord. How could she help enjoying it ? There were many young people there. Her own family was with her all the time, and when others failed her there was always Louisa Alcott next door, red cheeked and black haired, who could make you laugh even when, as Rose learned later, she did not feel at all like laughing herself. Next door there was the fun of private theatricals and charades and Mrs. Alcott's excellent cookies.

When Rose carried a package over for Louisa's birthday the pleased recipient sent Abby over with a paper on which Louisa

67

had written a verse of thanks, and called it the *Hawthorne Tree*.
Rose learned the last stanza by heart and used to quote it when she
came in sight of her house with its hedge and mulberry tree as she
walked up the highway :

> "Long may it stand, this friendly tree,
> That blooms in autumn and in spring,
> Beneath whose shade the humblest bird
> May safely sit, may grateful sing.
> Time will give it an evergreen name.
> Age cannot harm it, frost cannot kill;
> With Emerson's pine and Thoreau's oak,
> Will the Hawthornes be loved and honored still."

Mrs. Hawthorne thought this a touching tribute, but she shook
her head over Louisa. "If she only knew clothes as she does
verse," she mourned. For that morning she had met Louisa in
the town. "Oh, Mrs. Hawthorne, what a lovely blue bonnet
and what pretty white berries," Louisa had said in admiration.

"And," said the dressy Mrs. Hawthorne, "it was my royal
purple beaded with pearls."

Mrs. Hawthorne insisted that her daughters do a certain
amount of visiting among the poor of the town. Rose's lot was
old Abigail Cook who lived in a particularly airless cottage down
a very dusty lane. Rose would sit in a stiff chair and let the old
woman chatter to her about her ideas of the universe and Concord, and, without showing her feelings, would eat a large piece of
mince pie which Abigail had made out of the apples on her one
tree and a few other ingredients, surmised by Rose to be pepper
and molasses.

Then Abigail read to her a chapter from her very greasy Bible,
sniffing at times with a nose charged with snuff. It would have
been much pleasanter to take food to Abigail or read to her instead,
but that was not what Abigail wanted, and it had early been impressed upon Rose by her mother that courtesy was one of the
greatest of human traits. It was not what you wanted to do for
the sick poor, she told her girls, but what they wanted to do or

have you do, that mattered.   And you must never make them feel there was anything distressing to you in their appearance or actions.

This last was her father's conviction too.   "I remember when I was very young," he told them, "I said one day to a woman who came to our house, 'Take her away.   She is ugly and fat and has a loud voice.'   I was so sorry when I realized that she had meant to be kind to me.   She *was* fat and ugly, but I should not have said it."

Feeling that he could well afford it now, Hawthorne set about enlarging the Wayside, which was much too small for his family, who loved each other, but also were much addicted to privacy. Mr. Weatherbee and Mr. Watts brought their plans for enlarging the house, and their estimate was about five hundred dollars. They set to work, and of course before they finished, the bill was thrice that because Hawthorne kept thinking of more and more improvements.   It took the best part of a year to build, and there was no chance to do much writing with the noise of saw and hammer always about the house.   The children rather liked the racket and were sorry when it was all over, but Hawthorne breathed a sigh of relief when evening fell and his family were quiet about him, while he read Scott's novels aloud, and the latest numbers of the *All the Year Round Journal* conducted by Charles Dickens.

A parlor was added to the house for his wife so that she might keep in it her most beautiful keepsakes.   It had a white marble mantel and a paper of gray and gold.   Over the windows of both rooms Hawthorne put little pointed gables of wood and they graced the windows too.   The dining-room needed no altering ; as Hawthorne had said, "The sunshine comes in warmly the better half of a winter's day."

Upstairs a room was added for Una over the library and a spare chamber over the parlor, each with its quaint gables.   The spare room had a very high ceiling because a tower was built over it.   This last was Hawthorne's pet project, one that had been in

69

his mind ever since he had for a short time owned the tower at Montaulto. High steps led to it from the hall, with a small cupboard built half way up. It had windows on all four sides and deep cupboards. Someone persuaded him to try a tall standing desk, but after some weeks of using it and finding it very uncomfortable, he went back to his own desk. Up in this tower he could shut himself from the tumult of life and be alone with clouds and birds and the sun, or listen to the rain on the tin roof. He spent up here now all the time he did not actually give to his family, or the time when he walked the hill path.

One afternoon, however, he always gave to the Saturday Club in Boston, one of the few social gestures he made with pleasure. He and Emerson and Judge Hoar were the three Concord members, and on the last Saturday of each month they met to dine at two and talk and talk until the Concordmen had to run to make the one train that would get them home that night. Emerson expanded at these meetings and enjoyed them greatly. No one could tell whether Hawthorne did or did not, for he spent most of the time looking shyly down at his plate and said little.

All the other evenings at sunset he walked along his path, the crooked little path he had worn among the ferns and the berry bushes. At the parlor window his younger daughter often watched him, knowing content and security because he was there. In the dim light he seemed to her to be pacing some great amphitheatre, stopping to meditate now and then, perhaps a point of plot, then pacing on again, with strong firm steps. But his mane of hair, his family noticed, was getting whiter every day.

When the Wayside was quite finished, Mrs. Hawthorne, coming home from the village, found herself standing in front of it, beautifully painted now, a pleasant home, a haven, and she knew a feeling of uneasiness as there flashed into her mind an old proverb : "When the House is built, Death enters it." She shook away the morbid thought.

7

In 1862 Hawthorne went to Washington to meet President Lincoln. The papers recorded that he had been received "with special graciousness," and his family was very proud of him. Mrs. Hawthorne wrote him while he was away to be sure to give Mr. Lincoln her love and blessing, "if you find you like him. Tell him I like his message and I think a man shows strength when he can be moderate at such a time." Later in the letter prudence overtook her. "Perhaps you had better give him my regards instead, my highest anyway."

Hawthorne wrote an article about his visit for the *Atlantic Monthly* called "Chiefly about War Matters," to which some objected because they felt he had handled only the lighter instead of the heavier aspects of the strife. Back home again he said to Emerson, "It is regrettable that I am too old to shoulder a musket and a joyful thing that Julian is too young."

But Emerson was feeling far from friendly when he saw the *Atlantic* article and found that Hawthorne had attacked him for his speech on John Brown, about whom, when under sentence of death, he had said, "He is the new saint waiting his martyrdom who if he shall suffer will make the gallows glorious like the cross." The *Atlantic* itself was a bit uneasy about the article and put in many foot-notes of disagreement. "We are compelled," the editors wrote, "to omit two or three pages. The sketch lacks reverence and it pains us to see a gentleman of ripe age falling into the characteristic and most ominous fault of Young America."

"It is odd," Hawthorne had written, "when one measures our advance from barbarism and we find ourselves here." The *Atlantic* had put an indignant note here : "We have heard of twenty Quakers in a single company of a Pennsylvania regiment."

Hawthorne was very busy with the *Dolliver Romance* now. It was being published as a serial while he was writing it, but he found time to pen words of passionate conviction about the War now raging. "Had I my way," he wrote, "I should let no man under fifty years of age go to war, such men having already had their share of natural pleasure and enjoyment. I would add a premium in favor of recruits of threescore and upwards, as with one foot in the grave, they would not be so likely to run away."

Concord was a different place now. The War had changed so many things, made men critical of each other's opinion instead of listening with the old pleasant tolerance. It gave no chance for quiet and thoughtful talk of the sort they used to have when they met to discuss philosophy and art. Hawthorne's sympathies pulled him one way and his party the other. "It may be a wise idea to fight, but we should afterwards be prepared to prepare our black citizens for future citizenship," he said to Mr. Sanborn when he came for Christmas dinner with them, very zealous to free the Negro and having not given much thought to what would happen afterwards.

That year Thoreau died. Emerson spoke at the funeral and Alcott read in his deep beautiful voice from Thoreau's writings. The coffin was completely covered with wild flowers. Hawthorne had lost his best friend in Concord. He grieved deeply, and for some time found it almost impossible to work on the new novel. He would stand looking down the Lexington road toward Walden Pond, always a spot of beauty but dearer than ever to him now that its guardian spirit was gone. It was not altogether that he missed his conversation, delightful though that had always been ; he missed even more the delight in silence which they had shared.

Sometimes on hot June days the air was hazy, and they wondered if perhaps it might be the smoke of distant battles. When on Sundays Una insisted on going to church, the rest sat on the hilltop and read books about peace. Once Rose was allowed to give a short talk from the verse on the Sermon on the Mount about peace.

Louisa Alcott ran in on the Hawthornes early one morning in wild excitement. "I have been accepted to go to help with the soldiers at the Washington Hospital. Tell me what shall I take to read to them ? What would they like best in their wounded condition ?"

"Dickens," said Mrs. Hawthorne promptly. "He is always the story-teller. And he is grave and gay by turns."

They all agreed that Dickens would be best, but Julian and Rose voted for games, too, and ran to get some from their store. Una went home with Louisa to help her mark her clothes with indelible ink, and at noon Rose went over with some blancmange sent by Mrs. Hawthorne for busy Mrs. Alcott to use for dinner, since she would have no time to make anything. She found herself caught up in the excitement.

"I want to be a nurse too," she said, throwing away in a second the intention of being a great writer like her father or a wonderful beauty like Mrs. Fields.

Louisa paused with David Copperfield in her hand ready to tuck it in the little round topped trunk. "Oh, child, I hope this terrible War will be over long before you are old enough to be a nurse." Then seeing the disappointment in the little face, she added, "But we need nurses in peace time too, darling. Perhaps some day you can be a peace-time nurse."

But after six weeks at the front Louisa came home. Rather, her father, hearing she was ill, for once forgot his arbors and his educational theories and went straight to the hospital to get her. Only the week before she had written the relatives in Concord,

"Till noon I trot, washing faces, dusting, sewing bandages, rushing after pillows, sponges, brooms, till I would joyfully pay all I possess for fifteen minutes of rest."

"Then she isn't finding time to read them Dickens," said Julian sadly.

"Oh, well," said Mrs. Hawthorne, "she can give them affection and that is more than books. Don't you remember the day she came by here and called in to us, 'I love everybody in the world'?"

And now here she was sick, their bright smiling Louisa. She would say little of her experiences. Only once she said to Hawthorne, "I know now what war is. It doesn't bear talking about."

One day when troops came marching past the Lexington road, the young Hawthornes helped Louisa and her mother to give cake and lemonade and cookies to the tired dusty boys halting at their gate. The soldiers cheered them lustily. Then someone heard a faint sound behind them. Louisa was weeping bitterly. She tried to regain her composure, but toppled over in a faint.

When the second fall of their stay in Concord came, Hawthorne was persuaded to take a short trip to the seashore with Julian, and Rose and her mother promised to see that Una did plenty of resting and they did plenty of weeding in the garden which by early September had fallen into a deplorable state. The trouble was that the Hawthornes weeded very hard on one day and not at all on many. As a result the melon and cucumber vines were utterly invisible, and it was only by faith or deep delving among the mammoth weeds that they could find them. Even the beans were lost to view, and as for the corn, when by intensive search they found forty whole ears, they took them over in triumph to the Alcotts who were at tea. Of course to the Alcotts tea did not mean tea. It meant apples or some other fruit, and on this occasion it was new spruce beer. But Mr. Alcott received the corn with honest thanks ; according to his dietary creed, anything that grew above the ground was edible, as were not those wretched vegetables beneath the earth with no direct benefit of sunlight.

The morning after Hawthorne had gone, and Julian with him,

74

they promised themselves they would surely weed, and then Mr. Bull came from next door with a new kind of grape he felt sure was going to be very successful and would make his fortune. He also brought over a bouquet of roses in which they counted at least ten colors. And that afternoon the Emersons gave a party out under the trees, with marvelous food and a parrot swinging from her cage in a tree scolding at them. "Mrs. Emerson," wrote Mrs. Hawthorne to her husband, "looked like a lady abbess in her black silk with a white winged head dress."

But that evening Rose and Mrs. Hawthorne weeded conscientiously, talking about the rest Papa was having with sea breezes instead of this hot Concord air. Una, who was not permitted such strenuous work, went off to get the mail and then sat down near them. Rose wheeled away barrel loads of the giant weeds and shouted when some long lost vine or plant appeared. But finally she carelessly cut her thumb on a sickle, so they adjourned to the seat under the tree, and Mrs. Hawthorne read them the story of the *Miraculous Pitcher,* and Una sat straight up blissfully aware that had her father been there he would have made her lie down.

"I think it the loveliest story of hospitality I ever read," said Mrs. Hawthorne, closing the volume as she heard steps on the path. Two ladies were tripping over from the Alcotts', Mrs. Emerson and Mrs. Hawthorne's sister, Elizabeth Peabody.

They all sat chattering and it was obvious that the guests were waiting for something, but Mrs. Hawthorne talked blithely on, hoping after a while they would tell her what they had come to tell her. Finally at about seven o'clock Elizabeth asked abruptly, "Why don't you have tea ?"

"But my dear Elizabeth," cried Mrs. Hawthorne in dismay, "we had tea hours ago. Oh, I am so sorry," and she and Rose bustled about and managed a poor meal of bread and butter and cheese. Their hostess shook her head at the meagre array. "And here I have just been reading the *Miraculous Pitcher* to the children. There was a much better hostess than I am."

When they had gone, Rose and her mother took a walk up the

hill along the little winding path where half way up there was still clinging to its tree an arbor that Bronson Alcott had built for his girls. "A sentimental journey," Mrs. Hawthorne said, but she sighed as she spoke. She was glad there were few evenings like this when looking up from a window she saw no tall figure pacing there.

The letter that Rose brought in next morning's mail made them all laugh. It was written by Hawthorne to his Onion — dreadful nickname for so lovely a creature as Una. He and Julian were having a splendid time. There were no comforts whatever in the small lodging house, but the view was so good no one minded. And there were great art and literature about the place too. "We have found and are deep in *Pearls of Grace drawn from the Depths of Divine Love* and there is a life of Christ with portrait !"

When they came home again he seemed a little better. By dint of locking himself in the library and pulling down the blinds, he managed to keep his writing going, but it was obvious that his health was suffering more and more. Rose coming in one day to show him a new party frock, was startled by the shadows in his face. He smiled at his big girl in the white muslin frock with short ruffled sleeves and blue sash and tweaked one of the shoulder bows. "You look all pearl and rose," he told her gaily. But Rose went from the room troubled at heart.

He would allow them to take but little care of him ; in fact he worried more about his wife when she had a cough or about Una's occasional illnesses than about his own. But his family grew more and more worried. "The splendor and pride of strength in him have succumbed," wrote Mrs. Hawthorne, "but they can be restored I am sure." Yet in her heart she was not so sure. "Of course he is very delicate and nervous and must be handled like the airiest Venetian glass."

As the War dragged its weary way through the nation's length and sapped its strength, so Hawthorne's energy seemed slowly to ebb. He had been happy and well when he came home from Europe. Four years later he was dead. And all those years had held troubles, personal as well as national. He found he had much less money than he had thought he would have. Julian, now at Harvard, was an added expense. He had spent more than he intended on the Wayside. Remembering English perfection, he had wanted his home like that, and it had cost money. Besides he had loaned a large sum of money to a friend, not a cent of which had been returned.

Making up his mind about the War had been very hard, too. As far back as 1857 he had declared, "If we must choose I would go for the North. But we are no country really, not in the sense in which the Englishman has a country. And I have no leaning towards the Abolitionists." But when the South fired on Fort Sumter, Hawthorne like other Democrats came out for the North and for Union. In 1862 when Franklin Pierce paid him a visit in Concord and they talked about the War, Pierce saw only ruin if there were not union. But Hawthorne thought they should fight only for the Northern slave States and let the South go its way.

The dedication to *Our Old Home* had caused trouble too. Realizing that the book would never have been written had it not been for his Liverpool appointment, he felt it a small thanks for what had been given him, to dedicate it to Franklin Pierce. Even his publishers were worried and wanted him to dedicate it to someone else, some one more in favor in the North. But, "The public," he wrote, "must accept my book as I think fit to give it or let it alone." So the page stood. But Emerson cut out that page with his penknife before he read his copy.

To General Pierce himself Hawthorne made his position clear. "I am willing to agree with you in supporting the Compromise of 1850. But on the other hand my feelings — all my feelings and my sentiments are with the Negro. I feel most kindly towards those poor fugitives and I wouldn't put them back. But I am almost as reluctant to urge them forward."

General Pierce was always wanting to discuss the economic results of the loss of the South. But Hawthorne shook away such argument. "Whoever is benefited by the results of this War, it will not be the present generation of Negroes who must battle with the world on very unequal terms."

In the winter of 1864 Mrs. Hawthorne stood looking one day at the trees outside the window heavy with ice and snow, and at the white hill back of the house. The path was empty and suddenly it seemed to her that it would always be so — that spring would find it empty too. And that same day Julian, home from college for the week-end, was reading aloud to his father from Longfellow's *Evangeline*. He came to the scene where the woman's weary search is at last ended beside the little hospital bed.

"Thousands of toiling hands [he read] where theirs have ceased from
        their labors
Thousands of tired feet where theirs have completed their journey."

Suddenly he felt something dreadful in the air, and it required all his strength to finish reading to the end. He glanced up to see his father looking at him with the blue eyes that now were sunk deep in the cavern of his face, smiling reassuringly.

That evening he and his mother concocted a little plot with Mr. Ticknor's help. The latter had for some time been anxious to have Hawthorne take a short trip with him, going to Boston en route, and stopping to have Dr. Holmes give him a good examination, although Hawthorne was not told that part of the plan. They knew that, though he had refused to see a doctor, he would feel differently about an old friend.

He smiled sadly at Mr. Fields, when they stopped off to visit him, who with difficulty concealed his concern over his friend's altered looks, and said, "Why does nature treat us like little children ? I think we could bear it if we knew our fate."

Dr. Holmes, coming to his hotel, was startled too at the change in him and could offer very little help and very little hope either. He could scarcely believe that the shrunken figure was Hawthorne's and that the feeble step was his firm tread. Hawthorne could tell him little of his symptoms, a "boring pain" and "great weariness," but his appearance spoke for itself and the way he

78

talked with a calm detachment.   He said later that Hawthorne looked like a man who did not care to live any longer, but who was putting up a brave fight because of those who wanted him to live.   However, he felt a short trip would not do him any harm, so the two men set out for Baltimore.

Next day terrible news came to Concord.   Mr. Ticknor had died suddenly in their hotel room, and the only result of the trip that was taken to help him was that Hawthorne came home with nerves more shattered than when he had gone.   Even Una's caresses and Rose's smiles could not move him now as he sat brooding and silent in his study or in the library.   It was Franklin Pierce who, having heard of his illness and come to see him, made what sounded like an excellent proposal.   They would take a short trip through New England together, going only as fast as Hawthorne wished to go and returning whenever he wanted to come home.

Rose stood at the gate to watch them go.   Julian was back at school and Una, having a cold, was watching from the window upstairs.   Mrs. Hawthorne was to go along to the station.   Her husband looked very old and like a "snow image," but he was unbending and erect as ever.   Mrs. Hawthorne walked beside him to the carriage, and for once her calm was broken.   She sobbed as she walked along.

That evening she sat in the little library which she had arranged for him, where everything, books, chairs, papers, spoke of him.   And Rose, coming in to find her, was alarmed by the broken, hopeless look on her face.

With the next day came bitter news.   The two men had stopped for the night at Plymouth, New Hampshire, for Pierce saw that his friend was worse and he intended to send for his wife the next day.   But that night, not being able to sleep because of the howling of a dog in the courtyard below his room, he went about midnight to see if all was well with his friend and found he had ceased to breathe.

He died on the day near the end of the War when the Army of the Potomac was marching from the Rappahannock to the James.

The news sped to Julian, who went at once to tell Professor Gurney that he must leave for home and why. The latter shook his head when he heard it, and said sadly. "Only a few months since Thackeray died, one of the best men of England, and now we have lost the best man in America."

Nathaniel Hawthorne was brought home — it was on Rose's thirteenth birthday — and placed in the Unitarian Church for the burial servies, and many came to look at him for a last time. Mrs. Hawthorne and the girls decorated the whole building with flowers from the Wayside and from the yards of their grieving neighbors. The afternoon of the burial was fair with sunshine. "The one bright day in a week of rain," commented Longfellow to the widow as he came to the church with yet more flowers. In his eyes was remembered sadness, for it was only two years before that his wife had met her tragic death.

The coffin was carried through the blossoming orchards of Concord. All the way from the church the birds sang continually. The banks along the road were blue with violets. The elms were putting out young leaves ; and Holmes said later that as he looked at them, the leaves had that passing aspect Raphael loved to put in the background of his sacred pictures. The sun and air were warm and living. At the gates of Sleepy Hollow Cemetery, as Mrs. Hawthorne was driven up in her carriage, were his friends standing, Longfellow and Whittier and Holmes, Emerson and Channing, Hoar, Agassiz, Lowell, Alcott. Franklin Pierce scattered flowers into the grave and the unfinished *Dolliver Romance*, which Rose had found that morning in the little cupboard on the tower stairs, was laid on his coffin.

Near the Hawthorne plot was the grave where lay five-year-old Waldo Emerson, "the hyacinthine boy for whom morning well might break and April bloom," and where an earlier Emerson had cut on his stone, "*Quis non me habet fidem, ille quamvis mortuus esset vivet.*" Thoreau, dead these two years, slept not far away.

That evening Longfellow sent one of his daughters with a copy of a piece of verse he had just written for the *Atlantic Monthly.*

Rose took it from her at the door and brought it to her mother. She asked Julian to read it.

When he had finished, she asked him to read the last stanza once more and the boy's lips trembled as he repeated :

> "Ah, who shall lift that wand of magic power
> And the lost clew regain ?
> The unfinished window in Aladdin's tower
> Unfinished must remain."

PART II

1

Despite its bereavement, the household went its accustomed way. Though there was something of the indomitable spirit of Nathaniel Hawthorne in all his children, they might easily have grown, during this time, gloomy and self-centered had it not been for their mother's undaunted courage. A very few days before her husband's death she had written to their friend Horatio Bridge : "My faith has been cut in its central life. I cannot conceive myself as surviving any peril to my husband. But I would not complain because I know that God must do right and that He is also love itself."

Of course she did survive ; she knew she must. There were Julian and Una and Rose left to her care. There was some of her husband's unpublished work which his publishers were urging her to put in shape. And there was her faith in God and her firm belief in a future life.

When Mr. and Mrs. Bridge came down for a brief visit a few months after Hawthorne's death, they were pleased to see how well the household was progressing. Julian was finishing his first year at Harvard and came home for Saturdays and Sundays. He was at the Scientific School there, for his father, with that same vehemence he had shown Rose when she announced she was going to write stories, had begged his son not to be an author.

"Be an engineer, my boy," he urged. "Be something really useful. Don't, I beg of you, turn into a writer."

But Mrs. Hawthorne was not so sure he would ever be an engineer ; she knew how he hated all mathematics and how he loved Latin and was friendly to Greek which was hardly an engineering basis, but she felt, too, that his father would after all want him to do what he could do best. He was very aesthetic and so full of a lack of worldly conventions, that she was afraid he would not advance far in the dusty arena of life. But that, she thought, might keep him unspoiled for the next world, and she hoped he would at least make a living in this one.

Rose, grown so fast that she was a head taller than her mother, played the piano for the guests and showed them some of the drawings she had been working on in the school at Lexington she was now attending. Incredible as it seemed to Mrs. Hawthorne, she was now fourteen, and Una was twenty, slim and tawny-haired. Today she sat there quietly sewing for the soldiers, for the War that had helped to shorten Hawthorne's days was still not ended.

Mr. Bridge expressed the hope that Hawthorne's Journals would soon be offered to the world. Mrs. Hawthorne said, "I work at them daily. The *Atlantic Monthly* is anxious to publish portions of them before they go into a book. Oh, it is as if he were speaking to me when I read his papers. They will be his best biography."

"Mother says," Una's voice came across the room, "that he left no bird or leaf or tint of earth or sky unnoticed. His diary will show people just what he was like." The vivid face was alight, but Mrs. Bridge felt somehow uncomfortable. This girl was too intense, too lovely, too delicately apart to be happy, it seemed to her ; or if she did know happiness it would be an ethereal, selfless sort. "I am fortunate to have had him for a father," ended Una, stitching away at the coarse blue stuff.

"We were all fortunate to have had him," added her mother. "Pain passed away when he came. Poverty was lighter than thistledown with such a power of felicity to uphold it. It is often

86

cold without him, but I always held it all as if it were not mine, but God's, and I was always ready to resign it. That has made his death possible to bear, but — " and the tears fell for the first time — "not easy."

But the house was as cheerful as ever, bright inside and out with flowers. The children spoke of their father as if he had stepped into another land for a while, and the Bridges went home reassured, remembering their hostess's words of the evening before, "My king is gone and the cottage is no longer a palace. But I have an eternity, thank God, to know him, or I should die of despair."

Mr. and Mrs. Higginson came to spend a night at the Wayside, and he told his wife as they went up the walk that going to see Hawthorne had always made him think of what Keats said when he went to Burns's home : "He felt as if he were going to a tournament."

The family gave them a pleasant evening. Rose, at her mother's request, sang for them "Consider the Lilies" and "Break, Break, Break." "It is not singing but eloquence," commented Mrs. Hawthorne, when Rose had gone from the room.

"From you the eloquence," said Mr. Higginson. But to his wife when they had gone up to the guest room under Hawthorne's tower, he spoke with concern of her white hair, her pale cheeks.

The death of her father was the first, perhaps the greatest, shock, of Rose Hawthorne's life. It was not merely that the child had lost her father, she had lost her idol. Always impatient of even small disappointments, this sorrow bowed her deep in grief. She was perplexed about life and living in it, and Mrs. Hawthorne found her very difficult to deal with.

It had always been hard for Rose to take any sympathy kindly, and, if now her mother spoke to her out of her own gentle faith, she put it aside impatiently as something of no actual value. The only reality was that terrible aching sense of loss, that woke her up in the morning and went to sleep with her at night. At the same time her physical health did not seem to suffer, and this,

87

too, troubled her. She ought not to be so well in body when her heart was so sick. She hated the gay young Concord people who tried to take her with them in their outings and parties. Thoreau, who had so loved seeing children about him and had planned many a gay excursion for them, was gone now, but Emerson did his best, from tea parties on the lawn to swimming parties at Walden. Rose went to them only if she could find no excuse for not going.

Finally Mrs. Hawthorne decided to send both girls to Dio Lewis's Seminary for Young Ladies in Lexington, a few miles away. Una went for only a short time, but Rose enjoyed the school so much that she was allowed to board as long as she wished to and was happy there. It was really a school of physical culture, far ahead of its time. It delighted Mrs. Hawthorne who hated doctoring anyway and welcomed such a substitute. The girls wore simple outdoor clothing, blouses and skirts that were very short for those days. Studies and health education went hand in hand. Una had benefited by her brief stay, and the effect on Rose was to make her again the gay happy girl she had been at first.

It was then unfortunate that during Rose's second year there the school burned to the ground, and Mr. Lewis decided not to rebuild. But for some time Mrs. Hawthorne had been evolving an idea, an inspiration really, and was almost ready to announce it to the family.

She was placidly happy in her children. The great love of life and joy in all things concerning it which she had shared with her husband, was hers no more. But she was content steadying her children, seeing to her home, spending hours on the precious journals.

"The children are all so bright," she wrote to her sister, "that my life is a thanksgiving for them. When they are settled in life I should like to fall asleep as he did, if God please."

In 1866 Longfellow had suggested to Lowell that he write a life of Hawthorne, and the latter, much intrigued with the idea, set to work.   But he met with an obstacle : Mrs. Hawthorne would allow him no access to the notebooks, so he gave up the idea altogether.

From a literary point of view, this was perhaps unfortunate and from an historical viewpoint as well, for Hawthorne's wife had her own ideas of what should be printed and what not.   Una and Julian came in one day as she was deep in her work and very inky about the fingers.   She was smudging out some lines from one of the diaries.

"Mama, what are you doing ?   Blotting out something ?" asked Una.

Mrs. Hawthorne nodded.   She turned to them.   "Children," she asked, "did you ever hear your father use any unpleasant word when he might have used a pleasant one ?"

They shook their heads.

"Well, there are some words and sentences here that I am sure he put in for the effect, and because he thought the world would never see them, perhaps even to tease me and shock me a bit if I read them.   I shall have to leave out a bit here and there."

Julian looked slightly alarmed.   "But, Mama, you are not changing his own sentences, are you ?"

"Never the idea," his mother assured him, "merely here and there the words."

The Peabody elegance, the niceties of the language of Boston of that day drove Sophia Hawthorne to change more than she admitted she had.   She blotted out whole phrases she could not approve of.   "Quick tempered as the devil" became "very quick tempered."   "Swap" she made "exchange" and "cloak" even became "chlamys," in her eager desire to have her husband show only his best face to the world, the one that was least like the seafaring Hathornes.

Besides there were people still living whom he mentioned in the diaries, sometimes not too kindly ; it would not do to hurt their feelings.   Her modesty made her eliminate herself from the pages.   When Hawthorne wrote, "Had my wife been with me," she made it, "Had I not been alone."   So the notebooks turned

89

out to be a labor of love rather than a document of Hawthorne, and the smudges in the books kept the world from knowing that Hawthorne in his diaries wrote sometimes with realistic male gusto.

If the children guessed something of what she was doing they did not interfere. They realized how she grasped every bit of beauty from these pages. "Listen, children," she would say, looking up from her work, "your father says here : 'A stray leaf from the Book of Fate picked up in the street.' It is a whole poem in its imagery."

She would read them entire passages sometimes. It was when they were listening to the account of a man to whom Hawthorne talked and had befriended, although he hated to be near a man so diseased and dirty and uncouth, that Rose shook her head in disgust.

"How could he ? And why did he anyway ? There are plenty of people who wouldn't have minded doing it and he did."

"But, my dear, it showed the very highest principles for he was so very sensitive to the slightest deformity or ugliness of disease."

On a pleasant Sunday in spring when they were all at home together, Mrs. Hawthorne looked around at them all and said, "Children, I have a plan. Why don't we go abroad and live in Germany for a while ? Julian will be all through school very soon. It will be a long time before Mr. Lewis' school will be ready again. And then Una and I need a bit of stirring up, too."

The traveling Hawthornes had stayed in one spot a long while this time. They were ready, all of them, to be on the move. Besides, no matter how hard they tried they could not feel the house was really home without their father's presence. The walk on the hilltop was empty no matter how many walked there. The tower was a lonely spot too. It would be good to see other scenes and other cities ; and Una had confided to Julian only last week that their mother did not seem so strong as usual ; the change would be very good for her.

"When will we go ? When will we go ?" demanded Rose,

pleased at the idea of being out of uniforms and away from classes, perhaps forever.

"I had thought of Dresden where Julian could perfect his German and perhaps the rest of us could pick up some too. I studied it years ago, but have forgotten most of it."

Una visited her friends the Higginsons in Brattleboro before they went abroad. She wrote back to her mother, "I love the spring. I must have been born with spring in my mouth, not a silver spoon." But she came back even sooner than she had intended from her woods and her walks with her friends, eager as the rest to try new worlds.

Once again followed by the good wishes of Concord friends, fewer now than on the day when the Hawthornes had left for England, they sailed for other lands. Una had with her a periwinkle plant dug up from the ground above her father's grave, and Mrs. Hawthorne carried a few slips of ivy from the yard.

The atmosphere of Dresden was the sort they all enjoyed : gay and sunny, but with Old World cadences, with the ancient safeguards of home and land that their father had always taught them to hold important. Rose liked this happy, free society much better than Concord. The outdoor life, the pleasant concerts in the Grosser Garten, were delightful, and so was the Kaffeekuchen in the Säschische Schweiz, obligingly translated by Mrs. Hawthorne — who in her youth had studied this heavy tongue along with reading the Bible in Hebrew and Plato in Greek — as the Switzerland of Saxony.

The pension was interesting too with its German chatter, its students come to learn this guttural language. Everyone at the long tables talked or tried to talk it, and soon the Hawthornes were venturing phrases too. Julian, who was enrolled in the Realschule, found two boys slightly younger than himself who had been in Germany long enough to help him, and American enough to understand what he was trying to say when he became stuck.

He presented them to his mother and sisters. They were

91

Francis Lathrop of New York and his brother George, sons of Dr. Lathrop of New York, the latter a tall angular boy of seventeen with a mop of black hair and a pleasant smile. Both could speak German fluently and George offered to teach the two girls, especially after he had seen Una. No one could blame him for this sudden and immediate fascination, for this older of the Hawthorne daughters was now at her loveliest. Everyone turned to look at her on the street, though she went her tall, serene way, noticing no one at all. Her coloring was enough to attract attention, especially in beauty-loving Dresden ; the tawny hair, the warm color in her cheeks, the upright carriage, the faraway glance. "Harp-souled," her mother called her, and it was an apt description.

Rose sensed George's interest in Una at once, and that night teased her sister about this conquest. But Mrs. Hawthorne shook her head and bade her stop.

Francis Lathrop found little time for talking German even to the pretty Hawthorne girls. He was anxious to get to Leipsig as soon as possible so that he might study art at the Royal Art Academy. But he used his spare time drawing the two girls, trying to get the tints of their hair with every pencil he owned, but never quite succeeding. "You need an old master to paint you, not a raw American dauber," he said in disgust one day when the fifth attempt had not pleased him.

But the girls thought the likenesses excellent, and were not at all surprised when George came in one day fairly bursting with great news :

"Whistler has seen some of Francis' work and he wants him to come to work with him in London — in Chelsea — imagine that."

They hurried now, all together, to do the things they had meant to do earlier, visit the little restaurant where the Lathrop boys had discovered marvelous Mohrenköpfe, go to the museum where Francis had worked copying paintings, spend some time in the Grosser Garten. Rose was attended by the two older boys, for George stuck close to Una, and she, the soul of kindness, never repulsed his boyish affection.

It had been very cold in Dresden that winter even for Concorders accustomed to icy blasts. Una wrote to the Higginsons that the winds there shook "even the ponderous stone mansions." But spring was beautiful, and she wrote that she loved the city, the dreamy artistic life, but she felt a bit selfish to be doing nothing but enjoying herself. "But I am fulfilling the duties of the moment, and so am content," she wrote Miss Higginson.

None of them cared especially for the German people, even though they loved the German city. Una never really came close to the language either. "My little jokes," she lamented, "were never made to tear themselves to pieces with these monstrous syllables." She was no fonder of the Germans' attitude toward their women folk. "They are careful of their horses, but not of their women. Do you know I have seen them put drags on the wheels when there is no hill at all, but they actually let women push when there is a hill to be climbed."

On this second trip to Europe Mrs. Hawthorne found she had lost much of that old passion of hers for museums and palaces ; she was content to sit in her sunny room in the pension that overlooked the red roofs and shady avenues of Dresden, working now at a book of her own. She called it *Notes on England and Italy*, and that was exactly what it was ; jottings she had made through the years in England and Italy, often in the form of letters to the Peabodys. She had to be persuaded to do it at all by publishers and family too, and in the end she refused to put down her given name. She used instead on the title page the name she was so proud to call hers : Mrs. Nathaniel Hawthorne.

The gay days came to an end. Francis went to London to Whistler's studio, and perforce young George had to go too, tearing himself away from his beautiful pupil with much grief, to Una's slight embarrassment and Rose's huge amusement.

Even though they had not expected to do so, it was not long

93

before the Hawthornes, too, decided to go away. The Franco-Prussian War was making things very difficult for foreigners, and although none of them wanted to go back to America as yet, they did want to live in some land not torn by strife. Recollections of the war between the States were still fresh in their minds. It was decided that Julian was to go back to New York for further study, and the girls with their mother would remain in London for a time.

The English boarding house was very different from the gay, noisy pension in Dresden, but they all liked it. Mrs. Hawthorne was going through the proofs of her book, and the girls left the authoress to herself while they roamed about the London they had been too young to enjoy when they were there before.

As they walked together one day, they took a wrong turning on their way home and found themselves in a narrow little street of dirty houses and sickly filthy children. Rose pulled her sister to come away from this unpleasant place, but Una stood looking at them.

"Rosie, some day I'm going to help clean up children like those."

"What a job," shivered Rose. "No one as pretty as you are ought to touch such dirty children. Let other people do it."

"Papa would say they are our children too ; that the reason they are so dirty is our fault too," said Una thoughtfully.

Rose looked again at the gray rags, at a hand clutching a gray piece of bread, and then back of her at the gray houses. She hugged her sister's arm. "You darling ! You are like Papa — just exactly. He'd make all that awful grayness look gold, and you do, too. But for today, for now, anyway, let's leave it dirty and go home."

Their mother was out when they reached home, but when she did come in, she had several interesting bits of information. She had met in the street just now — they could never guess — Mr. Browning !

"He found me unchanged," she said. The girls looked at her proudly — her dress of delicate black lace, the jet coronet on her

94

white hair. "And he is coming to call next week, as soon as he returns to London again."

But the other news was even better. It was a little note from Francis Lathrop who had just learned they were in London. He and George would call that evening to pay their respects. They were unaffectedly glad to see their Dresden friends again. Francis had found work with Whistler rather difficult, and was now with Madox Brown and Burne-Jones, helping to make designs for stained glass windows. And he promised to bring the girls two scarves which he had made for them in William Morris' studio.

They sat talking together in the little parlor. Rose threw a glance now and then at George, whose black eyes and bright color she had always privately thought superior to the quieter coloring of Francis. Each time she found him studying her with a slightly puzzled look. She wondered why he was not looking at Una, especially since she was particularly lovely tonight in gray silk, the very color of her eyes.

When the boys had gone, Una broke into a laugh. "I told you," she said to her mother, "that it was really Rose he liked. I just looked like her and was older. Anyway, now I don't have to worry about the child any more. He was quite a care at times."

Rose knew that George's glances had strayed to her a great deal all that evening, but she was sure Una was exaggerating. Then, a few mornings later, the post brought a letter for her. Not a letter, really. It was a poem. And it had a title : First Glance. She read it with a beating heart.

"A budding mouth," ran the words, "and warm blue eyes ;
 A laughing mouth, and laughing hair ;
 So ruddy was its rise
 From off that forehead fair.

"Frank fervor in whatever she said ;
 And a shy grace when she was still ;
 A brief elastic tread ;
 Enthusiastic will.

"These wrought the magic of a maid
 As sweet and sad as the sun in spring ;

Joyous yet half afraid
Her joyousness to sing."

There was no name signed, but there was really no need of that. All day she felt her heart beating wildly, and at various times she would get the verses from her desk and read them over. George and Francis were to leave that day for a week's trip to the Lakes, and she was glad. She could never have met his eyes so soon after reading that poem!

Then for an aching interval they forgot Mr. Browning's promised visit, and the Lathrops, too, except as they could help in the crisis that was suddenly upon them. Their mother had a return of the pneumonia from which she suffered before, and this time it was apparent there would be no recovery.

She had said to them suddenly one day, "I don't know what is wrong with me. I have a sort of defenseless feeling as if I had no refuge."

They made her go to bed and called a doctor, but from the first there was little hope held out for her recovery. She tried sitting up when the girls came in, but soon that pretense stopped, and she lay day after day in bed. Sometimes her mind, that crystal clear mind, wandered. Noises troubled her greatly. She worried about Julian in New York, and was happy for hours when a letter came from him.

Rose and Una were in the parlor waiting the doctor's verdict on the day the disease reached its crisis. It was hardly a matter of days, he said, any longer — perhaps only of hours. The breathing was terribly difficult, almost agony at times. That night they watched together, or by turns, until morning. Una was half wishing Julian were with them, half glad he was not there to see their mother's pain. She fanned and fanned the poor fevered face, and Rose wiped away from Una's cheeks the streaming tears.

In a lucid moment their mother began to talk. "I am tired, too tired," she whispered. "I am glad to go. I only wanted to live for you two and Julian."

96

Rose went out for a short walk at Una's orders, and she brought back a little yellow crocus, the first they had seen that spring, and put it on the bed.   It was Sunday and the church bells were ringing ; the sun streamed in through the thin curtains.   The little crocus opened on the quilt in five points like a star.   Mrs. Hawthorne watched it open and looked up to smile at the girls, Una holding her hands and Rose standing beside her.   There was a brief struggle for breath.   It ceased and the bells had stopped and the silence was loud in their ears as Una put away her mother's hands and went downstairs with Rose.

When they put her in her coffin there was still a little wild flower color in her cheeks, and her white hair was brushed softly back under a white cap.   She lay in one of the lacy dresses she liked so well.

She was buried at Kensal Green, and Rose planted on the grave the ivy they had brought with them from America and which had flourished wherever they went.   At the head of the grave Una put the periwinkle she had taken from her father's grave.   The headstone said :

Sophia Hawthorne, Wife of Nathaniel Hawthorne

and the footstone :

"I am the Resurrection and the Life."

The Lathrop boys had helped with everything.   Letters poured in from friends in England and in America, a heartbroken letter from Julian, from Elizabeth Peabody, from old friends in Concord and Salem and Boston.

There were plans to be made now for the future.   The Wayside was no longer theirs.   It had been sold some years ago to a Mrs. Gray who had in turn sold it to Mrs. Mary Pratt to be used as a school for girls.   So there was no home to return to.   Julian had married and had a position in the New York City Department of Docks.   He urged them to come home as soon as they could make the trip.   George Lathrop had written him that he would himself escort the girls to America.

97

But Una decided not to go back, but to do instead what she had spoken about to Rose in the mean slum street a year ago. She had been recently received into the Church of England and she meant to do settlement work under the aegis of that church, devoting herself to the orphan and destitute children of the London slums.

She had a desire deep in her to go home. "All the galleries of Europe can't make up for the loss of friends," she had written to Miss Higginson. But something inside her told her that her duty lay here, with what her father had called, "the pale little progeny of the sunless nooks of London."

The one thing that had worried her was Rose. But that, too, was not a worry for long. On September 11th, 1871, Rose was married to George Lathrop in the little church of Saint Peter's in Chelsea. Una felt they were both too young — each was little over twenty — but they seemed to be so happy that she was reassured and content.

2

In New York the Lathrops found life interesting and full. Both Rose and George had aspirations to write, and here they were in the midst of a group of like-minded folk, only too glad to welcome the daughter of Hawthorne. Julian too was feeling the Hawthorne urge toward pencil and paper. "I'm finding," he told the Lathrops, "that it is easier and more profitable for me to write stories than to bother about the docks."

Mrs. Lathrop, George's mother, was herself a patroness of the arts, and at her home in Washington Square she gave teas and literary evenings to which the *literati* swarmed. She was very tactful about her parties. She said one day to little Mrs. McDowell, a bride of the winter and in New York for the first time from a quiet girlhood in Concord, "If you were giving a party, would you have authors and artists and business people all together or separately?"

"Oh, authors and artists alone," answered Mrs. McDowell with youthful assurance.

Mrs. Lathrop shook her beautifully coiffed white hair. "You are wrong, my dear. Alone they always argue and get into quarrels. Mix your parties, child, if you want them to be successful." She welcomed her son's wife into the family circle, glad to have George married, for she knew he had in him a certain instability that made it better he should know responsibility. Francis, the elder son, was very different.　Once before he had been called from his studies abroad to come home and help his father when business reverses came up, and he was with her again for the same reason.　He was to a great extent the breadwinner now with the painting classes he conducted at Cooper Institute.

She wished that George had married a girl who had less temperament, she thought, at times, but put aside the thought as unkind.　It had come to her after the evening when a guest found himself discussing the *Marble Faun* in a group of which the author's younger daughter was a member.

"Quite clearly Hawthorne was frightened by paganism and it drove him back again to the Calvinism on which he had been reared," he said.

"But his pity," flashed Mrs. Lathrop, "did not allow him to stay there long — if indeed your clever statement has any truth at all."

Who, the aggrieved guest wanted to know later, was the goodlooking red-headed woman who had told him off so decidedly ? But Mrs. Lathrop, past mistress of social amenities, soothed his feelings.

Almost from the beginning, the two found difficulties in their life together.　They loved each other deeply, without a doubt. But they were very young, and neither had any conception of what give-and-take meant.　No doubt, too, it would have been hard for any youth to live up to the image of a husband that Rose carried in her heart, that of her affectionate, adoring father.　The only marriage she had ever observed was that of her parents, a deeply happy one of deference for each other's opinion, of deep beautiful forbearance.

This one, it was clear, was not working out in the same way. George was insistent on having his own way and Rose, who had seen only the happiness of her parents' union, and whose father had died too young for her to notice that their happiness had been built on mutual forbearance, felt again that wild disappointment assail her that came always when things she wanted to have absolutely right went terribly wrong.

But she had been trained by her parents to try to sink her desires when she could, and she was very proud. These two qualities enabled her to take up a rôle that became more and more one of endurance with a difficult temperament, an attitude to life often unstable, a yielding to weaknesses instead of holding out against them. And besides, she loved George very dearly, and he loved her as deeply in return.

She had a reward for her patience one day when he brought home a surprise for her, a small square book with the title, *Rose and Roof Tree*. He turned to the dedication and gave it to her to read :

"I need give my verse no hint as to whom it sings for. The rose, knowing her own right, makes servitors of the light rays to carry her color. So every line here shall in some sense breathe of thee and in its very face bear record of her whom, however unworthily, he seeks to serve and honor."

She smiled at him as she turned to the first poem :

"Every year the sweet rose shooteth higher,
And scales the roof upon its wings of fire,
And pricks the air, in lovely discontent
With thorns that question still of its intent.
But when it reached the roof tree there it clung,
Nor ever farther up its blossoms flung."

During the next few years George contributed to various periodicals. Rose began to write, a tale here and there in *Saint Nicholas*, an article for the *Atlantic Monthly*, verse now and then. George also did reviewing for the newspapers. But after a few years of such haphazard work, it was a relief to them both when William Dean Howells, editor of the *Atlantic Monthly*, offered George a position as associate editor of that magazine.

He wrote articles for the magazine, too, and countless book reviews, including the books of his friends and Julian's novels, which came along quite frequently now. Often his review was of a book he found hopelessly old-fashioned, and then he found difficulty between inclination and duty.

"Rose, here is an oddity," He put in her hand a sturdy little volume, *"Mr. Gow's Good Morals and Gentle Manners.* It tells how to avoid homicide, plagiarism, chapped hands and vanity, and much else. Applied rules for all emergencies. But just suppose I were to do something that did not come under *Good Morals and Gentle Manners* ? Then what ?"

Rose was glad to be back again close to Concord to visit with the Hows, to go to Sleepy Hollow and supervise the erection of a memorial stone for her mother close to her father's stone, to talk again with her father's Boston friends. Una wrote that she was coming for a visit, and that too had been a brief joy. Una was as lovely as ever, but even quieter than she used to be. She looked much thinner ; evidently her work was not easy. But she was happy.

"Father was right, Rose," she said, "when he told about the poor baby in the poor-house ; you remember, the horrible little child that asked him to pick it up. They are ugly little things, some of them, but it is really our fault that they are so — our individual fault. That I see more and more. And what keeps me going on when things get very hard is to remember that he *did* pick up the child — and he hated to. You must read it all again some day in *Our Old Home*. Then you will see just what I mean."

But it was years before Rose was to pick up the book and read it with the eyes of the soul as Una had done.

In the group they visited in New York was a promising young writer, Albert Webster. He was fragile in appearance, and it was rumored that he had been threatened with consumption. Before many weeks had gone it was clear that the young writer and the quiet Una were deeply in love with each other. He wanted her to stay in New York until the next year when his duties would allow him to go back with her as his wife. But her own allowance of time was spent ; she knew there were all too few helpers, and that the vineyards were more than filled, so she kept her word and sailed back to England, leaving her betrothed unhappy, but hopeful of meeting in London and marriage within the year.

Una had not long been back at her work when a letter came to her from Rose. "Darling, I wish I could have found someone else to tell you this. I cannot bear to do it, yet I must. Albert was taken very ill and ordered to Honolulu for his health, as you perhaps know by this time from letters from him to you. But he never finished the voyage. He died on shipboard. If only there were someone with you, someone to help you bear it. Come back to us, darling. We all want you and we can comfort you with our arms and not with cold words such as these."

But Una stayed. There was nothing to take her back to America now, and in London, at least, she was needed. She wrote Rose not to worry about her, that she was staying with friends in a little Episcopalian convent near Windsor, that she was content and would soon be happy again, knowing as she did that her father and mother, and now Albert, would be waiting in heaven for her. "That hope, that assurance," she wrote, "should keep anyone content and willing to go through this span."

Rose forced herself to feel that Una was content ; in fact, she really knew she was, for in Una was something of that feeling of timelessness on earth that had been an attribute of Hawthorne, and days and years were to them not the exact things they are to most people.

And then, too, Rose herself had something else to take her attention even from her beloved Una. On November 10th, 1876, her son was born.

"His eyes are gray-blue like yours, Rösl," George whispered to her when they let him see her.

She smiled up at him. "All babies have gray eyes," she said. "Aunt Ebie told me that years ago."

"Well, they don't all have red hair to start out with, and he has. He is very like you, darling."

They had named the baby for his Uncle Francis, who duly came to see his nephew. He was hard at work assisting Oliver La Farge with the decorations for Trinity Church, and could not stay long even with a new and fascinating member of the family.

By the time the baby was a month old, Rose had admitted he was the loveliest child ever born, and that his eyes were going to stay gray-blue indefinitely. He looked to her most of all like a little cherub in Mr. Story's studio in Rome. Perhaps it was the memory of those childish days in the Eternal City that made her say suddenly one evening as George was digging into manuscripts, "George, I want the baby baptized."

He looked up in astonishment. "Why?"

"I don't really know. I just know I want it."

George was willing to please her. "All right. Where? We could take him down to the church Francis is doing pictures for if you like."

Rose shook her head. "No, I want him to be baptized in a church like those in Italy. Let's take him to a Catholic church."

George stared in surprise, but she pressed her point. "I was so happy those years in Rome, George. And the Catholics do things up so nicely — not cold and just dripping a little water, but they make a more supernatural thing out of it. They do something with a baby's soul, more than the other churches do."

So Francie was taken to the little Catholic church nearest his home and solemnly baptized in the most ancient of Christian forms and in the original Christian creed. The Latin words brought back to Rose the singing, the praying monks of years ago.

"*Dominus vobiscum,*" she said to George when they left the church. He put his arm around her in the carriage just as she had her arm curved around Francis.

"*Et cum spiritu tuo,*" he said softly.

Next day before he went to the office he put in her hand a piece of paper. "I wrote it for you last night when you and Francie were asleep."

Rose watched him go down the street, loving his swinging walk, his erect carriage, before she turned to the paper covered with lines in his slanting hand. He had named it:

"Today I saw a little calm-eyed child,
Where soft lights rippled and the shadows tarried,
Within a church's shelter arched and aisled,
Peacefully wondering, to the altar carried . . .

"Wise is the ancient sacrament that blends
The weakling cry of children in our churches
With strength of prayer or anthem that ascends
To Him who hearts of men and children searches."

The following year George was made editor of the *Boston Courier*. Rose was venturing further into the literary field, though Francie kept her very busy now. It was only for the most important social affairs that she would venture out evenings and leave him to alien care. But George persuaded her to go to a dinner at the Papyrus Club on ladies' night, and when she found out who was sitting at her right hand she was delighted. The gentleman leaned over to pick up her place card and handed her his.

"That is the easiest way, isn't it ?" he said.

But Rose did not need to look at the card to know that it was Dr. Oliver Wendell Holmes. He, however, was looking at her in a puzzled way.

"I had thought I knew you and could make certain from the card. I was mistaken I am afraid. Mrs. George Lathrop — no, I was mistaken. What was your name before your marriage ?"

"Rose Hawthorne."

He beamed. "There, I thought I knew you, but I didn't want to make a mistake. Suppose after all, you hadn't been you ?"

"I didn't often see your father," he went on, "though I did see your mother quite frequently. But it is such a pleasure to remember what a delight it was to suggest a train of thought to him, and how sometimes he wouldn't answer for a long time, but when the answer came, it was, you know, as if the mountain range had spoken. And how much he did for New England ! A light has fallen on the place not of land or sea. He has given a soft haze to our glaring New England, and it will never be harsh country again."

"But the people, themselves, with their odd characteristics, helped him," said Rose, glowing with pleasure at this praise of her father.

"And their surroundings show that too," declared Dr. Holmes. "Where else are the little doorways that hold the glint of sunlight so tenaciously like the still light of wine in a glass ? I hope," he added, "I shall not be doing wrong if I ask if you have you a preference among his books, that is, if you read them. Authors' children don't always."

"Oh, I read them all through when I was fifteen, except the *Scarlet Letter*. I was told to wait to read that until I was eighteen."

"I think the *Scarlet Letter* is his greatest. Some critic in the *Atlantic* said that in this book Hawthorne first made his genius efficient by penetrating it with passion. I think it is the one on which his future fame will rest."

Rose nodded. "I have thought so too."

"Concord is changed," said the doctor suddenly, as the company rose. "There are so many gone. But we miss most of all Hawthorne and Thoreau."

Francie throve lustily. From England came a silver spoon from his Aunt Una, and her letters were eager with questions about his health. His grandmother Lathrop rejoiced in her first grandchild, and his godfather came over to see him whenever he could spare time from the work in Trinity Church which was engrossing him.

Rose wanted her boy to have room to tumble and play. There was none in the little Boston apartment. Little by little she was formulating a plan in her mind, and when she suggested it to George, she knew in advance that he would like the idea.

"George, let's buy back the Wayside. Aunt Elizabeth says

the girls' school has been closed and the place is going to be put up for sale. It would be a fine place for Francie, and there would be room for you to write — and it would be home. If we do go away again, Julian would have a good place to put his family."

So it was decided, and when Francie was three years old, his mother was back again in the house which she had so hated after the stately homes of England, and to which she now returned like a homing bird.

Much of the Hawthorne furniture had been put in storage when the house was sold, and Rose put it back in the old house again. She went up and down, touching now the little shaving table that had been her father's, and now the little chair where her mother had been used to sit and go over her father's manuscripts for him. Downstairs were the shabby comfortable old chairs, and the polished brown table was back in the dining-room.

When their child was asleep, their first evening in the old house, she and George went for a walk up the hill. On the right, the Bull home was empty. Mr. Bull had produced the grape which enriched many, but to him it brought nothing except the joy of discovery. He had died recently in poverty. On the other side was the awkward house that Louisa Alcott had named Apple Slump. There, too, there had been deaths and many changes, but at the top of the hill the little path was still there, a bit overgrown with intruding fern and berry bushes, but still a path.

They paced up and down, following the crooked trail. "It is as if Nature could not bear to obliterate his footsteps," said George. Rose threw him a grateful look ; he could always be counted on to find the right phrase for things — the delicate phrase. If only everything about him were as perfect as this ; if only. But Rose put the thought away. One reason, one she hardly named to herself — why she had wanted to come here to live, was that George might, here in the country, in this quietness, get better control of the vice that was trying to control him.

To see him come home as he sometimes did, flushed and unsteady, struck terror to her heart. Here things would be much better, she knew.

But she had to admit that since Francie's birth he *had* been much better, as if making a determined effort to keep away from his enemy. This old Concord would help him, too, just as it would put roses into Francie's cheeks and give her the joy of being at home.

George was still musing about Hawthorne, not guessing her troubled thoughts. "Do you know, Rose, it seems to me in his last work he seemed looking down from a spiritual eminence over the world, as he looked on Concord from here, and subtly infused the essence of his concluding thoughts on art and existence from this height."

Up in Sleepy Hollow Cemetery the graves lay in the sunlight on the steep hill. Grass and ivy over her father's, and a little stone to show when and where her mother had died. Another tiny stone said "Garth." Here was buried one of Julian's children, dead when a baby. And close to her mother's memorial stone was another exactly like it :

UNA HAWTHORNE, DIED IN WINDSOR, SEPTEMBER, 1877
BURIAL IN KENSAL GREEN

Incredible still that statement. The letters from Una had been pleasant letters, accounts of her work and its success, little incidents of individual children, requests for prayers for her work. From friends who had gone to call on her in England, Rose heard that she seemed well, but that the tawny hair had turned quite gray. Tired out from too intensive efforts, she had gone for a short retreat to the little Episcopalian convent at Windsor for a rest. For some time she had intended becoming a nun of that order, and had no doubt been partly held back by Rose, who begged her not to take such a step.

But she must have let herself get too tired and too thin. And perhaps she did not care very much about living. An illness that had seemed so slight the nuns did not cable her family about it, proved fatal, and she died in her little cell and was buried, at Julian's orders, in Kensal Green beside her mother. That was the one thing that had lightened Rose's grief : the two who had loved each other so well were again side by side.

Miss Higginson said to her one day, "It was impossible that Una should ever have been happy," and with that view Rose had to concur.

Life went along pleasantly at the Wayside. Francie could play inside the white picket fence, and Rose sitting in the house, could watch the bright head bobbing up and down. Mrs. Walter Brown, when she came to visit Louisa Alcott, always stopped for a word with the child.

"Such a polite boy," she said to Louisa. "He never runs off as some children do when they are spoken to, but he is not forward either. He is certainly Hawthorne's grandson."

But little Walter How, a year younger than his cousin Francis, did not feel that way about him. He thought him a pretty big rough boy when his mother came over to visit with Cousin Rose while Walter and Francie were sent out to play together. But Francie was a big boy now, four years old, and Walter a small one, not quite three. No wonder the flying red hair and mischievous gray eyes filled him with something other than admiration.

Francie loved the outdoors. He loved all activity. He liked best of all to have his tall father lift him up high in strong arms.

"Higher," he would command, "higher up in the sky," and he reached eager arms toward the blue heavens.

George shook his head. "No, Francie, I can't lift you that far. Better stay down here with us."

Guests came often to the Wayside. The Higginsons came. Francis Lathrop came and stayed for weeks at a time when he could rest from his painting. There were still Alcotts and Emersons and Longfellows at Concord. And George liked visitors. He was a hale and hearty person, perhaps a bit too hearty for quiet Concord, but the younger men liked him and invited him to join the Saturday Club.

There was another club called the Social Club in Concord to which the older men belonged. It specialized in high thinking and simple fare, and the gentlemen who belonged to it called the other club, which sported an excellent dinner at each of its meetings, the Stuffing Club.

George was also much in demand for odes and verses for occasions for which he had a decided flair. At a dinner given for Dr. Holmes in Boston, the little doctor had been much moved by the ode George had written in his honor. George also wrote the words for an ode sung at the 240th annual celebration of the Ancient and Honorable Artillery Company, and it was later reprinted by the proud Artillerists.

But he really preferred to dine with his wife to all these others, much as he enjoyed their company. He came back from one important dinner with a verse for Rose which he had written on the back of his card when the rest were listening to the speeches.

> "But most," it ended, "when vis-à-vis the opposite gender
> Is represented, with the repast to blend her
> Dear personality, when in one purée
> Our spirits mingle. Ah, that is the way
> When Love to Savarin stoops in sweet surrender —
> I love to dine."

3

Francie was five years old when one evening Rose met George at the door as he came up the highway. He stared at her worried face.

"Has anything happened to Francie?" he asked in quick fear.

She shook her head. "Nothing has happened, but he seems to be sick. He is feverish and won't play. I called the doctor and he is with him now."

Francie lay in the room that had been built long ago for Una, and for once he did not even notice that his father had come home. The doctor looked at him with a troubled face. "There is quite a bit of fever. It may be scarlet fever but I hope not."

George hurried over to the bed. "Hello, Francie, how are you?"

"I'm hot," said the child complainingly. "Take me outdoors, father."

"I'll hold you up the way you like to — you'd like to do that, wouldn't you?"

There was a small smile. "Way up in the sky," he murmured. George made a move to pick him up, but the doctor shook his head. And besides the child's eyes had closed again, and he showed no further sign of interest.

Through the night they watched him, both of them. By morning Rose had made up her mind. "George, we must take him to the city — to someone who knows about fevers.   Perhaps a hospital would be better for him where he could get the very best care.   George, nothing will happen to him, will there ?"

George smoothed back her hair.   "Of course it won't.   He just has a little fever the way children do.   But we'll take him right away if it will make you feel better."

But within a week two desolate people were following a small white coffin up Sleepy Hollow Hill.   They felt there could be no end to their grief.   Rose grew thin and wasted until George decided the best thing to do was to get her away from home, away from her memories, far away to some place so different that the memories might become background and not her whole existence. He persuaded her to take a trip with him to Spain.

She hesitated at first.   Spain did not seem the country she would select.   But she looked into George's eyes, clouded with grief, and felt in a sudden rush of love and pity that she would go anywhere with him if it could take that look from his eyes, if it would lift his shoulders again and give back wings to his spirit.

And that very morning she had found on his desk scribbled verses and read them with tears falling for every line she read. For them both the memory might some day grow less keen, but just now it was a knife that stabbed and stabbed.   George's little verse brought back the worst stab of all.   *The Child's Wish Granted,* he had put as title.

"Do you remember, my sweet absent son,
  How in the soft June days forever done
  You loved the heavens so warm and clear and high ?
  And when I lifted you, soft came your cry —
  'Put me way up — way up in the blue sky.'

"I laughed and said I could not — put you down,
  Your gray eyes filled with wonder beneath that crown
  Of bright hair gladdening me as you raced by.
  Another Father now, more strong that I,
  Has borne you voiceless to your dear blue sky."

When the Lathrops returned from their trip, Rose seemed herself again.   George brought back with him the manuscript of a new book, *Spanish Vistas,* which Scribner's were to publish.   It was put in a red and gold cover that Rose said made it look like an ancient Book of Hours.

At the first meeting of the Stuffing Club, George was asked how politics were over in Spain.

He laughed.   "Well, a man asked me one day if I were an Englishman, and I told him no, I was an American from the North, from the United States.   His face lighted up.   'Oh, then you are a Republican,' and in an undertone, 'I am too and a firm believer in republicanism.'   I asked him if there were many in Spain belonging to that party, but he only said, satirically, 'Party, my dear sir ?   In Spain there is a separate political party for every man.   Sometimes,' he added bitterly, 'two.' "

"What interested you most there ?" they wanted to know.

"One thing was the benefit given for the Society for the Prevention of Cruelty to Animals — it was a bull fight.   And also I liked the cry of the *Sereno* in the streets — the night watchman, you know.   In English it goes like this : 'Hail Mary most pure, three o'clock has struck.' "

George sang it for them as the *Sereno* had done, and the Saturday Club applauded, electing him *Sereno* for the Club with no delay.

They were at the Wayside for only a brief time, though, for memories crowded in too strongly now.   They sold the house to Daniel Lothrop, the publisher.   This time Rose left the furniture, too, selling most of it to the new owners.   She and George took rooms in the village for a while until all transactions were completed.

"Lathrop ? Lothrop ?" said the new owner.   "We ought to be related, ought we not ?   Surely one little vowel couldn't spoil our being relatives as well as buyers and sellers of real estate."

"I don't know just how we acquired that vowel anyway," said George.   "Our family name was Lothropp.   The first man in this country was a Concorder, or almost one, by the way.   He was a Church of England minister who renounced his orders in 1620 because he did not like the growing fussiness of that church's ceremonies. But Laud's Tomlinson got after him and arrested him and shut him in prison. He got away somehow and turned up at Scituate where he was town preacher."

"I'll leave you my mother's little table," Rose was saying to Mrs. Lothrop, "if you'd like to have it. It belongs here with the other things."

"I'll love to have it and take the best care of it," promised Mrs. Lothrop, "and I'll use it to write on too."

For once again the Wayside was to house a writer. Under the pen name of Margaret Sidney, Mrs. Lothrop was writing her series of *Five Little Peppers,* and the flying pens of the Alcotts and Hawthornes were going to have another successor.

In New York where the Lathrops went to live, they found plenty to divert them. It was the period when the house of the Richard Watson Gilders was functioning as a meeting place for artists and writers, probably the only really literary salon America has ever possessed. Here Rose met many of those who read and loved her father's work, men and women who could really appreciate it. There were many, too, who, though in the beginning her chief merit was that she was the daughter of a great man, learned to appreciate her for herself, for her cleverness and delightful wit, or who were attracted by her grace and charm, like the young poet who said she was a "peach blossom in the sun."

George was doing a series of travel sketches for Harper's. Both were writing poetry. Rose was busy with a series of articles which were to be called *Memories of Hawthorne,* and which the *Atlantic Monthly* had ordered. And George was busy with an especially ambitious scheme, one which in those days of easy pirating, was badly needed. In 1883 he founded the American Copyright League, and was its secretary for several years. He drafted a copyright law to protect authors against pirating, and later, when the International Copyright Law was passed, it was in all its essentials just as George had written the earlier one.

In 1886 Jeannette Gilder came to the Lathrops with an idea

she had long considered, namely, the compilation of an anthology of living poets, the authors to be left free to select their own work. She wanted the Lathrops' assistance. Both George and Rose approved highly of her suggestion and George said, "It's a splendid idea. Dead poets get any amount of charity and generosity. I think a few palm leaves for the living are decidedly in order. Only don't forget, you two, that American poets are under the Puritan ban. They can write about the fireside and the home and war and patriotism, but other emotions can't be put into verse — not published verse anyway. Poets in America certainly don't have free speech."

Rose offered to help too, but she was so busy with her ordered work that the other two did most of the selecting and correspondence with the poets. *Representative Poems of Living Poets* was published with a long preface by George, a very long one, but George did them well and they were the fashion of the day. At Rose's suggestion, poems by Emma Lazarus were included. She was a beautiful Jewish girl who had been so moved by the sufferings of her people that she had forgotten the transcendentalism of Emerson for the reality of pain ; Rose had seen some of her verses, and admired them especially.

At the head of each author's selections was a cut of his autograph instead of a picture. The volume won very favorable comment in literary New York.

With this book out of the way, George could set to work in earnest at the new edition of Hawthorne's works which his publishers were bringing out, the very complete Riverside edition, for which George was to write the various prefaces and do the general editing. It was a task he thoroughly enjoyed, and to which Rose brought him valuable aid.

"You know," he said to her one evening, looking up from the proofs, "one important thing in this work is its quality of revived belief. He was so definitely a man with faith, and his faith went out always to what in life is most beautiful, and this he found only in moral truth."

Rose nodded. "I have never heard what he stood for phrased

115

better, George. I'm so glad they picked you for this. You understand him as very few do."

He smiled. "There are two ways in which people can admire a great man : silence and speech. I choose speech."

George's literary activity during these years was prodigious He wrote many novels. *An Echo of Passion* and *True* attracted much comment, the latter partly because of its unusual chapter headings — *Her Eyes were Gray* was one — often in the form of sentences, a new idea for the eighties. *Gold of Pleasure* was another, published in Lippincott's and, to their amusement, sandwiched between *Is Alaska Worth Visiting ?* and letters of Horace Greeley. *Afterglow, In the Distance, Somebody Else,* all had an excellent sale.

Rose, who read them all for him, particularly liked the ending of *In the Distance.* She had awaited the reading of it with interest, for George told her that the last speech in the book was his declaration of love for her.

"You know," it ran, "I thought I could never be certain of any ideal thing. I've changed my mind now, for I'm touching the rainbow and know it."

He wrote a novel too for the publishing firm of Roberts, one of the *No Name Series* which were original novels by well-known American authors but published anonymously. Each book bore the motto : "Is the gentleman anonymous ? Is he a great unknown ?" from *Daniel Deronda.* No one guessed for a long time which was George's, but as it was variously attributed to Holmes, Higginson, Aldrich and Scudder, George felt complimented rather than neglected.

Rose's friendship with Emma Lazarus dated from an evening at the Gilder's home when she saw the tall beautiful girl with the face of a young Rachel and asked her hostess who she was. She learned that she had written the well-known poem, the *New Colossus,* which may be found today on the base of the Statue of Liberty. Her father, Moses Lazarus, was a member of one of the most cultured Jewish families in the city, a merchant of

wealth and prominence.   Rose read the sonnet, an impassioned
piece of verse that called the Liberty in New York harbor "Mother
of Exiles," and ended

> "Send them, the homeless, tempest tossed to me :
> I lift my lamp beside the golden door."

After that first meeting they walked and talked much together,
often leaving the rest of the company and strolling about the
Square deep in conversation.

Emma had made the acquaintance of Emerson some years before.   She had liked his lofty aloofness of thought, and much
of her own earlier verse was of the transcendentalist type.   She
treasured the letters he had written her, had dedicated one of her
little books of verse to him, and remembered with joy a brief visit
at his home in Concord.

"He was very kind to me, even about the dedication of my
flighty verse.   But nowadays, somehow, his ideas seem to me
not so practical or ideal as they did then."

"Mrs. Gilder tells me you have written poetry recently about
your own people.   I can't seem to put it with that earlier verse.
How ever did you come to write such a thing as the Liberty sonnet that Mrs. Gilder showed me ?"

Miss Lazarus turned a sombre face to Rose.   "Years ago I
could not convince myself that the disaster to my people in Russia
and other countries concerned me in the least.   We were safe
and sheltered here.   That seemed enough.   I even wrote an
article called, 'Was the Earl of Beaconsfield a representative
Jew ?' and it was published in the *Century* and people thought
it very good and true.   But it was not.   It was nonsense.   And
it was the last thing of that sort I ever wrote."

"Something must have roused you mightily — to judge from
that sonnet."

"Something certainly did.   The story that followed mine
in the magazine caught my attention.   It was by a Russian,
Madame Ragozin, and it was a defense of the Russian atrocities
against my people !   My own people, Mrs. Lathrop !   It was

117

the first time I had ever realized I belonged to them. I forgot Emerson. I forgot everything except that my people were in need of help. I hated it too. I hated going down on Ellis Island. The people were often dirty, but was that their fault, I scolded myself. The more I studied about it, the solution did not seem to me to be merely to pour them into this country, either. They needed a land of their own, not merely being tolerated in alien lands. Something I read in George Eliot gave me an idea that might work : a restored and independent nationality for them, perhaps repatriation in Palestine."

Rose thought how her own father would have enjoyed Emma Lazarus. "How has your idea been accepted ?"

She shrugged her shoulders. "I have tried hard to tell people of my idea. There is a great indifference. I am afraid people must suffer, each for himself, before they understand suffering. Until they suffer, they can never really comprehend."

Rose nodded. "Do you know, Emma, I feel sometimes I should engage in something to help people. A married woman loving children as I do, and bereft of them, must, it seems to me, fill the void in her life with works of charity."

George came home with a copy of the *Atlantic,* his eyes twinkling as he showed Rose the review of Julian's book on his father and mother. Mr. Higginson had written it and had found the volume far from satisfactory. "There is too much of little Julian's feats of swimming and his torn garments in it. It is nearly one hundred pages before we find out where Hawthorne was born, and then it is somebody's letter on page ninety-eight."

"But of course," said George, "there was need of this sort of a book. My own was too guarded and delicate and so unsatisfactory as biography."

Rose was laughing as she read. "He is annoyed because Julian mentions my being married, but doesn't say to whom."

"Higginson is right about one thing though : there is no mention of Mr. Fields. How could anyone write a book on Hawthorne and leave out the man who first appreciated the *Scarlet Letter* as he did ?"

For several years George was literary editor of the *New York Star,* a post from which he derived great satisfaction.   Julian was in newspaper work in New York too, having been made literary critic on the *New York World,* but after five years of New York, the Lathrops were ready for country life and began to look for a place to settle.   Francis, making one of his infrequent visits, gave them an idea.   They saw him now much less than formerly, for he was a very busy man.   He had painted a large oil for Bowdoin, Nathaniel Hawthorne's alma mater.   The painting of Light of the World on the reredos of St. Bartholomew's was the work of his brush, as was the Apollo over the proscenium at the Metropolitan Opera House.   Critics spoke of the pre-Raphaelite influence of his work, but they admitted, too, that it possessed the personal stamp of imagination and an excellent instinct of design.

Francis enjoyed visiting the Lathrops and was happy with them.   He wished only they could be happier with each other, these two.   He himself had never married, and had his New York workshop in a tower apartment in the old University Building in Washington Square, where Winslow Homer had lived. It was he who suggested that they go up to New London which at that time was a sort of suburban Athens.

It was a happy inspiration, and the Lathrops acted on it. Rose liked the change — change always delighted her, and George was pleased, for he would be among relatives he was fond of and friends who knew and liked him.   People were usually fond of the jovial George ; and up at New London lived H. C. Bunner of *Short Sixes* fame and Walter Learned, at that time editor of *Puck*.

Two people in the group became close friends of the Lathrops : the Chappells, Alfred and his young wife Adelaide.   The latter proved an excellent companion for Rose, and both Rose and George were greatly drawn to the serious Alfred, who had been studying for the Episcopalian ministry, and had suddenly during the past year, given it up completely. There were rumors in New London that it was Rome that was alluring him, but that would have been so incredible a thing for a Chappell of New London — turning papist ! — that most people put it aside as idle gossip.

But Adelaide said to Rose one day, "That story about Alfred going to Rome is true. He was received into the Catholic Church a month ago, but he has promised his family he would wait some time before he told people about it. But he wanted you and George to know."

"But why under the sun does he want to go into the Roman Church, Adelaide ? Surely there is nothing for an American in that institution."

"I don't know either," agreed Adelaide, "but he is afire with fervor. I could not even have thought of trying to stop him. I only wish I could follow him, Rose, but I can't. I'll go with him to his services if he wants me to ; I like them myself. But I can't find my way to their altar. I simply can't."

"But why should you ?"

"I don't know but I wish I could. He is so happy. Perhaps some day — "

"George, did you know that Alfred Chappell has really gone over to Rome ?" asked Rose.

George nodded. "He told me today. I don't know why, but when he talks about it he is like a crusader. It is so true for him that he can almost make a person feel it must be true for everybody."

"Oh, you know how Alfred gets excited about a new idea."

"Yes, I know, but this is different. He isn't excited, Rose. He is as calm as a still deep lake. He makes it sound so real — so necessary."

"Oh, please don't," began Rose, then stopped. Into her mind from the past, pictures came trooping. Saint Peter's with the people kneeling and a little girl stepping carefully among them.

A tall balcony with a white figure on it, fingers extended to the throngs below. Her mother taking her to the Convent of the Ladies of the Sacred Heart to hear the nuns singing. A great cathedral with an organ pealing. A vivid picture of a little girl in a garden running headlong into a tall man pacing there, a tall man in white, who put his hand on her head and said words she could not understand.

The New London life was very pleasant. With the Hawthornes' delight in moving about, which was shared by George, they lived in various places in the town. At first they stayed at the Crocker House, then in an apartment in the Harris Building, and then in a house on Broad Street. Finally they built a home of their own on Post Hill with a big studio to work in.

Rose was a temperamental housekeeper. She had been that from the beginning of their married life. Now she took cooking lessons and became an excellent cook — when she felt like being one. She could keep the house looking polished and neat — when she wanted to. Her rooms were always beautifully arranged, with the artistry that was natural to her. But when she grew weary of lifting the dust, it might lie there as long as it liked. When Rose grew weary of housekeeping, she hated it with a great hatred.

They entertained and were entertained a good deal. George was a person who made friends easily, a good conversationalist, and a merry host. His gay breezy way of talking sometimes irked Rose in whose veins ran the thinner and less tumultuous Peabody blood.

"George, George," she would say, half under her breath, when his sallies grew too gay for her. And there were people in New London who resented this, feeling that Rose was dimming his gaiety. But perhaps it was something else that was troubling her. She knew so well what sometimes caused this excess gaiety. The old craving was oftener with him nowadays, making him difficult to handle if she tried to remonstrate with him when they were alone.

But she loved him. His mind could meet hers so exactly.

121

She loved his appearance, the clipped Van Dyke beard, the small ears, the straight nose, the thoughtful eyes. Everyone, not only his wife, considered George Lathrop a very handsome man.

To the little New London world she was a gracious hostess, moving among her guests, or the center of conversation when she was the invited guest. She was not, said George's cousin, Emilie Learned, as she sat watching her, exactly beautiful, but she moved with a beautiful grace.

"At last I know of whom it is that she reminds me," said Miss Learned, "and why it is such a joy to see her move about. She walks exactly like Ellen Terry."

When it was repeated to her, Rose said it was the greatest compliment she had ever received. Cousin Milly's compliments were often very beautiful. For a birthday gift she sent Rose a great bouquet of rosebuds and hawthorne, and Rose sat at the breakfast table enjoying their beauty and reading the little verse that was one of George's gifts to her.

How sweet, how thoughtful George was, and how much he loved her. She sent a sudden little message to heaven. "Keep us happy — or at least keep us together." She put the verse in a drawer with the rest of his poems to her, and felt happy in having him, and them, through him. But those who knew her best were noticing how often an early physical characteristic of hers occurred now : the pupil of one eye became much larger than the other, something which happened only when she was excited, or nervous, or extremely worried.

Alfred Chappell liked talking to Rose about her father. He had just read the *Marble Faun,* and was amazed at the author's knowledge of things Catholic. "How splendid to have grown up under him," he said, as the four sat together at dinner. It had been one of Rose's good housekeeping days ; the food was excellent. And George was happy but not exuberant.

Rose shook her head regretfully. "I hardly grew up under him. I was just fourteen when he died. I always regretted having come on the scene so late because by that time my father's fame had grown, and so I never shared the fairy tales and things they did at Lenox and Concord. It sometimes made me feel like a stranger who had come to the feast too late."

George, who was working on the new edition of his father-in-law's work, and was steeped in his philosophy, remarked that *Our Old Home* showed a marvelous conception of the Catholic ideal, and felt that it was only the early Concord pull that had kept him from the Church, since his spirit knew what his mind apparently would not grant. Alfred thought that no doubt Rome, itself, had focussed Catholicism for him, and Rose agreed, telling Alfred how the paintings Hawthorne saw in those Italian days made him appreciate Catholicism, and removed prejudices which Puritanic traditions had made almost a part of his nature. "Of course," she said, "our friends there bowed down utterly to Catholic art, and my father, too, felt that every religious school of art that departed from imitation of the old masters, forfeited holiness in depicting the Holy Family."

At the Church Street house of the Bunners, Rose felt always at home. There they vibrated still to the Concord tradition. They read the books of the "Concord Pleiades" and could talk about them understandingly. There had been talk one evening of the many men who had made the little place important, and someone quoted "The shot heard round the world."

Mrs. Lathrop, overhearing, interposed, "And don't ever forget that the shot fired round the world of course returned to Concord on completing its circuit."

"Did you know Emerson well, or was he too remote to let himself be well known?" asked a stranger in the group.

"Oh, he spread over Concord like the American eagle. I used to love meeting him striding along the Lexington highway, that long yellow thoroughfare that stretches its little papyrus strip of history to Lexington. When we met he smiled and I smiled. We were a great force and a small girl, but he never made me feel like a small girl. His smile was wonderful, he

123

always wore it like an extra feature, and it was always there. But he never laughed. I heard him tell my father once that a laugh was merely a muscular irritation — a pleasant spasm."

Mr. Bunner pulled a book from the case and turned the pages until he found what he wanted. "Here it is, in his own words : 'The best joke of all jokes is that sympathetic contemplation of things by the understanding from the philosopher's point of view.'"

"So you see," said Rose, "he did have something to smile at always. The only time I saw it disappear — and Mr. Emerson, too, if he could get away in time — was when Mr. Alcott was seen coming up the path, or was announced as approaching. You could hardly blame him. Mr. Alcott was a dear, he was a lamb in chains, really. But my mother's eye would get a darker gray when she saw him coming, and that happened only when she was making some sacrifice. The thing that troubled my parents was that he often brought his own verse with him, and the dear child of his Muse was likely to be an *enfant terrible*."

"Last year at Concord," put in a guest, "I walked in the wood back of the Wayside. Someone pointed out a lopsided arbor and said it was one Mr. Alcott built and left hanging there all these years."

"Oh, those arbors," mourned Rose. "He was always finding in his walks bits of branches that he knew he could use for building. And the neighbors felt nothing in the woods was safe while Mr. Alcott prowled in them. And then the arbors he built usually broke in the middle. But it is really not fair to laugh about him. My Aunt Elizabeth would scold me roundly, for she found him a great educator and learned much from him. And for all his carelessness, it was he who went straight after Louisa when she was sick in the war hospital. I loved to watch him striding among his apple trees, looking like a close relative of Pomona."

The group welcomed this talk about their idols. One woman leaned forward. "But you haven't said a word about the man I loved most of them all — Thoreau."

Rose's eyes misted. "My father loved him best of all too. He used to scare me at first. His eyes were tame with intellect, and at the same time liable to be wild with the loose rein — a startling combination, I assure you, which at the time I could not understand. But later I learned more about him. I learned he wore the hair shirt of sacrifice to self-denial. He really was happy when he was disciplining the flesh, and he did it gaily as the saints do, and he went to nature's peacefulness as the saints do, too. I must tell you one thing about him that I just remembered. When he was very ill, his last illness, in fact, my mother sent me over to him with the little music box she had bought during her first year at the Manse, and people with him said he loved to lie there and listen to the tinkling tunes dream forth. And really when he died it was as if an anemone had dropped among the ferns and mosses."

She looked around at the absorbed group. "You must forgive me for talking such a lot about him, but he was nearest to my father of anyone in Concord. After his death the Walden woods rustled his name when we walked in them."

4

The eighties turned into the nineties. The Lathrops lived now in New London, now in New York at the Hotel Albert. Always they were part of the literary life about them. In 1887 George, together with Henry Edwards, had dramatized Tennyson's *Elaine* and it was played with great success in Madison Square Garden.

Rose was glad of its success for various reasons, one being that success made George happy, and also kept him away from his enemy. She wrote to Cousin Emilie Learned : "Yesterday I spent looking at a great many papers for all mention of *Elaine* and cutting out the same for George's collection. Then I called on Mrs. Presby (Annie Russell, you know) and went to dinner at Mama's which was over at eight o'clock. We are very jolly about *Elaine* which so far could not be more crowded or more flatteringly noticed. Saturday evening we went again and they were all acting better and with great zest, and I cried and thrilled with the fervor I felt at the matinée."

In 1888 Rose had published a book of verse herself, called *Along the Shore*. The title was taken from one of George's poems :

> "All day along the shore
> Shout the breakers, green and hoar."

The dedication read : To George Parsons Lathrop.   Directly
under his name was a dedicatory poem :

> "There is no price, best friend, for greatest need,
> Laid on the altar of our true affection.
> Wild flowers of love for me must intercede :
> And lo, I win your unexcelled protection."

She leafed the pages through, wanting to see, yet dreading to
look at one poem — the little one for Francie.   She was almost
afraid to see the words in print.   But now that they lay before
her, they did not hurt at all :

> "I loved a child as we should love
> Each other everywhere ;
> I cared more for his happiness
> Than I dreaded my own despair.
> An angel asked me to give him
> My whole life's dearest cost ;
> And adding mine to his treasures,
> I knew they could never be lost.
>
> "Upon the shore of darkness
> His drifted body lies ;
> He is dead and I stand beside him
> With his beauty in my eyes.
> I am glad I lavished my worthiest
> To fashion his greater worth ;
> Since he will live in Heaven
> I shall lie content in the earth."

Francie was so safe, so cared for.   The God whom Sophia
Hawthorne had remembered, the God of the little church to which
they had taken him to be baptized, was, she knew, taking care
of Francie.

The Riverside edition of Hawthorne's works which George
had edited, was selling very well.   Scribner's had published his
new book of verse, some of them a reprint from the earlier *Rose
and Roof Tree*.   He was very busy with orders from magazines,
and Rose, too, sat often at her desk spilling ink for editors.   She

127

had done a little illustrating, besides, especially for Mrs. Horace Mann's book for children.

Life went easily for them. They did not have a great deal of money, but neither ever needed very much. Their temperaments often clashed, but it was very evident that Rose wanted to be, and stay, the good wife and helpmeet. The shadow of his weakness sometimes stepped out as reality, and then for months it would become only a shadow again.

The child they never mentioned even to each other. But among the papers on George's desk she found sometimes scribbled lines that she read with an aching heart. She had thought hers the greater grief. She wondered about that now, and sent a little petition, almost a prayer, for the soul of the child buried beside his grandfather in Concord.

No one in New York ever heard them mention him. But the Chappells guessed sometimes the grief still in them when they saw George looking at their own pink-cheeked son, or when Rose held the child closely in her arms.

Alfred and George had many long talks together about the Catholic Church. There had been a time in Boston when George had been quite swayed in that direction by the arguments of his friend John Boyle O'Reilly, but not enough to be convinced. Alfred, however, was so serenely happy as a Catholic, that George's interest was again aroused. Years ago, he told Alfred, only a short time after his marriage, he had gone to see Orestes Brownson to discuss Catholicism with him. Brownson had received him at ten in the morning and did not let him go until six in the evening.

"Not with his glittering eye did he hold me," George told Alfred, "but with his bold and brilliant tongue."

When he went to see him a second time Brownson read him Emerson's *Threnody* on little Waldo's death, and he cried unashamedly over it. George had been told that Brownson was a rude rough man, but he did not find him so. But neither he nor O'Reilly had sufficed to show him the necessity of Catholicism,

128

though George felt that Brownson formed a close link between transcendental thought and that embodied in the Catholic Church.

George read countless books about the Faith and talked them over with Alfred, while Adelaide knitted and Rose listened intently to all that was said. They discussed the Church's mighty art, and agreed that it surely emanated from the Divine Spirit. Rose said that if art were all that were needed to make a convert, the people her father and mother knew in Rome would certainly have been converted. "They bowed down utterly to Catholicism because they agreed that without it the great art they saw and lived for would simply have never been."

Alfred hoped that some day he might see the actual Rome as he now saw the spiritual city. Rose thought he should if he could. "Rome is the theatre of the greatest human effort both in the ranks of Satan and of God. She is so visibly mourning her sins at the feet of those spiritual victors, Peter and Paul."

But George felt that Rose was too moved by the heart in her ideas. He wanted his mind to feel the necessity, but Rose shook her head and insisted the heart was terribly important. "It stays the same, George, in all ages, so that the commonplaces of a thousand years ago are still effective as ever today."

And George thought a bit guiltily that that was just the sort of thing John Boyle O'Reilly used to say to him about it — that he had an academic interest in Catholicism and needed a rousing one.

They went to Mass sometimes up on the hill at Saint Mary's church, a sombre structure that seemed at first to George an unworthy receptacle for such greatness as he was beginning to feel Catholicism held. But Rose saw not so much the difference in beauty as the likenesses: the lamp that flickered, the ancient Latin that had seemed such silly stuff to the little girl in Rome.

But it was the reading of the Gospel in English that held them most. They knew many of the passages, but somehow here they were actually the Words of Life. And people knelt reverently here, just as they knelt on the floors of the Roman churches

129

where a small Rose had stepped carefully among them, half wishing to kneel too. A great content stole into her, an assurance that all would come out as it should, and glancing at George, she saw his absorbed face and knew he felt so too.

In 1891, in the church of the Paulist Fathers in New York City, George and Rose Lathrop were received into the Catholic Church by Father Alfred Young. There was amazement in Concord when the news reached there. Of course by this time even Concord was better used to Catholics. There had been for many years a mission in the town to take care of the spiritual needs of the Irish who lived there. The Universalist Church on the Common was for sale, and the priest who had the Concord mission decided to buy the building for his flock. The fact that he had no rectory was soon remedied ; across from the church next to the site of the old Indian weir was an aged building that had belonged to the sheriff and had once been the village lockup. This, too, was for sale, so the enterprising priest converted it into a rectory.

Concord was startled at first to find not only one but two Catholic institutions on its Common, but the only outer differences were a gold cross on top of the New England meeting house and many more people about the Common on Sunday mornings. They soon became accustomed to these sights.

In New York and in New London the news was taken more lightly. Everyone found reasons, of course, ignoring the obvious one. Some said it was merely the result of the Chappell friendship. Some said it was because Rose hoped to hold George in line better with some restraint of authority over him. These latter were unaware of how much the religious thought of Sophia Hawthorne had affected her daughter, or did not realize how his study of Hawthorne's work had affected his son-in-law.

And no doubt everything had helped. But it was only Alfred Chappell who, when he heard the news, exclaimed, "It is the grace of God." That was the answer the others had not thought of. Even Hawthorne would not have said it. But Sophia might well have said it and Una too.

130

Their literary activities changed now, or rather increased. George helped in the founding of the Catholic Summer School at New London the following year and lectured here. His wife, too, occasionally gave talks to groups of Catholics and non-Catholics who were interested in studying the Faith. George was of help in establishing an Apostolate of the Press and lent his pen to its services and needs.

When Christmas of 1893 came it was a lonely one for them both, for Rose had left George and it was evident she did not mean to return. Temperamental differences had at last won out. As one friend said, they were the original two of whom it was said that they could not live together nor apart.

But it was also true that for many years Rose had tried to be a good wife. She had made attempt after attempt to pull George away from his intemperance. She had failed, and she had fled from her failure. She knew with what horror her father and mother, her neighbors in Concord, her whole world in fact, viewed the sight of a woman leaving her husband. But despite all that, she went. She spent a lonely holiday in New York, and George's was equally lonely in New London.

In the early spring a package came for Rose, and when she unwrapped it, she found a new book of verses by George. It was dedicated "To Rösl," the little name of Dresden days. The pages as she read them through her tears, held many of the earlier verses published long ago. There were some about Francie, the one about the child who wanted to be lifted to the blue sky. And the other longer one he had called "The Flown Soul."

> "For which of us indeed is dead ?
> No more I lean to kiss your head
> The gold red hair so thick upon it.
> Joy feels no more the touch that won it,
> When o'er my brow your pearl cool palm
> Crept softly once. Yet see my arm
> Is strong and still my blood runs warm.
> I still can work and think and weep,
> But all this show of life I keep

Is but the shadow of your shine ;
Flicker of your fire, husk of your vine.
Therefore you are not dead, nor I
Who hear your laughter's minstrelsy.
Among the stars your feet are set ;
Your little feet are dancing yet
Their rhythmic beat, as when on earth
So swift, so slight, are death and birth."

She packed her bags and went with him again. Francis Lathrop and their friends rejoiced about it, and hoped with all their hearts that the reconciliation would be a lasting one.

George had interesting news for her. Walter Damrosch had asked him to write for him a dramatic poem suited to grand opera music for the *Scarlet Letter* which he planned to produce. He had written much of it and they forgot their differences, as they always could, in the pleasure they found in literary work.

Little Pearl, it was decided, was to be omitted altogether. The elemental story was still there, but the plot alone was used. The words were so changed that scarcely two dozen of Hawthorne's own sentences were kept.

George planned to use rhyme and rhythm, feeling it was hard to express emotion in too limited a medium. He felt that the book had great cultural value, and thought that one of the greatest values of Hawthorne was that he came to a practical country and showed the world that that country had a high beauty, too. He would prove by this drama how some of these ethical gentlemen who said Hawthorne was artist but never teacher, were really only confused thinkers.

Through some of their friends among the Paulists they were asked to write together an account of the founding of the Visitation Order in America at Georgetown. As they read into the history of the Order, they feared there would be too much to write rather than too little, and after they had read only a partial account of some of the early difficulties and triumphs, they decided on their title : *A Story of Courage.*

132

The Lathrops were to be allowed to go through the convent itself, something which had been permitted to no outside visitors,
save necessary physicians and workmen, for over twenty years.
Feeling in themselves a certain constraint, they presented themselves at the door on a bright spring day.

The convent was a brick structure with a great garden stretch-
ing out behind it.   Georgetown College was near at hand, over-
looking the Potomac.   Arlington rose green beyond the river.
Next to the convent was the much larger Academy for Young
Ladies, and between them stood the chapel with mullioned windows and a quaint balustraded belfry spire on the tip of which
stood a slender cross.

They stood before the green door set so deeply back that one
could be sheltered there while waiting for the door to open, and
rang the bell.   A panel in the dark wall was drawn back, and the
face of the portress appeared.   She had been informed of their
coming, and showed them into a little parlor that was really a link
with the world, for it was outside the bounds of the actual convent.
Across one side of the room was a strong wooden grating, and beyond that another room with a chair, a few pictures and one other
object that fascinated them both.   It was a tiny, an unbelievably
small air-tight stove.   "I am sure," whispered Rose, "that its last
warmth emerged from a silver birch stick fifty years ago."

A door in the room beyond the grating opened and the Mother
Superior came in with her assistant behind her.   The Lathrops
felt suddenly, as George phrased it later, as if all their worldly
wisdom and ordinary knowledge had taken flight and were of no
account whatever.

Certainly such feelings were not purposely caused by the
Mother Superior, who welcomed them graciously and then said,
"You would certainly be excommunicated for this if you had not
received a special dispensation."

They were taken first to see the refectory, plain tables placed
at three sides of the wall and a reading desk for the sister who read
aloud during meals.   On the fourth side windows looked out on
a garden with box borders, and a statue of Saint Joseph in the

centre. The sisters told them what their meals consisted of, and how on Saints' days they always had desserts. "In fact," said the Mother Superior a bit apologetically, "we have very good meals, often, I am afraid, better than those of people who have taken no vow of poverty." But the list of viands sounded very poor to the visitors ; bread and coffee for breakfast, and for dinner bread and meat and a vegetable, with now and then molasses with the bread.

They were shown the burial vault where lay the second Archbishop of Baltimore and some of the earlier sisters. Little black crosses fastened into the earth showed where the nuns rested. In the convent garden was laid out the new graveyard, less than ten years old. Here Rose found the grave of an old friend of Concord days, Phoebe Ripley, who was Emerson's niece and one of the young people who went to all the parties for young folks in Concord with the young Hawthornes. They were told that in religion she had been Sister Jane Frances and a directress of the Academy for several years.

The Mother Superior took great pleasure in showing the Lathrops over the grounds. She gathered for Rose a bouquet of early rosebuds and ivy and showed them the pecan trees grown from nuts, so the story ran, sent by Thomas Jefferson to Georgetown. She showed them the Academy playground, the farmyard, the meadow where the cow belonging to the convent grazed, the steam laundry, and then brought them to the veranda of the nuns' house, where they were urged to have a cup of tea and some food lest they grow too tired.

Later they met the sister who had been very close to Phoebe Ripley, and Rose was glad to find in her a sympathetic and friendly person.

"You must have been a great solace to Phoebe," said Rose, "since she could have with her none of her own dearly loved sisters, and there had been no sympathy at all with her religious views in her own home — bitter opposition, in fact."

They were taken into the long choir, a spacious room fitted with dark stalls on either side for the sisters to sit and kneel and

134

chant their office and hear Mass.   They were shown the assembly room where the sisters gathered for their recreation, that is, for pleasant chat and for knitting or sewing.   "We try," they were told, "to obey the rule of Saint Jane de Chantal : 'Let the hands be employed whenever possible.' "

Little tables stood here and there and simple chairs of a quaint outline, chairs which Madame Iturbide, once Empress of Mexico, and now buried in the convent vaults, gave the community long years ago.   The music rooms for the students were at the very top of the building, like big melodious bird-cages, said George, each enclosing a captive piano, and from the windows they looked out over all Washington, the brown Potomac, the white pillars of the Capitol with bronze Columbia on guard.

"It's very pleasant to look down on all that political turmoil from such a place as this, such a calm one," said George.   "Perhaps Liberty down there can now and then exchange glances with the spirit of sacrifice and self-control up here."

The Mother led them down the stairs again to the little parlor where they said goodbye to her.   She had entrusted them with a very valuable thing, the manuscript records, the Annals of the Convent, the contents of which they were to arrange for use in their book.   She had a slightly troubled look in her clear eyes as she stood there, and it turned out to be a fear that perhaps she had not made them see the convent as it lived in her eyes and her spirit. "It is all very old," she said, "and plain, but we love it.   It is our home on earth and," she hesitated again, "we think it is a little above and more than earth."

Back in New York they began going through the Annals, simple blank books for the most part, in marbled paper, or covered with brown wrapping paper or dark cloth, all penned by sisters in the past and giving the full history of the dauntless group that had formed the Visitation Order in America : the story of the five women who first belonged to it, known in the city as the Pious Ladies.   Four sticks of wood were allowed a day for each stove ; beds were covered with snow rather than with blankets ; brooms were made out of weeds ; only one chair, and that was reserved for the Superior ; the one candle in the convent was that used in the choir.   And through everything a charming humor ran, for all these things were taken with gaiety and were not very important anyway, when the love of God was so much more important, and they had that.

There were stories of the sisters.   Wilhelmina Jones, daughter of a Commodore in the War of 1812, who was very angry when his cherished child became a Catholic through her friendship with Father Fenwick, a Jesuit, and who finally won her back to the Episcopalian Church.   Later she went to see Father Fenwick in an attempt to convert him from the dangers of popery, but several visits brought no change in that gentleman's convictions despite her arguments ; in fact, it was Father Fenwick who, instead, brought Wilhelmina back to the Catholic Church and she became Sister Stanislaus.   Her brother threatened to burn the convent if she did not come out.   Her father sent a man late at night to impersonate her dead mother by wailing "Wilhelmina Jones — come out — come out."   The interested people of the town joined their shouts to the supposed ghost's, but Wilhelmina did not come out.   The Annals spoke of her with great affection as "Sister Stanny" and told how she, being of an impatient disposition, was wont to call herself "The Holy Father's little snapping turtle."

They read the story of Sister Mary Eulalia, who had been Julia Pierce, born of an old Boston family.   She told a tale on herself, duly chronicled by the writing sister.   After she was received into the Church, she realized she had no friend to whom she could speak of her happiness ; there was no one in the Boston of 1844 who would rejoice with a Catholic convert.   Then she remembered the family laundress was a staunch Catholic, and hurried off to her.   Throwing her arms around her, she exclaimed, "Oh, Mary, we are Catholics !"

There was Sister Mary Emmanuel, born Virginia Scott, daughter of Major General Winfield Scott, who had been received into the Church in Rome where she had been at school, and who lived only long enough to make her profession.

They had more material than they needed, and they set to work at their book, sorting the best, though they decided it was all good.

The volume was duly finished and published, a handsome green volume with a Celtic cross in gold on its cover. So far as its purpose had been to tell the story of the Order, it was successful. As a means for keeping George and Rose together, it failed. It seemed nothing could be of help. Nothing could keep them together any longer, not even the great love Rose had given him for so many years, not even the devotion George had given her. Before the year was out, Rose had gone again, and this time she did not return.

Down in Concord they shook their heads when they heard about it. "If the child had lived," said those who knew them both, "it would have been different."

5

During those first difficult months, Rose busied herself with her work on the memories of her father which she had nearly ready to put into a book. She went occasionally to Concord, and sometimes dropped into the Wayside for a talk with Mrs. Lothrop, or Mrs. How, her cousin. She must have been very lonely during those days, for she was in all truth entirely alone now. Una and her father and mother and Francie — all were asleep and only she was awake with her pain. She tried to remember that she was a Catholic, and she thanked God for her faith. Without that she would have been utterly bereft. It bound her as by a bridge with the dead ; she remembered, and echoed her mother's words : "I have an eternity to know them or I should die of despair."

In Concord she stayed with Mrs. How in Hubbard Street. Young Walter, grown a big boy now, slept in a room near the kitchen, and he was wont to listen to his mother and Aunt Rose talking out there by the hour. But it was very tiresome talk for a boy — all about Unitarianism and Catholicism, and Walter fell asleep to the sound of their voices, the click of their knitting needles, the soft insistent tones of his mother's voice, the argumentative voice of his aunt.

Mornings while the Hows were still asleep, Rose went quietly from the house to early Mass at Saint Barnabas on the Common.

Surely to anyone who knew her, it was an astonishing sight : the daughter of the Hawthornes taking her way through the town of Emerson and Thoreau to the Catholic Church, kneeling in the midst of the little congregation of early worshippers. The altar was plain ; the statues were of plaster and paint. She knew no one of those among whom she knelt. But here was that which could restore her soul, which could feed her with love and hope for the days ahead. She prayed for them all, for the Chappells, for Francie, for Thoreau (it would have delighted him), for George.

There were days when she decided to go back, and there were other days when she knew she could not, would not ever again. But she felt, too, that she must not merely waste her time ; surely God would soon find something for her to do, would fill her idle hands with work for Him. She would go back to New York and talk to the Paulists, offer her aid wherever it might be needed.

She went once more to Sleepy Hollow and saw that the ivy over the graves was weeded, over Francie's headstone, and little Garth's, and the memorial stones. She sat in the sunlight, with Concord in front of her, the waving trees over her and all about her the people she had known and loved. Nearly every head-stone she could see held the name of a friend of her father or of her own. Not one of them was left to listen to her problems or help her.

Back in New York again she hunted up the address of her seamstress to take some dresses to her for alteration. At the door of the rooming house the landlady told her the woman was no longer with her ; she had been found to be very ill with that terrible disease — cancer.

"I had to put her out quick. You know how it is with me. The other boarders would have left me if they found out she had it. They would be afraid to catch it."

"Where can I find her, please ?"

The landlady wasn't quite sure. "To a hospital they took her, and then I hear the money gave out she had saved. I guess she is at the Island now, maybe.   Bellevue won't keep 'em either, you know."

Rose did not know, but she had heard enough to make her feel shaken and ill.   It was cancer that had a few years ago carried off Emma Lazarus, not yet forty, with a brilliant life before her.   She heard the low lovely voice saying earnestly, "You must suffer to care, I am afraid.   Until you suffer you cannot quite understand."

Rose had gone up to her house several times to see her when she lay very ill, but still unsatisfied about the world and her people. The marks of the disease were hidden, but pain had drawn the red lips thin and made them pale ; pain had shadowed the great brown eyes.   There was in the room, too, an unmistakable odor which Josephine, Emma's sister, told her later always accompanied the disease.

Rose had tried hard to act naturally, but she shrank from that odor though she tried not to let Emma see it, Emma, surrounded by all the comforts that wealth could give her, food, warmth, medical care, love of family ; yet the inexorable enemy was daily making her a little weaker through the pain of an illness that money and love could help but could not cure.   Rose had gone back time and time again.   She was glad of that, remembering Emma's saying long ago at the Gilder's home, "You stir me up with suggestions — you give me hope."

Walking through the bright day of a New York spring, Rose was beginning to realize that the world held shadows much deeper than her own.   Here was the seamstress, a gently bred woman whose only crime was that she had an incurable illness and that her money, saved up through years of sewing, was spent in trying to get well.

She asked questions of people who knew more about such matters, a nurse of her acquaintance, a settlement worker, and she learned how little was done for such cases after they were pronounced incurable, how they were turned away at just the time when they most needed care and kindness, how they were finally doomed to be sent to the Island and left there until death should end their sufferings of body and mind.   She went out to the Is-

140

land to find the dressmaker, to make her last hours at least a bit easier. She learned the woman had died some weeks before and had been buried in the grave the city gives its poor.

In Rose's heart was horror and pity. A fire was lighted in her that burned more brightly as days went on. She would have to do something, she felt, toward preventing such inhuman regulations for those who are too forlorn to protest. For out on the Island she had seen others, cancer sufferers, and it had been no pleasant sight. She turned away shivering from the bandaged faces with the wounds often partly visible beneath them, turned from the odor that rose from their uncared-for bodies.

She sat in her room one evening, remembering the death of Emma Lazarus from the grim disease that was beginning to alarm the whole nation by its swift rise. That death had been hard enough, even though surrounded by love and all the comforts wealth could give. Never for a moment had Emma been made to feel unwanted, or that her death would be a relief to all concerned. And what made the difference between her and these inmates of the Island ? It was the love of those who were with her, who were related to her, her friends who brought her flowers, her family who spent their wealth upon her.

She remembered Una in the London street, the day she had been urging her to come away from the dirty gray children. Una had said that their father's book, *Our Old Home,* had made her realize that all the world is responsible for their grayness, their misery.

In the bookcase were ranged her father's books, the splendid edition of them which George had worked so hard editing. She felt a moment's panic just then. Perhaps she was mistaken. Perhaps she should give him one more chance. But some inexorable thing in her told her that that road was closed forever. And something made her leaf through *Our Old Home* until she came to the account Una had spoken of, the story of the little workhouse child.

"It might almost make a man," she read, "doubt the existence of his own soul to observe how nature has flung these little

141

wretches into the street and left them there, so evidently regarding them as nothing worth, and how all mankind acquiesces in the great mother's estimate of her offspring. For, if they have no immortality, what superior claim can I assert for mine ? And how difficult to believe that anything so precious as a germ of immortal growth can have been buried under this dirt heap, plunged into this cesspool of misery and vice. As often as I beheld the scene, it affected me with surprise and loathsome interest much resembling, though in a far intenser degree, the feeling with which when a boy, I used to turn over a plank or old log that had long lain on damp ground and found a vivacious multitude of unclean and devilish looking insects scampering to and fro beneath it. Without an infinite faith there seemed as much prospect of a blessed futurity for these hideous bugs and many footed worms as for these brethren of our humanity and co-heirs of all our heavenly inheritance. Ah, what a mystery."

So she had felt in the street beside Una. So she had felt before that array of broken and diseased bodies at the Island.

"Slowly, slowly, as after groping at the bottom of a deep, noisome, stagnant pool, my hope struggles upward to the surface, bearing the half drowned body of a child along with it, and heaving it aloft for its life and my life and all our lives. Unless these slime-clogged nostrils can be made capable of inhaling celestial air, I know not how the purest and most intellectual of us can reasonably expect to ever taste a breath of it. The whole question of eternity is staked here. If a single one of these helpless little ones is lost, the world is lost. How superficial are the niceties of such as pretend to keep aloof. Let the whole world be cleansed or not a man or woman of us all can be clean."

She came then to the passage about the little workhouse child. Hawthorne had been shown through the poor-house by the governor and in the children's ward he felt a tug at his coat. Turning he saw a hideous little face, covered with scurvy, holding out red diseased hands to him, asking to be taken up and held. He hesitated a moment, then stooped and held it close to him as if it had been one of his own children. "Young as the little thing was its pain and misery had endowed it with a premature intelligence, insomuch as its eyes seemed knowingly and appealingly to stare out of its sunken sockets, as if summoning us one and all to witness the deadly wrong of its existence. At least so I interpreted its look, when it positively met and responded to my own awestricken gaze, and therefor I lay the case, as far as I am able, before mankind, on whom God has imposed the necessity to suffer in body and soul till this dark and dreadful wrong be righted."

Last of all she found the passage she had opened the book to find : "No doubt the child's mission was to remind him that he was responsible, in his degree, for all the suffering and misdemeanors of the world in which he lived, and was not entitled to look upon a particle of its dark calamity as if it were none of his concern : the offspring of a brother's iniquity being his own blood-relation, and the guilt likewise a burden on him, unless he expiated it by better deeds."

She marveled at the grasp her father, untaught in the Faith, had of the fundamental principles of Catholicism. She put the book back in the case with the others and one fell out on the floor. It lay open at the story of the *Miraculous Pitcher*. Suddenly, as in a photograph, she saw a picture from the past : her aunt and Mrs. Emerson, waiting for a tea that was not served ; her mother's dismay, the story of the *Miraculous Pitcher* open on the table just as they had stopped reading when the guests came in.

The open page caught her eye. "Human beings owe a debt of love to one another, because there is no other method of paying the debt of love and care which all of us owe Providence," and a bit farther down, "Providence put me here, I hope, among other things in order that I may make amends for the inhospitality of my neighbors."

She went on her knees, the tears raining down her cheeks. "God help me," she prayed, "to help them." For she knew that somehow she must take from those faces on the Island and the others who would be sentenced there to die, or who were dragging out their lives in dark rooms, hoping only to escape notice until they died, the look of fear and dread, even as her father had felt he must take it from the child in his arms.

By the next day she had thought things out. She went first to see Emma Lazarus' sister with her plan for she had heard that she had tried some sort of work of just this kind. But Miss Lazarus strove only to dissuade her.

"My dear, it is a hopeless task," she said. "You know I opened a small hospital for the cancerous poor in memory of Emma. It started well, nicely equipped, good nurses. I thought it would be the beginning of proper care for these people. And it failed. Perhaps some great institution will take care of the situation some day, but a small place? No, it can never succeed."

"But we can't wait for that," cried Rose. "We dare not wait. There are no free beds in hospitals for them. They lie in damp basements and no one comes to see them. They die of exposure and hunger and lack of medical care. Or, if they are not left neglected, they are shifted around until they get to the almshouse on the Island. Even then they have to wait their turn to be admitted, sitting, in their condition, at the end of their illness often and not the beginning, on a hard bench where draughts chill their bodies just as unkindness chills their hearts."

But Miss Lazarus was not to be persuaded. "It will not work."

"But why not? Why won't it work just as other hospitals for special diseases work?"

She considered. "Mostly I think," she said slowly, "it is because of the nurses. They will not stay with the work. We paid them well, gave them short hours, everything we could. Something more than paying wages will have to be done if such work is to be successful ever."

"But you see I won't be paying any wages to myself. It will be a one woman sanitarium. And perhaps there will be only one room. I haven't much money, but I can start with what I have."

144

"You may be right. There must be a special stimulus of some sort. Your religion may accomplish it for you where the best secular one can't. But it is terribly tiresome work, my dear. There is no cure ahead ever, as in some hospitals. Think twice before you begin."

Rose lifted her head defiantly. "I have thought once and I have decided. I shall begin tomorrow."

Miss Lazarus smiled at her. "How Emma would love to hear you talk like that — with such determination. 'Send them, the homeless, tempest-tossed to me,' Emma wrote that. It would do for a motto for you if you insist on going ahead."

"I have my motto," said Rose seriously. "It is from Saint Vincent de Paul : 'I am for God and the poor.' "

"Yes, that is better than Emma's. I wish I could persuade you to give up the idea, my dear, but if you won't, then let me know when you are ready to start. I'll send you some money to help you."

6

Rose packed her books and her clothing and stored them. She bought the necessary hospital wear, the cotton stockings, the blue dresses, and went up to Central Park West to present herself at the doors of the New York Cancer Hospital and begin there the three months' practical nursing course they were allowing her to take.

On her way she pondered the news that had come to her that morning. The arrangement of the *Scarlet Letter* in opera, upon which George had been working, and which Damrosch was playing in New York, was proving very successful. She was glad for George's sake that he was meeting with success. And then before the doors of the hospital, she forgot everything except the present and the future inside those doors.

The Head was waiting for her in her office. The rules of that day were not so strict as they are today, so that Rose's application had been quickly accepted. Besides the hospital was glad to get the services of a free nurse, even if only a practical one, to help with the one ward from which nurses fought to stay away, where they had to be shifted frequently because of the horror of the work.

The Head rose smiling. "Mrs. Lathrop, I believe ? I have been told just what it is you wish to do. But will you forgive me

for asking you why under the sun you want to do work like this ?
Have you any special reason for it — is someone dear to you ill
with cancer ?"

Words surged to Rose's lips.   There were so many reasons, so
very many.   But would they be ones which this woman would
understand ?   "There are several reasons," she began lamely, but
the Head, seeing her hesitation, decided it was probably just a rich
or bored woman's fancy and she would get over it soon enough.
She led her to the door of a long circular room.

"This is the room where you will be at work," she told her and
left her to the nurse in charge of the ward.

It was a little late in the day for changing dressings, but there
was one left which had not yet been taken care of.   The nurses
always left her until the last because she was a face case of par-
ticular unpleasantness.

"You'll help me ?" asked the nurse.

The patient waited smiling.   Above her eyes and below them
were stretched pieces of adhesive tape.   The eyes twinkled from
these white bars, and they were blue and gay.   The rest of her
face was very attractive and her curly brown hair was nicely arranged.   She came toward them with the air of one about to do
them a favor, as if she were welcoming this newcomer to her ward.

With this gaiety before her, with the tapes still covering the
ravages of the disease, Rose was entirely unprepared for the horror
that confronted her when the tapes were pulled away to disclose
a face half eaten away by the disease.   She shivered as if with a
chill, but the nurse was watching her, evidently all ready for this
rank outsider who dared invade a professional field.   And the
eyes of Mrs. Watson, the patient, were on her too, silently begging her not to admit how terrible it really was.

Rose opened the eyes she had closed in involuntary shrinking ;
then she went to work, as the nurse directed her.   It was a
thorough initiation, and she did not flinch until it was completed.
No doubt later dressings were as bad, but she could keep her eyes
open on them after that first case.

When the strange Mrs. Lathrop had retired that evening, the

147

Head called to the nurse in the Incurable Ward. "Well, did she last all day or only part of it ?"

But the ward nurse did not smile at the sally. There was a look of amazement on her face. "She lasted all right. I thought she was finished when she got a look at Mrs. Watson's face with the bandages off it. I heard her draw a deep breath and she got pale, but that was all. You know what Mrs. Watson looks like with the bandages off."

Rose in her little room was at that moment remembering some lines from one of her own verses — strange how these things that had been more or less literary exercises came back to one as truth :

> "To his heart it struck such terror
> That he laughed a laugh of scorn."

In the weeks that followed she grew very fond of Mrs. Watson, who was the joy of the ward, giving it its laughs by her Irish cleverness. Her lips were bright red, her chin softly rounded, her expression intelligent. It was incredible to realize what lay under those bandages.

Rose was watching her one morning as she went around the big circular room, built so that all the beds faced the big pole in the centre. "It is like a circus tent," she told her, "and you are the entertainer." Someone had sent in a charity package of underwear of a very old-fashioned sort, and Mrs. Watson had put on some of it and was dancing round among the beds. From the ring that faced her, women who would die before the month was out, laughed until the tears came at her grotesque appearance.

The new nurse walked into the Incurable Ward one day to find Mrs. Watson all ready to go out. She was amazed to learn that so dreadful a face case was allowed on the streets, as Mrs. Watson, arrayed in all manner of garments, stood beaming at her in a state of embroidered elegance. She was adjusting over a very large black hat a very large black veil, so that through the black there gleamed here and there white touches — a sight to haunt the timid passer. Mrs. Watson bade her a solemn goodbye.

"But where are you going, Mrs. Watson ?" asked the new

148

nurse. "And are you well enough to go out alone ?"

"I've a small grandson in the Catholic Protectory, and it's every month I go to see him." Rose told herself that no doubt the children there must be supposed to have iron nerves, probably because they were the offspring of hardship, or they would certainly have been alarmed at sight of Mrs. Watson.

"I've the basket ready to take to him," and she pushed it forward to show her nurse the pile of things she had been able to save or beg from patients in the private rooms, cake, messy fruit, even some slabs of pie, all lying companionably together.

"Here is twenty-five cents to buy some candy," offered Rose.

"It's you have need of your money, dearie ; I'll not take it. There is plenty here for the young rascal," and away she floated out of the door of the ward and disappeared round the corner of the hall. It was the time to the minute when patients were allowed to go out, and she would have to return on the minute too.

She was back right on time. But she was not the same Mrs. Watson. She was weary now and dusty, and the veil was all twisted around her hat and the hat twisted around her head. The basket was empty except for one odd object ; the end of a boiled pig's ear it was, she explained to the baffled Mrs. Lathrop, as she exhibited it proudly to the ward.

"I stopped by to see my sister that's a widow and little she has to live on, but it was a good supper she gave me of pig's ear. And she sent back this bit for Mrs. Smith after me telling her how fond she is of it."

Mrs. Smith's face lighted up at sight of the tidbit. She was the sickest woman in the ward. She ate the bit of ear with much relish.

The next month, the last of her stay, Rose came in the ward to find that Mrs. Watson was not there. She had grown so accustomed to watch for her welcoming smile when she came in the room, nerving her for the horrors to come, that she felt a sense of loss. She had been for some time on night duty and therefore had not known what went on during the day, and she felt immediately apprehensive that there had been a fatal hemorrhage,

149

for the doctors had been expecting that. Her dressings were being changed three times a day now.

But she was not dead. When Rose learned what had happened to her she was sick at heart. The little dressmaker had been dead and buried before she learned about her. Mrs. Watson was not dead, but she had been sent to the same fate that was the dressmaker's. The kind old woman whose only crime had been that she had a dreadful disease from which no recovery was known, had been sent away the moment it was absolutely certain there was no chance of cure, as was the hospital rule.

But where had the poor soul gone ? She had only the sister to go to who was very poor herself and caring for three small grandchildren besides. On Rose's insistence the hospital gave her an address where she might be reached. Rose wrote several letters, but none was ever answered.

A few weeks after the going of Mrs. Watson, Rose was ready to go, too. She knew a great deal more than when she entered those doors. She knew now the real horror of the disease. She knew its hopelessness. And she knew what she had only suspected, what she had been told after the dressmaker's death : for the cancerous poor there was no place, no refuge other than the careless oblivion of a pauper's home, the namelessness of a pauper's grave.

She knew, too, exactly where she was going : to the slums of the lower East Side, where the disease was rife, and where the victims received little or no care. She went through her small store of jewelry, sold what was not too dear to her, and wrote a note to Miss Lazarus to tell her that she was starting her home for cancerous poor. The latter promptly responded with a check and an appeal to remember what she had told her regarding the impossibility of helping that work, urging her to find something to do that had some slight assurance of success. Rose smiled at the letter and cashed the check, and with that sum and her small savings, went out to find a place for her cancer home.

Down on Scammell Street she found three little rooms and a

pantry which she felt she could afford and which were in the very heart of poverty. She bought two iron beds, a chair, a table, a few medical supplies, some material for bandaging. She cleaned the little rooms as best she could, but she saw she would have to paint them to make them cleaner and brighter. But she would have to be careful of what she spent. She found she had just twenty-five dollars left after she had paid her rent and bought the furniture and supplies. Then, considering her immediate environment, she discovered that on each side of her there was a stable, and she found on looking out of her front window that in front of her was a third stable.

Her first night was alarming to her. The noises, the shouts and shrieks seemed unending, and she was frightened, until close by her window she heard the voices of children at play and that steadied her.

Before two days had gone she had accustomed herself to the noise, but it took that long. Morning and night the horses clattered on the paving stones. A barrel organ would send out its strains and out streamed the whole neighborhood, the younger and noisier part of it, to dance to the music with shouts and yells. The shrieks of the drunken, the squalling of children, hungry or beaten, came to her ears. Cats yowled by night and dogs barked by day. To Rose, who had lived always in the quiet country or in well behaved parts of cities, this bedlam was unnerving.

But when she went outdoors everything was different. She saw then why the poor stayed outdoors when they could manage to do so. The dank dingy houses had nothing to offer, but outside there was air, good clean air, especially mornings and evenings. And down by Water Street there was the river. There were ships dipping and greeting the shabby trees of Corlears Park. At sunset Brooklyn Bridge was a marvelous sight, and the sunrise there, was, so Rose thought, like a pageant, soothing to the soul as dawn on the Alps. And the moonlight, the soft cool breeze at night, were to her messages from God at the end of day that could, if not blot out, at least bless the poverty and disease of the day.

She went out often in those first few days on Scammell Street to catch a view of water and sky, hoping that those around her were cheered in their dirt and poverty by this panoramic loveliness, but more and more aware that they did not notice it at all. The river and the trees and the mornings and evenings of looking at them helped her to keep going. When she walked in the early morning there was the circle of God's heaven about her and about all the people there, even though she realized that perhaps those around her did not notice them at all ; but she felt that the cheerfulness of it all must be influencing them without their knowing it. And then the ships, the masted schooners that went in such a solemn way to and fro from their moorings. They seemed to be, she thought, on important errands, hurried errands like her own, but doing it with such a dignity that she found herself trying to emulate their gait.

"Lady, you living here ?" a voice, apparently coming from the ground, asked her on a morning ramble. She glanced down at a child of seven or so, holding in her arms a small baby, both dirty, ragged, smiling.

"Yes, I am," she said, "but do look out for that baby. You ought to hold his head — see, like this," as she took the malodorous little bundle carefully in the crook of one arm, while the child watched gravely.

"It's not her baby anyway," another young person came forward in a businesslike way. "She wants to hold him all the time because her baby died last week," and she took possession of the infant who placidly allowed all this shifting about, holding him at an even more dangerous angle than the temporary mother had.

Mrs. Lathrop watched them move off, still wrangling for possession of the bundle of rags, watched that uneasy head gyrating again toward the ground. "It is their toy," she thought, "a cheap and easily procured one." But she was glad that the children of the neighborhood were accepting her as one of them ; she knew that if children are kind to you in their mean streets, they really love you.

Often when she walked home, in the days that followed, faint-

152

ing with over-strained sympathies and energies, children from the tenements about her own would cluster around her with the sincerity of children toward a person to be trusted, and she felt strong again and able to meet her difficulties. She remembered her father's remark as he watched sadly the children of London slums mothering those still smaller ; he said they must derive such a sense of responsibility immediately from God.

During her first weeks at her new work, Dr. Miller came to see her and offer his help. For two whole years he gave his best efforts to her. And later Dr. Coyle from Henry Street helped her not only with the house patients but with the sick in their homes. Later still Dr. Shiels of the same neighborhood offered his services.

At first she had wanted no doctors at all. Her simple reasoning was that the patients were incurable and beyond a doctor's care, and that she was merely making those comfortable whom the doctors had done their best for and given up. But criticism had sprung up. Her friend, Dr. Storer, of Newport, wrote to urge her to continue in friendly relations with the medical profession, especially with those in New York who were engaged in cancer work. Also he suggested she would find it well to consent to frequent inspection by the Board of Health, since that was really essential to what was becoming rapidly a public charity.

In addition to the kindly doctors of the neighborhood who came to help her, from uptown came an energetic young physician, Dr. James J. Walsh, who was equally interested in the tiny sanitarium and the women who ran it. He, too, promised them any help they might ask of him, a promise which was filled over and over as the years went on.

Somehow the news of her enterprise was heard of in newspaper circles, and the editor of the *Times* sent one of his reporters to get the story : "Daughter of Hawthorne — wife of Lathrop who was a *Sun* editor — looks like good stuff."

It was the first of October. In the country, and up on Riverside Drive, the leaves were golden and red ; clean breezes brought refreshment to those weary of summer heat. But, when the reporter got down to East Broadway and finally found number 1 Scammel Street, he saw no hint of pleasant autumn — only a dreary succession of tumbledown tenements ; he felt no autumn coolness, but only the stored-up heat of an airless summer.

He looked at the address to be sure he was right. Unhappily, he felt he was. It was a regulation tenement building, four stories in height. The narrow hall and the stairs were black with dirt ; the shaky baluster by whose help he mounted, was sticky from hands that had used it before him so that, after one touch, he preferred to risk the rickety stairs. The ceiling above him had patches where the plaster had broken off, and the reporter ducked involuntarily when he saw a piece just over his head apparently ready to fall directly on him.

When he reached the second floor, an odd sight met his eyes : a freshly painted snowy door set defiantly in the grime of ages, and on it a sturdy iron knocker. He knocked and the door opened almost immediately to disclose a woman with a mass of red gold hair wound round her head, whose blue eyes looked distinctly disappointed at seeing him.

"I'm the reporter from the *Times* whom you promised to see."

"Oh, yes, come in. I thought you would be a patient whose bandages I was to change. I've been expecting him. I hope he gets here," but though they both peered through the gloom of the hall, it showed no one coming up.

A few boxes were placed here and there in the room, so the reporter sat on one of them, after placing the only chair in sight for her. "Now," he said, "would you mind telling me your purpose and your aims in taking up this work, Mrs. Lathrop ?" his eyes on the painted white walls, the little holy pictures, the small saint in plaster on the table along with a roll of bandage and a shears.

"Oh, I have wanted for a long time to do something to help people. These cancer sufferers seem to be among the most neglected of all. Their own families sometimes won't take care of them."

"You are beginning in a small way," he said tentatively.

She laughed at that. "Yes, it is small. I would like a place large enough to establish a small hospital ward, but the landlords and the tenants objected, so I'll make house to house visits for a while and take only a few of the lighter cases here. I'm not really started yet, but next week, when my drugs and bandages get here, I'll really get to work."

"Won't the expense be heavy if you take on more ?"

"Well, I have a very small income of my own and some royalties to get it started, and my time and personal services won't cost anything. And I feel sure people will help me when they learn how really dreadful conditions are."

The knocker sounded. The door opened to let in a woman with a child in her arms, and back of her a man with dirty bandages on a gaunt face.

"This is the man I told you about, Mrs. Lathrop," said the woman, easing the child into her lap as she sat down in the chair which Rose had risen from. "He ain't so bad yet, but his daughter won't fix him up. Her stomach turns easy, and you see — " the man turned and pushed a bandage to one side. Mrs. Lathrop and the reporter both saw. She gave him a brief examination and told him to come back in the afternoon.

"I'll have some salve for you then," she promised, "and you may come every other day to have it bandaged."

The dull eyes were unbelieving. "Honest ?" he asked.

"Honest," she told him.

The loose, ill-put-on bandage creased under his sudden smile. "Then I guess she'll let me stay home."

He clumped out, and Rose turned again to the reporter. "I'm sorry I had to keep you waiting. Was there anything more I could tell you ?"

He was staring at her. "Are many cases as bad as that ?"

"That case was not so dreadful. You would see many worse if your paper sent you up to the Cancer Hospital on One Hundred and Sixth Street. It is a splendid place, and it is a shame the people of the city don't support it better."

"But will you take cases as dreadful as this, continually ?" he asked.

"I plan to take anyone who comes," she told him cheerfully, "provided of course they have no money to pay for help, and that the doctors have assured them they can't recover ; and my work will be carried on along lines generally adopted by sisterhoods who do charitable nursing."

"You're Catholic, too, aren't you ?"   He looked at the pictures and statue.

"That fact," she told him seriously, "is my one great asset for my work."

He waited for a moment at the door.   "I wish you all the success in the world," he said earnestly.   "I hope you get your ward, and perhaps some day a whole hospital.   I wonder have you any special phrase I could use in my story and say it is your motto — you know what I mean."

She considered only a moment.   "Yes, you can say it is a sentence from Saint Vincent de Paul : 'I am for God and the poor.' "

Back at his desk the reporter began his story :

"The daughter of Nathaniel Hawthorne, Mrs. George Parsons Lathrop, wife of the editor and author, has taken up her abode in the tenement house district on the East Side of the city.

"Mrs. Lathrop is still on the sunny side of middle age, and retains much of her early beauty of face and figure."

It sounded so inadequate, but neither the *Times* nor Mrs. Lathrop would want to have him burst into a rhapsody about her clear gray-blue eyes nor that marvelous head of tawny hair.   This was to be a dignified story.

"She says," he wrote on, "she will continue her ministrations as long as her health and strength are spared."

Two incidents came up during the next few days that took toll of the emotions she was husbanding out of regard for her work.

She saw from her window a long funeral procession going past, turning into Water Street as she was on her way to get some fresh

156

air on the river front.   A young man, watching it also, said to her, as she paused for a moment and said a Hail Mary for the departed soul, "Gee, but they're giving her a good send-off !"

"Who is it ?"

"Mother Sherwood."

She was shocked to hear that, for the woman whose body was being carried along had only recently been speaking to her.   It was Mrs. Sarah Sherwood, who for years had worked in the Water Street Mission, and of whom Rose had heard it said that she could enter the vilest dance hall on Cherry Street and the place would become quiet.

"My dear," she said to Rose, "this is no place for you.   Until they know you, you always have lots of trouble.   The old Fourth Ward is no place for a lady like you."

"But you stayed — "

"Yes, I did ; but it took time to make them let me stay."

"Oh, I have plenty of that.   I'll stay too."

Mother Sherwood had patted her and smiled at her.   And now she was here, followed by dozens of those who had made things hard for her at first.   She had stayed and won.   She said another little prayer for the dauntless woman, as the procession, caps and hats off, moved slowly down the narrow street.

The other incident involved her friend, Susie Swift, capable and hard-working Brigadier in the Salvation Army.   Father Doyle of the Paulist Fathers sent a note about her that made Rose speed to find her.   Miss Swift, she knew, was on the brink of becoming a Catholic, and now here was Father Doyle writing that it was doubtful if Miss Swift would be baptized right away.   She thought she would wait until she came back from London, and she was sailing the next day.

"Oh, my dear," she said to the obdurate Miss Swift, "you know how I live.   The Scammell Street house is not a comfortable place ; but if you don't know where to go for the moment, to think, to breathe, oh, half of all I have is yours rather than that you should put off for one hour what is the most wonderful thing in the world — the receiving of Our Lord."

157

"I feel I should wait until I come back from England," objected Brigadier Swift, turning from the appeal of Rose's tear-filled eyes.

"I'm not worrying so much about your being baptized. Your long ago Episcopalian one was probably a good one, and Father Doyle has been trying to convince me, teasing me, I am afraid, that if your ship goes down you will have had the baptism of desire. But that wouldn't comfort me at all — nothing will until I know you have received Our Lord in Holy Communion."

"Rose, go away. I may go to be baptized this afternoon. And I still have my small room to go to."

Rose took her arm impetuously. "Come now — come with me !"

But Brigadier Susie, who did not by any sweep of fancy dream that she would one day be Sister Mary Imelda Teresa, O.P., shook her off.

"I will not. If I do, I go alone."

Rose stood up. "Very well, since you are so determined. But I shall go back and set every one of the Catholic patients, I am on my way to bandage, to saying the Rosary for your intention, or for my intention, perhaps I should say."

Late that evening Susie Swift came down to Scammell Street to see Rose. She brought her the news that she had been baptized that afternoon, and would go to Mass with her in the morning.

7

For some weeks Rose took no patients into her house. She went to visit them here and there, going to addresses which she had brought from the hospital, cases dismissed as incurable. She dressed the poor in their own homes, thinking with regret of the clean hospital beds where they should be lying, instead of among those who would often be only too glad to have them die. And in the eyes of the sick poor, she could see that they knew it too.

No sooner was she well established in her rooms than she had to seek other lodgings. The row of shanties was being torn down to make room for a public school, but near at hand, at 668 Water Street, she found new quarters, as tumbledown as the others had been, and as much in need of paint.

Meantime relatives had been coming down to see that nothing really terrible had happened to her. George wrote her to forget this idealism and come home again ; he wrote that he could not bear the thought of his wife in such danger of disease. What there was of the Hawthorne and Mann clan around New York tried to tell her how her strength would not be able to keep up to what she was trying to do.

She answered them all in one way. "I can't do much," she told them, "but I am going to carry out my idea precisely as I at first received it, fresh from the fires of compassion, and I am going to do it as best I can."

Of course this stopped much of the arguing, since no one could really say just how far she could go. And perhaps they were beginning to see that here was no sentimental idea ; that she was bringing succor to a need that had had very little help.

"Anyway," she insisted, "I shall keep on until some at present unidentified personality does it better."

One friend used one day a phrase that kept haunting her. "But Rose, they are so boring, so uninteresting. How can you bear to be with them all the time ?" She was not content until, late that evening, she wrote down all the thoughts that question had roused in her during the day. She put it with the remark of one who said she could not see how the people down here could ever "go into a church the morning after one of their lurid nights."

"Of course the poor are uninteresting," she wrote, "like a long dusty stretch of road with no tree or hill ahead. They are the human race devoid of illusions, bare of superficial attractions, standing as sinners imprisoned by circumstances before the tribunal of spiritual and intellectual joy. Even if they are loathsome or despondent or unresponsive, they are ourselves in a different guise. If we the fortunate did not neglect the unfortunate, they would not be walled in behind circumstances over which we are powerless or imprisoned in ignorance and sin.

"And then, too, suddenly, in all this weedy confusion of cruelty and grossness, there will spring up some flower of loveliness. The poor, I have learned, can feel and do heroic things. And if we go deeper and deeper into our relations with them, we will at last find ourselves standing beside them and acknowledging ourselves guilty of every misdemeanor attributed to those shackled with the handcuffs of misfortune.

"As for their sinful lives, I used to think such things about them too. But lately I have made up my mind that the so-to-speak semi-depraved poor are an open book, and we see just what they are writing of their lives every day, while the semi-depraved rich are a decorously closed one. There is a truth, or at least an observation for people to carry around with them. The rich have so many chances at legitimate pleasures too and the poor so few. Watch how they enjoy the least thing that falls to them. I have learned not a great deal in my short time down here, but I have learned this, and I learned it while sitting at the bedsides of the poor. When I set their agonies beside those of the rich, and their sins against those of well-to-do souls, and when I study the two orders of suffering and misdemeanor, I see more and more that I must reverse all my ideas. And I feel vaguely that missions for the rich, free lectures for the debonair fledgings of wealth, should be the next thing the world must have to accomplish social betterment.

"If anyone wants to know how extremely similar the poor are to friends and enemies uptown, they may well give a week to studying them. It would take but that long to sweep away all the carefully devised barriers placed between us and common sense. The impulse to ignore them is more worthy of jailers than of cultivated citizens."

She put the sheets of paper away in her desk. Some day she would find a place to print them.

It was the daily press which brought her the first house patient. The story in the *Times* was responsible for various sums from sympathetic readers, and some bundles of clothing and bandaging supplies. It also brought her a patient whom she was only too willing to take into her home.

Rose stepped out of her clean little rooms to an autumn day of wind and racing clouds in a deep blue sky. The postman had left a letter for her from a woman who had read about her in the paper, and who asked for help — for complete help, in fact ; a home to live in. "Maybe you remember me from the hospital," she wrote. And it was signed "Mrs. Watson."

She went out gaily from the shabby building, afire with the thought that at last her life work was beginning. Later, much later, she was glad that she had known so little of what she was attempting to do ; she might have lost courage to go on. She was going to do what she felt she ought to do, what God was wanting her to do, what her father would bless her for doing, what Una would help her with were she still here to help. But Una, she knew, could help powerfully. She sent a prayer to her sister, and then on impulse, added another to Saint Rose of Lima whom long ago in Rome Miss Elizabeth Hoar had called Rose's patron saint.

She was going to bring her old friend from the hospital home and make her comfortable until she died. Perhaps, she dreamed, as she hurried along, perhaps she would not even let her die. She flew along with the wind to find Mrs. Watson. She had, of course, a few qualms about this novel intention. Those few rooms had been merely intended for herself, to be used as a *pied à terre*, a clinic, so that she might study the poor about her and try to live as they did before she actually started a hospital. Yet here was a patient, and no doubt there would be more. Well, there was no use in brooding ; there was just one thing to do right now, and that was to find Mrs. Watson.

She found her very much changed, thin and pale and depressed. She was having her face dressed only twice a week now, and she had to walk to the dispensary where they did it. She had only house slippers and no stockings and so she had caught a very bad cough. When it racked her she held her poor head as if to keep it from flying apart. Rose gave her the address on Water Street and bade her be there within the hour.

Meantime she looked in her purse and saw exactly one dollar and a half. Half of that she spent at the druggist's. Then, at home, she prepared a bed and hot water for her guest, who arrived well within the stipulated hour.

"Mrs. Watson," she greeted her, "perhaps I shouldn't have let you come. Perhaps I won't have money for fires when it gets cold, or there may not be enough to eat. You know you are welcome to what I have, but it is so little I have to offer you."

Mrs. Watson took off the big hat and the veil, showing dirty dressings under them. "Dearie," she said, with some of the old charm in her voice, "we were good friends in the hospital, and we'll be good friends here, and it will be a real pleasure to starve and freeze with you, that it will."

Rose felt her eyes fill with sorrow when she looked at the poor wreck muttering such sentiments, and at the same time she felt a respectful joy to think that if the woman needed help as much as she obviously did, she should be the one to bring it to her. And she had learned by this time that absurdity and misery are inseparable, and that grotesqueness especially delights to mock the desperate plights of man. But that was no reason for neglecting them.

Mrs. Watson exclaimed over the rooms. Rose had the floor painted a warm tan, the trimmings of the walls were white and there was a big old-fashioned fireplace where a fire glowed. "It looks like heaven itself," said Mrs. Watson simply and reverently.

She proved herself as much helper as patient in a short time. Rose was so young at the work, so new to the sort of people she had to deal with, that Mrs. Watson's background proved a valuable one. When Rose came in from calls that had worn her out, Mrs. Watson had tea ready. When someone knocked on the door, Mrs. Watson answered, ponderously and importantly, and, as with Rose, so with her, there was no difference in attitude whether the one who knocked was moneyed charity or moneyless charity case.

Rose confronted her after a few days with a steely eye. "I won't be back till evening. I know the floor needs scrubbing, but I'll do it in the morning. Don't you dare touch it — promise."

"That I will promise you," said Mrs. Watson promptly. "Not a bit will I do, never you fear."

But Rose, hastening home, did fear it ; there was always the danger of hemorrhage in a case as far gone as this if there were too much exertion. And there was Mrs. Watson, surveying proudly a very fine job of scrubbing. "Sure it was my profession for years, dearie," she said, "and I'm feeling fine, and there is your coffee on the hob," she added tactfully.

They had to cook gypsy fashion on the open hearth, because

there was no stove. There might not have been coffee or fire either, that day, but a providential check sent through the *Times,* took care of it.

Mrs. Watson was invaluable, too, in that she immediately knew just whom Rose should see and whom she should not. And when the day was over, and if Rose had no calls for evening dressings, she would sit by the fire and sip something hot while her patient, doing a bit of mending by the lamp, told fairy tales of Ireland, done with dramatic verve, even though sometimes interrupted by a groan of pain which could not be quite muffled.

But there was much less time for stories as the tale grew of the place where a beautiful lady dressed cancer wounds for nothing, if you didn't have the money to pay the doctor. One room had to be entirely devoted to those who came. Rose put Mrs. Watson's bed in her own tiny room, that somehow miraculously expanded to take two beds. The only window abutted on the stable wall a foot away, but at night there was a blessed gush of cool air that revived them. The friends who came to see her had remonstrated with her for putting the sick old woman in the room with her. But Rose explained why she was glad to have to do it.

"It will give me the chance to show the doubters that this is not a contagious disease, as so many think it is."

Those who had come down to see if they couldn't cure her of her fatuous notions, gave up completely at this happy thought. They went away without Rose and with lighter pocketbooks.

Julian, too, had helped call off these well-wishers. "Let her alone," he counseled ; "see how happy she is about it all. She has given up everything else and cast her cares on the Lord, and she feels a deeper satisfaction in this life she is leading than she ever did with the pleasant trifles of the world. In this new state of mind, all the ordinary satisfactions of life are trivial to her. Best let her do her work."

But to a former acquaintance of the Lathrops who asked how Rose was coming along with "her new pose," he answered with restrained anger, "It is not a pose. She is a plain hard-working

164

woman, and she is diligent and faithful in her work — and she is finding plenty. She wants no praise, but also she deserves no blame."

She was happy — anyone could see that. Behind her lay loss and defeat, years of brave effort that seemed to her to have accomplished nothing. She herself could not realize that those years of loss and forbearance had made her able to make her own the pain and suffering of those she now worked with. Her father, perhaps, set the thought firmly in her mind, but its accomplishment was due in no small part to those years when cheerfulness was her defense and her stay. Now that strength, stored through difficult years, was there to be given to those who had none. If her success were shown in no other way, it was shown in the way it was mirrored in the eyes of the gaunt sad women who came to her to be helped a little with their pain, or to learn how to die.

In the morning, before she started on her rounds of dressing, she said to Mrs. Watson with a lift of her head, "Every day I am proving that impossibilities can be done ; and every day God sends me a gift over and above other things as a reward for temerity, sometimes a sun ray and sometimes a smile."

And that same Mrs. Watson at whom the visitors from uptown had gazed in dismay, aghast that this should be the daily and nightly companion of the elegant Mrs. Lathrop, turned out to be an even better gift than sun ray or smile. She quite simply and literally saved Rose's life when she, overworking even her strong body by too much exposure to all weathers and too little sleep, fell ill with pneumonia. Her nursing day began at five-thirty in the morning and ended at eleven at night ; then often she wrote appeals for help until past two. She woke one midnight in great pain shivering with cold, burning with fever. Mrs. Watson ran for the trained nurse who lived on the next floor and who had been keeping an eye on the careless Mrs. Lathrop.

Relatives and a doctor brought by them insisted on good care for the sick woman. But above the physical care, it was Mrs. Watson who brought the spiritual care. Rose had considered herself a good Catholic, faithful to her duties of prayer and Mass, but it was the sick old Irish woman who showed her what a Catholic really is. Every evening of those hard weeks of illness, Mrs. Watson came and knelt beside her bed for twenty minutes while she said the rosary for her, with her heavy clinking old black beads. In Rose's hand she would put the relic of a saint, and when the prayers were over, Rose lay serene in the knowledge that all would be well through the night with her after that offering of prayer and pain.

"How pleasing," she reflected, as she lay there, "in the sight of the Lord of Crucifixion must be Mrs. Watson's motionless figure !" She saw how there was something holy in that peaceful hopefulness, and at the same time, that resignation, to the will of God. She saw that here was one who had actual true faith in the supremacy of God, who knew that He was strongest and knew best.

Rose Lathrop came back to her work in excellent health. In fact, she was inclined to view the whole thing as a period of enforced rest that would give her extra strength for troubles ahead. She came back to more and more knocking at the door. More and more people were asking to be taken in to stay. And, since enough money had come in to warrant the move, she decided to rent larger quarters on Water Street, large enough to take six staying patients. There was a living-room that served also as dispensary, and that, sometimes, had to be used as a temporary bedroom if one too many patients came in, as she had an unfortunate habit of allowing them to do. And there was a kitchen and a real stove. In fact, as was the case with many old tenements, the main entrance led through the kitchen itself.

She was hurrying one morning to bandage a patient in neighboring Cherry Street, when a man came up close to her.

"Nickel for a cup of coffee, lady ?"

She stopped for a moment, realizing that she had just enough carfare for both ways for her later visits. She would willingly have walked but she had not the time.

166

"I haven't any," she was beginning ; then as she looked more closely at the old man, "Are you sick ?"

He nodded. "Sort of."

Her practiced eye had seen the tragedy. "Is it cancer ?" she asked gently.

He nodded again. "They's no place to take me," he said, as if explaining his plight. She knew how very true that was.

"I tell you — you wait in the park till I get back. It's nice and warm there on the benches. I'll try to get you a room then — or something."

He hesitated. "Sorry, lady. I can't."

She was astonished. "Why not ?"

"I got a partner," he jerked his head toward the corner where a bent man with a dirty bandage around his head was waiting — to share the cup of coffee, she thought. "He's got it lots worse than me. He can get it dressed every week at the dispensary."

She felt suddenly shaky with the need of making an immediate decision. "Both of you wait. I'll get you some sort of room. I'll find you something. Tell him to wait too."

But when she came hurrying back the bench was empty. Why had they gone ? Perhaps, she thought sadly, because they saw she had too little to help them ; perhaps because they knew how hard it would be to find quarters where cancer patients would be taken ; perhaps they saw in her an enemy who would send them to the Island.

Inside her burned a fierce resentment at conditions, and she made an equally fierce vow that some day old men like these should be her guests, in a big house where they could be warm and contented until God finally called them home. In her small quarters she could take only women. She had no money as yet to open a place for men, for that would mean the expense of men nurses too.

Shortly before Christmas of that year a diffident knock came at the street door. "I'll answer it, Mrs. Lathrop," offered the nearest patient. Rose wanted to suggest that someone else

167

should go, for this patient was rather a sad sight as portress, in her short red skirt with an undershirt hanging out. But it was too late.

"Come in, come right in," she heard. "A young lady to see you, Mrs. Lathrop."

The young lady was standing rather uncertainly in the doorway, which was that of the kitchen. She had not liked the look of the slattern at the door, nor the look of the woman she saw inside ironing. She started to step back, apologizing for having made a mistake, when from inside she heard a bright voice call, "Do come right in." The face beyond the door was as bright as the voice, and a crown of tawny hair set off the nurse's dress. She stepped in.

"I am Mrs. Lathrop. I can talk to you in just a moment," and she went back to bandaging the leg of an old woman who groaned about it until the matter was finished and she was dismissed.

"Now what can I do for you ?" The visitor handed her a letter silently.

Rose read it. "From Father Kent Stone !" she exclaimed. "What a pleasure to hear from him." Rose's friendship with him dated from the early days of her conversion. He had been one of the interesting convert figures of a slightly earlier day ; an Episcopalian minister, President of Hobart College, he had, shortly after the death of his young wife, become a Catholic and joined the Paulist Order. Later he became a Passionist and was known throughout the United States and many other lands as missioner and founder of Retreats of the Order.

The letter stated that this would introduce Miss Alice Huber who was in New York studying. Father Stone thought that perhaps she might give Mrs. Lathrop a little of her time for this very worthy charity she had undertaken.

Miss Huber, however, having had a look at the place, was beginning to wonder how she might extricate herself gracefully from the situation and go back again to her study of art, which had been her real reason for coming to New York. The old women were not any too clean, to put it politely, and one of the patients, a fierce looking old lady, planted a stick in front of her and stared at her like an annoyed old hawk. The neighborhood through which she had come had been one to daunt the bravest.

But the woman in the middle of the room, who sat talking so cheerfully about all sorts of things, music, books, the beauty of the river nearby while she serenely bandaged another patient and gave her cheerful words of comfort — Miss Huber paused before she refused her help too quickly. She might come for just a few hours once a week, she decided ; she could not bear to disappoint Mrs. Lathrop entirely after Father Stone had written of her desire to be of help.

Her hostess went to the street door with her to give her definite directions about taking the Grand Street ferry. She stood there with misery and disease around her, the one cheerful object of it all. And Miss Huber felt pity fill her heart and take the place of repulsion : she knew affection for this woman's bravery instead of distaste for the misery.

The following Tuesday she came back as she had promised. The dressings filled her with horror, though Mrs. Lathrop could have told her they were not nearly so bad as had been her first patient up at the Cancer Hospital. And when two hours were up, she simply could not tell that anxious woman, looking up from her work with a pleading look in her eyes, that she would not come again. She promised instead, and was astonished to hear her voice promising, to come two afternoons a week instead of one. Within a few months she had decided to throw in her lot with Mrs. Lathrop, and came to live with her on Water Street.

She almost regretted it at times. There was no time for reading, no time even to write a letter. There were groaning patients very close to them at night. The noises of the neighborhood were like one large continuous sound beating always on their ears. They had no money for anything except the simplest food, and the most necessary medical supplies. They used boxes to sit on, and they ate in the kitchen with the patients who were well enough to be up and about. There were bugs in the walls, and the heat of the summer was intolerable. The bedroom which she and Mrs. Lathrop shared was a tiny one, and opened directly into the patients' room with no other exit. And the poverty around them was very hard on a sensitive spirit.

"When I first came down here," said Mrs. Lathrop musingly to her young helper one evening when after a long day of dressings and complaints and knocks at the door, they sat down to a cup of tea, "the poverty was so terrible that I thought it would break my heart. It seemed to me that I would lose all sense of order if I stayed near people under its merciless régime. And then after a while I began to see the alleviations, the brightnesses which a kind Creator sends even into the shadows of destitution."

Alice Huber shook her head as one who found these brightnesses rather faint. The sights and sounds were proving violent indeed for the girl from the quiet Kentucky convent school. This was very different from singing in the choir for the love of God, or painting pictures for the convent chapel.

Mrs. Lathrop poked up the fire and poured Alice Huber more tea. "In the evenings the low cross streets were ended in the west with orange and gold and rose. And the sunrise, if someone had to see me for a very early call, had all the gaiety I needed to keep me in my path."

Alice Huber shook her head despairingly. "I could stand the dirt, I think ; you can clean that up if you try hard enough and get enough people to work at it. But the noise — the noise."

Mrs. Lathrop laughed. "I think the poor like noise — I really do. Or perhaps, as some of our friends say about teas, they detest them and yet keep on having them. Perhaps that is it ; there seems no other explanation."

For the people of the little Cancer Home the noise around them began from four in the morning until after midnight ; there was usually a little lull then which Mrs. Lathrop surmised was for naps. But during that lull, the pet parrots put an end to peace by their whistling and foolish remarks. As for cats, she had learned how to handle them long ago.   There was only the first serenade from them to disturb the patients.

"After that," she said with relish, "we use ammunition on hand to frighten them away, always hoping it will miss the feline, and always shutting our eyes for the moment when the missile hits the tin roof and we add to the clatter.   To tell you the truth, I have learned not to mind the singing and talking and laughing, but I can't get used to the crying of the children nor the drunken screams and the swearing."

Alice Huber shivered.   "They stay out in the cold until you would think they'd freeze."

"Of course they do.   They show good sense ; and don't ever think the children suffer outdoors unless it is bitterly cold, and even then they can dance and keep warm if only there is an old organ around with its master forcing lively airs from its reluctant jaws.   I defy anyone to be more cuirassed against cold than a pin-cushioned child, battened up with ragged layers of habiliments.   But the inside of the homes !   Oh, my dear, I wonder if there is anything more dreadful than the indoors misery of a dank twilighted hungry relentless landlord-visited despair ?" And she punched the fire to emphasize each adjective.

"But they could stop drinking and use the money for food or rent ; or gambling it away on the street — you've seen them," insisted Alice Huber with excellent logic.

Mrs. Lathrop shook her head violently.   "Now don't you be like so many people expecting the poor, just because they are poor, to be the saints of the world.   I can see, of course, how pleasant it would make it for the conscience of the world if they would only be kind enough to take on their shoulders the dual burden of ill luck and self-conquest.   And anyway what makes you think beer is harmful really ?"

Alice Huber tried to say that that was not just what she had said, but Mrs. Lathrop swept on : "The harmful part about it is that what they sell down here is no doubt abominably impure. I think the German beer gardens with their cakes and sandwiches and music from the classics would do a lot of good for our poor

171

here in America if someone charitably inclined would build a few such gardens. Only," she added as an afterthought, "they would have to electrocute the false concocters of unreal beer first."

It sounded beautiful the way Mrs. Lathrop put it. It sounded, in fact, too beautiful to be true. "If you had seen the group of boys I saw this morning with really big sums passing, right on the sidewalk with all the youngsters watching them — "

"Oh, that," and Mrs. Lathrop came over to the side of virtue with a swoop, "I could never defend that gambling. Those boys are sink pots of wickedness, and I suppose will all end in States Prison. What interests me is how the largest and healthiest policemen are so singularly blind about it all. My dear, I haven't talked so much for an age. Do get me those extra bandages for Mary Daly. I promised her I'd get there first thing in the morning and it's a long trip. You'd love her if you knew her. I don't know what old Tim Daly will do when she dies."

She said good night, leaving her assistant with a strange feeling of being privileged to work with one of the true saints of the world who would be acclaimed one day by an understanding nation.

8

City officials who handled charity work were of course interested in the work of this unusual charity worker, and came down now and then to examine it. She was showing one of them around her small domain one day, with its inadequate equipment, its poor beds, and he said to her in utter bewilderment, "But, my dear Mrs. Lathrop, they should be in an institution, these people. They are not for individual charity such as yours. Send them to the Island where they will be cared for and give yourself to something that will care for those who are going to live and be of use." Mrs. Lathrop had volumes ready to tumble from her lips in answer to this outrageous suggestion, but she contented herself with asking, "Do you notice the faces of our patients ? They look happy. Do they look happy on the Island ?"

"But, my dear Mrs. Lathrop, what does it matter whether they look happy or not ?"

"They will live longer if they are happy and cared for," she said, in order to make him understand better. "You might be interested in hearing about one old patient we had. The doctors said he would last only a few days after he got to the Island, but we took care of him instead, and do you know what happened ? He lived three months."

The amazed official did not dare make the obvious statement

that came to him, that had he died there would have been room for another sooner. Instead he shook his head in admiration of this patient whom love made persistent in hanging to life.

"You see," she told him, "we plan to make this work so thoroughly and affectionately gentle that even the poor can praise it."

"But," the baffled official turned the conversation, "do you really think that this is needed when the government does not think it large enough to be institutionally supported ?"

"Even a nucleus of kind hearts is better than nothing," she flashed back, "and even fifty beds for them are better than so many cellar holes. I had a letter yesterday from a woman in France to whom I had sent an appeal, and she writes that the doctors there told her the cancerous poor should not be nursed at all, but allowed to die rapidly. Christ differed from them, I am going to tell her. His touch was never withheld from loathsome flesh. In this field of the daring imitation of His compassion, tepidity is more unwise than even usual. It reminds me of what Faber said : 'There are sacraments for sin, but for lukewarmness there are none.' "

Back in his own office again, his associate asked the official what sort of place it was Mrs. Lathrop was running down on the East Side.

"I don't know," he said in honest perplexity. "I went down to see if she had any new theories worth trying out. You should see the place : grinning old ladies, two good looking women taking care of them, statues and saints' pictures all around, and when I asked her why she wasted her time on cancer patients when she might be helping us up here with an established thing, she began telling me about the Good Samaritan and Christ saying, 'Go thou and do likewise.' Anyway something like that. Just one of those idealists. 'They all crack up before long."

And that night Mrs. Lathrop, still angry at the stupidity of officialdom, sat down to get some of her anger out of her system and on paper. Everyone was asleep or at least at rest. Alice Huber slept the sleep of weariness across the room. The pen

174

flew as she told the official all the things she had not been able to tell him in person.

"So long as the poor are squalid and otherwise unattractive, we refuse to inspect their needs, unless they live in a foreign country like Armenia, or elsewhere, which makes a difference. What I would assert is that pity and justice might lead us to care for the incurable poor, if we allowed ourselves to admit that pity and justice have no caste or predilection, no taste for excitement, no weakness for charm. If the public knew what our experience knows of a department of suffering, a charity for that suffering would begin to develop. I assert that a great home is needed for such a charity, that of nursing incurable cancer. Persons who ought to know the truth say that the incurable poor are amply cared for by hospitals already at work and that the providing of more beds and more nurses for non-paying patients and incurables would be impertinent activity. Hospital and dispensary aid for the poor continues to be unfeeling and superficial as is well known to people at hand, though denied by those in charge.

"There are no free beds in hospitals for incurable poor. The sick poor work, however desperately ill, if they can find work. If they cannot find it, they are blamed as lazy paupers, and they sink down never to rise again. A high official in a large charity (so-called) told me that it was difficult to find a case of genuine destitution. Two dollars a year is reported as too much for each family calling for aid in one American city. One would think America a very poor Mecca. Their report is like that of a charity visitor who was allowed by some rich ladies five dollars a month among fifty families, to supply tea and clothing as required.

"We are at work for those sick who get ten cents a month or nothing unless we plead for them."

She felt, as she folded the sheets, that she must write and write paragraphs like these until she could make people understand.

The winter was a bitterly cold one. They kept the patients in bed but the two women who had to be up and about at all hours nearly froze. So long as she had room for the cases that came to her, Rose Lathrop was gay and hopeful ; and it was the pity and affection for her that held the art student from Louisville to her task, when perhaps her spirit might have quailed had she realized what was ahead of them both.

175

As she sat drooping with fatigue one night, Rose Lathrop, who had just had time to open her day's mail, looked up annoyed. "That fallacious feeling people seem to have that one must rest, rest, rest. That is what my dear relatives are telling me again. It is all nonsense. Action is what makes muscle, and the spirit of life enters into us when we take a vital part in life. Let me tell you that I think lots of people suffer from rest."

Alice Huber strove to sit up very straight and look as if she were not sitting at all. Rose went on :

"They said I'll get aches and illnesses. Why, headaches evaporate if we have to exert ourselves for those we love, or anyway we forget the pain, which is the same thing. My advice to those who try to advise me is that people ought to labor in comfort and health instead of sitting down to lassitude and sighs."

"But if you are careful of your health, then you can be more useful to your patients," argued her associate.

"How could my life blood be expended to greater advantage," demanded Rose Lathrop most illogically, "than in fighting the forces against health in the world ?"

But Alice Huber began making her a cup of tea, thinking that a safer answer, and in a half hour Rose was feeling able to write the little article for the *Christian Herald* which they had requested : tell them just why she had gone into the work, they asked.

"I am trying," she began, "to serve the poor as a servant. I wish to serve the cancerous poor because they are avoided more than any other class of sufferers ; and I wish to go to them as a poor creature myself, though powerful to help them through the open-handed gifts of public kindness, because it is by humility and sacrifice alone that we feel the holy spirit of pity."

"I shall have to let Willie come down from the Protectory to see his grandmother," announced Mrs. Lathrop one morning. "She can't make that trip any more and the poor soul wants to see him. We'll try to keep him a week or so if possible."

So Willie was brought for a visit. His golden curls had long

176

been familiar to them all, for Mrs. Watson kept one of them in a little box tied to her wrist, like a relic, and pulled it out to show people at least once a day.

Willie arrived, chaperoned by an officer from the Protectory. He was a handsome healthy child, but Mrs. Lathrop, looking at him as he was introduced to her by his admiring grandmother, thought that in his deep blue eyes she detected depths of mischief — if not worse.

She began to teach him his catechism, while proud Mrs. Watson sat listening to his solemn and correct answers.

"He likes to study it better than be idle," she said, wiping away tears of pride. "I taught it to him long ago, and he remembers it that well."

It took much less than a week for Willie to become famous for his ill-doing in a neighborhood that thought itself first in the field. He built fires on the shed roofs, he threw bricks at people, and Mrs. Lathrop said it was only their guardian angels that averted the missiles from their heads. Sometimes in the big room now known as the Relief Room, little boys had to be mended who had been damaged by the playfulness of Willie Watson.

The nurses gave him little pictures of saints and he thanked them very politely, stole what more he could find, and sold them all. He was always sorry for his sins, and he made a very good impression on a priest who had been called to do something about Willie's soul and whom Willie convinced it was in fine condition. Immediately after the priest had gone, Willie built an extra large fire in the woodshed. Even Mrs. Watson, who had been used to refer to him as the Angel when he was still at a distance in the Protectory, now said apologetically that anyway he was a good-hearted boy. But unfortunately in her affection for him, she sometimes tried to excuse his petty thievery, and her beloved Mrs. Lathrop grew hard toward her on these occasions.

At last after four days of this, Willie played one prank too many for their frayed nerves. "Either we send Willie back to the Protectory, or we shall have to bring the Protectory to Water Street," said Mrs. Lathrop, so Willie went back.

But he had wrought more havoc than merely in the neighborhood or in the house. Old Mrs. Watson, grown wavering in her mind now at times, was yet clear enough in her thinking to make Rose feel that she had here missed a wonderful opportunity to save a soul. She had not risen to the heroic heights expected of her and which, Rose felt uncomfortably, Mrs. Watson would eagerly have scaled had she been in her place.

Not that Mrs. Watson ever said this openly, but she made the tender conscience of the woman caring for her even more tender. It was long afterwards when Rose Lathrop had become experienced in her work, that she realized that by her sternness toward the old woman, she was only proving the fact that charitable acts and laborious services are no better than tares when the spirit does not speak to the soul we serve in full and humble accord.

She had had little experience with the care of souls, yet she did feel vaguely ashamed and felt that she was falling short of an ideal. When Mrs. Watson died soon after, she sat by the coffin and wept, feeling dimly that she was only a poor friend to the people she had come to help, and that she had judged where she had no right to, and had perhaps judged wrongly. Mrs. Watson had never hurt her, had prayed for her over and over, had helped her physically and spiritually.

"I wonder," she said sadly to Alice Huber, "if perhaps I did not hurt her spirit more than I helped her body?"

But Alice Huber reassured her, telling her that she had done her best, that only an angel could have measured up to Mrs. Watson's idea of what should have been done for Willie.

Rose Lathrop shook away her tears. "Perhaps," she said, "God has special clauses of mercy for those who try to reach heaven by Alpine climbing, and fall, instead, into crevices."

9

Not long after she had moved to Water Street Rose heard of the great success of George's adaptation of the *Scarlet Letter* in the Damrosch opera. She was glad of that. She had kept in touch with his condition through some of the Paulist Fathers and knew he was not well. This success would make him better. But she had really closed that chapter of her life when she went away for the last time. She had deeply searched her own heart and made sure she had done the best she could during all those years, that she had been right to go away completely at the last.

In the middle of the spring word came to her from Roosevelt Hospital that George was very ill and was asking for her. Could she come immediately, the message said, since the end was imminent?

"I am going uptown," she told Alice Huber. "My husband is very ill."

She dressed hurriedly, discarding the uniform she usually wore nowadays, tossing over the contents of a closet until she found a blue suit and a blue hat with roses on the brim. She adjusted it on the red gold of her hair, found a pair of gloves not too badly worn, and hurried uptown.

She knew enough of death by this time to realize that it was staring at her out of George's eyes. She laid her firm warm hand

179

on his dry, fumbling one. His fingers closed around hers.
His voice was very weak, and she bent close to hear him.

"Father Young has been here."

She nodded, her eyes tear-filled. They did not matter now,
these tears that fell on George's hand as she bent over him. His
eyes widened in the old charming smile. "Rösl," he said, "forgive me for the years."

The years of patient endurance, the difficulties, disappeared.
A boy and a girl stood in little Saint Peter's, astonished at the
magnificence of life, at their daring in meeting it thus boldly
together.

"Not all the years were hard, George — only some of them."

"And Francie was so sweet — his hair like yours — " He
looked up at her shining crown. His eyes caught the blue hat
with the pink roses.

"Did you wear it on purpose ?" he asked.

She nodded again. His eyes closed and he seemed to be
asleep after his effort to talk. She sat beside him, her hand
lightly on his. Now and then he opened his eyes to look at her,
but they drooped again after a moment. There was deep content in them. Once when he seemed quite awake she said,
"George, I keep a verse of yours in my heart to say when things
are too hard :

> "Fear not, though thou starvest,
> Provisions are made ;
> God gathers his harvest
> When our hopes fade."

He looked very aware for a moment. "All my verse was
for you, Rösl. You know that. But you aren't really terribly
poor, are you — not really hungry ?" He looked at her anxiously.

She shook her head. "No, George, of course not."

After some time a nurse came and touched her shoulder. She
started and looked more closely at George, and saw that the
hurried breathing had stopped. She got up from her chair, and

someone took her arm and walked out of the room with her. Only then did she recognize Father Young.

She looked at him with frightened eyes. "I did my best, Father. Say for me I did my best. Say I was right to go away at the last. And George has had good care — he wasn't neglected."

He patted her arm and assured her she had been a good wife and to remember that under the circumstances that existed she had been given permission to leave George and take up her new work, that it was all in God's hands. He told her that George had received the last Sacraments that morning, and that he was spiritually at peace and now she had come and given him a last bit of earthly peace.

The doctors told her that his illness was cirrhosis of the liver and that he must have been suffering from it for a long time. They assured her he had had the best of care, and that nothing more could have been done for him than had been done.

Even had she been the type of woman who broods over the past, there would have been no time for it. Two new patients had come in that morning, and she saw there was much to be done for them when she reached home again. She took off the blue hat and the blue suit, got back into the uniform. In her thoughts she was putting forever behind her a boy in Dresden, a young man beside her in a little Chelsea church, an older man tossing in the air a bright-haired laughing child. They were safe now, both of them, and she could keep them always in her heart and in her prayers.

In uptown New York, in the church of the Dominican Fathers, Saint Vincent Ferrer, was stationed a young priest, Reverend Clement Thuente, one of whose duties was to visit the sick poor of the parish. Little old Mrs. Daly had been much on his mind of late. She had cancer, was terribly ill, and could no longer go to the dispensary to have her wounds dressed. He had been to see her last week and found her husband, just in from a hard day's teaming, trying to make his wife comfortable. It was a sorry job he was making of it, with Mrs. Daly smiling bravely at his efforts.

He decided to run up there today and see if he couldn't do something for her, have her sent somewhere for treatment, perhaps. But his heart sank even as he considered this. No hospital would take an incurable case, he knew, and no one wanted Mrs. Daly sent to the Island.

He knocked at the Daly door and was surprised to hear a happy voice say, "Come in." He usually just knocked and went in, expecting no answer. She sat up in bed looking very cheerful.

"How fine you are in here," he said. "And who put the bandages on your head like that so beautifully, Mrs. Daly ? It looks like a tiara."

Mrs. Daly smiled complacently. "It is a lady came in to do me ; twice a week she will come, and Tim says she is an angel from heaven. I tell him it is a red-headed angel then. And she brought me a bit of soup and started Tim's stew, with even a prato pared whole in it the way I told her he likes it. She is a grand lady, Father."

"She must be. Is she a nurse ? Where does she come from ?"

"She doesn't seem like a nurse quite, but she has the little case for the dressings. She gave me her name and address so if I should need her extra I will let her know."

Father Thuente looked at the address written in the vibrant, running hand :

Mrs. Lathrop, 446 Water Street

What a distance to come to bandage a poverty stricken woman ! Father Thuente had not too much spare time of his own, but he decided to go down to see this mysterious person.

That evening he went down to the East Side to find out who this woman was who had been ministering angel and cook, too, for Mrs. Daly. He went in the door of the tenement house whose address he had been given. After a few steps he hesi-

182

tated about even entering the building. It looked so unsafe. The stairs shook under his tread, but he reached the second floor with no damage done, and knocked gently on the door.

"I want to see the lady who comes up to bandage Mrs. Daly," he said to the old woman who opened the door.

"Oh, you want our directress. I'll get her," she said.

The woman who hurried forward at the name was evidently Mrs. Daly's red-headed angel. Her face was alarmed. "Is she worse?" she asked.

He shook his head. "I think she's better than she's been in weeks. And I hear you are the one responsible for it. I came down to see who you are and what you are doing. Perhaps I can be of some help to you, especially since I see you are Catholics," waving his hand at the pictures, the little shrine of our Lady in one corner, and the little statue of Saint Rose of Lima on the table. "She and I are of one family, you see. She was a Dominican Tertiary."

Something in his manner must have made her realize that here was one whom God had put in their way to help them. She told him their story. She brought in her helper, Alice Huber, and found that Father Thuente knew who she was. She had been educated by the Dominican Sisters in Springfield, Kentucky, and he spoke of pictures painted by her in the chapel there.

Father Thuente came down again and again, constituting himself their adviser. He learned that though they had no thought of affiliating with any of the established Orders, they were anxious to have a uniform of some sort, a semi-religious garb as protection in the rough neighborhood, and to give them a modicum of authority. They had, in the first months of their work together, dressed, so he heard from a priest in the neighborhood, in an outfit that looked rather Quakerish, and called themselves Daughters of the Puritans. It was a gray costume, with snowy caps with white strings tied under their chins, and they looked, so he said, like two anachronisms from old Salem.

In this garb, they told him now, they had gone up to the Cathedral, hoping to show the Archbishop what an excellent

183

dress it was, and wanting his permission to wear it. But they met, instead, Dr. McMahon, of the Cathedral staff, and he gave them one long look when he learned their purpose.

"He told us," said Mrs. Lathrop ruefully, "that it would be a much better idea if we went home and came back in our usual dress. He said he hardly thought that with that stage costume we would win our point with His Grace. He did, however, admit it was becoming," said Mrs. Lathrop with a smile.

They went home and waited a while. But it seemed so necessary to wear something in the way of a uniform to give them protection in their work that Rose went to Archbishop Corrigan about it, and he promised to consider the matter further. But "further" was too long for Rose to wait. She went up again, and this time went on her knees before him. He put his hand on her head and said he would consider allowing them to wear the semi-religious dress. They had made it by this time into something that looked almost like a nurse's dress, and had decided to drop the theatrical title of Daughters of the Puritans and call themselves, instead, Servants for the Relief of Incurable Cancer. This, she felt confident, would help with the Archbishop, and they hoped, when he heard this sensible title, he would no longer hesitate about letting them wear some distinguishing garb.

All this they poured out to Father Thuente, and he promised them his help. He became their unofficial spiritual adviser, and before long was appointed so officially. As for the garb they were so anxious to wear, he was not sure. But he picked up the little statue of Saint Rose of Lima on the table. She had their especial devotion because of her work among the cancerous poor.

"Why don't you," he asked them, "become Third Order Dominicans living in community ?"

They looked at each other. This would, indeed, be a solution for their difficulties.

"Will you speak to His Grace about it, Father ?" asked Mrs. Lathrop, and he promised he would.

When he came back a week later, he had the permission for becoming Tertiaries, but the habit was not yet permitted them.

184

He suggested, however, they decide what names they would take in religion. Mrs. Lathrop, using her official precedence, firmly insisted that of the two, it was Alice Huber who should take the name of their patron saint. So she became Sister Mary Rose.

Rose Lathrop meantime was wondering whom to choose for herself. She thought of Saint Columba, remembering the picture of her crowned with daisies in far away Italy. But somehow Saint Columba was not the one she wanted. In a book which she had been reading in a spare moment, she came across the story of Saint Alphonsus of Liguori. He had been a man of the world and fond of society. He had, at the height of his career, made a mistake on a case entrusted to him, and he felt he never wanted to enter the law courts again. Meantime he wondered what to do with his life. He prayed and waited, and went here and there on errands of mercy. It was while visiting one day a hospital for incurables and talking to the sick that he suddenly felt himself surrounded by a mysterious light ; the house seemed to rock, and an interior voice said : "Leave the world and give thyself to Me." He laid his sword before the statue of Our Lady after he left the hospital, and then and there determined to enter the religious state.

All this she mused over. There seemed certain parallels here, and he would make a wonderful patron for her, she felt sure, and a powerful one.

"I shall be Sister Mary Alphonsa," she announced.

The newly named Sister Mary Rose did not feel it was a very pretty name, but Mrs. Lathrop remained firm even though she, too, realized, it was not by any means poetic. And she became, in the tiny community of two on Water Street, Sister Mary Alphonsa.

She established immediately a few rules that were always to be carried out, whether they remained few or became a large community. She would have no experimenting on the incurables in her care, for, if they were really pronounced incurable, any cutting would be in the interest of science and not of the

185

patient. There was to be no aversion shown toward even the most diseased patient. There was to be no wearing of rubber gloves to show disquiet or fear of the patients. No money was to be received from relatives or friends of the patients, to avoid the harsh and well known result of pay patients ousting the destitute. "These things," she declared, "shall be anathema."

Years later a writer in the *Delineator* showed that these dicta were still being carried out : "Horror," she wrote after a visit to the Home, "is magnificently ignored."

PART III

1

By 1899 so many appeals had come from cancer sufferers who wanted to be taken into the Home that Sister Alphonsa, after having been forced to turn down many cases she wanted with all her heart to take in, felt they must find larger quarters. By this time, too, she was well into her letter-writing activities, an occupation that went on for years and years and was responsible for much of her success in raising funds. The Sisters never begged in person for their money. The begging, if it could be called such, was done by Sister Alphonsa, who put into letters to the newspapers, to friends, to possible donors, all the literary beauty and charm she had once put into her secular literary work. They sang, and they pleaded, these letters. They held sometimes a delicate irony, or a subtle humor, or a gay quip, and often an account of a small tragedy. Later, as an extension to her letters, she published for three or four years a little magazine named *Christ's Poor.*

There were some among her friends who mourned the fact that she wrote no more. They had not read, then, these articles and editorials and short stories that filled the pages of this tiny magazine. It was merely that now she was using her gift for God's work instead of for her own pleasure. But the beautiful phrasing, the deftly chosen words, were still there.

In her first number she listed some of the objects of the work :

a hope that perhaps later other incurable diseases could be taken in too ; the attempt to make sure that patients were not used to experiment with ("incurable cancer is now a matter of general and exhaustive study and the poor supply the material used") ; to prove it was not a dangerously contagious disease ; to engage the personal interest of women from different parishes. It was a cheerful little magazine despite the sombre reason for its being. Some of the numbers carried a department labeled, "Comical Sayings of Old Ladies."

In one of the first numbers she wrote a small apologia signed *"A Woman of the World."* "I have been indolent," she confessed, "self-indulgent, cowardly, for many years. I have labored with my hands and mind and affections for those I loved ; but for a long time it was rather against my will and with a longing for lazy delights or for intellectual pleasures. Since then I have had less of rest and pastime and I have not desired them. I have tasted of energy and love of my neighbor and of the elixir of self respect, and so I can no longer love and praise the merry hours of my life as I love and praise the hours in which we remember God.

"I don't believe there was anyone who loved fancy work, the reading of novels, painting, the theatres, chatting socially with friends about jolly matters more heartily than I have done. I remember that on the day when I realized there would be no time for me to paint in oils or water colors again if I attended faithfully to the work heaven seemed to be giving me to perform, it was as if a sword entered my bosom and I said, 'Oh, God, I cannot make that one sacrifice for You.' But all the same I knew I should make it.

"Effort would not deserve its high repute if it were not a transmuting of weakness into the activity of force, the evolution of semi-nothingness that is some degree of evil into life and honor. Effort is the precursor of courage ; it is the determination to be courageous, to throw off the half death of hesitation in our choice between a path of virtue and any sort of self indulgence.

"Good — very good people, fulfil their transient social duties,

190

make their houses look charming, embroider linen dainties for their tables, varnish the truth and succeed in keeping themselves and their friends well and happy, until God sends sickness, shipwreck, fire. Meantime while we embroider, paint, dance, there is an old story being told near us all. It is scornfully mumbled by an ugly witch in a dark cavern of daily truth. Whether or not the witch should be called human nature, or stupid economics, or sin, she is evidently unspiritual ; and her story, of which the gayest of us must have heard, is about crime and famine and forgotten souls.

"Forgive me for grappling with questions that are undoubtedly beyond any handling of mine. For if a woman desires a hearing for her thoughts at all, I think she may as well speak of the dearest interest a woman has in this world. Now I hope I shall never cease to believe that, as it was in the time of the three Marys, the chief interest of woman is to follow Christ, and lead the children to Him.

"Conscience, which is born omniscient, knows almost too much and tells us that dreadful thing, the unvarnished truth, even though we bewilder ourselves with little pastimes so that we may not hear the chilling voice of unswerving courage.

"No matter how selfish we are, let us learn the art of generous activity. It is ever so much more absorbing than china painting or a boat race. But it takes more than four years to graduate from its schools. Yet remember this : 'What is hardest to do, is sweetest to see done.' "

This is all of the past that *Christ's Poor* contained ; the rest was of the present and the future, and it was for that future that she used the little books. She wanted no musicales at expensive hotels which would cost sixty percent of the profits, nor fairs which took money and strength too. Her letters, her little magazine, were her means of raising funds. And prayer — that was the mightiest of all.

When Sister Alphonsa, considering the many pleadings from sufferers and the few beds for them, decided they must have more room for more beds, she sent out a fleet of letters, and they

191

brought in such excellent results that it was decided to move to new rooms on Cherry Street, to a comfortable old-fashioned house where they could take in at least twelve patients. This naturally increased in a few months to fifteen, since the Directress could not bear to turn away certain cases, not when she knew that if she did not take them, they would leave her to go to poverty and neglect and uneased pain. But this house was really a house compared to the hovel they had left round the corner on Water Street or to the first little rooms where even yellow paint could not disguise the tenement's decay.

People were learning more about the Home, too, and there were frequent gifts of clothing and fruits, of furniture, of wine. Notes came from religious and clergy, wishing them success in their new work. These filled the Sisters with pride ; they, too, were what Sister Alphonsa called "the Servants to Divine command." The priests of St. Teresa's church on Henry Street came to attend to the spiritual needs of the Home.

One of the real charms of the new house was that there was a roof garden where chairs and cots and awnings could be put, and the patients brought up to have their fill of sun and trees and park and river. It was merely a square railed off with a few chairs, and a palm and an awning, but it brought brightness to dull eyes and put a bit of color into sallow cheeks.

There was a postulant now, too. The more practical Sister Rose had not always felt sure there were going to be others than just themselves in the work, but Sister Alphonsa had been serenely sure of it. "We are carrying out the simple command of Christ to harbor the harborless and to do it with love. You know what the doctors of the Church have said : that Christ would have become incarnate and submitted to death to save one soul. Then wouldn't it be strange if a few women could not be found willing to give their lives to carrying on a charity like this for consoling a few souls ?"

"But promise me just one thing," Sister Rose capped this logic, "that you won't take any more patients until we have more nurses, or at least one empty bed." This, of course, Sister Alphonsa was willing to promise, and Sister Rose could only hope for the best.

But the promise was broken only a few days later. A knock came at the door in the early morning. The patient who was brewing tea opened the door to a tall shabbily dressed woman in dingy black. The nurses who by this time could detect the disease easily, saw that this was undoubtedly a cancer case, even though no wounds were visible, or bandages.

"What can we do for you ?" asked Sister Alphonsa hospitably even while Sister Rose was looking at her warningly.

The woman leaned against the door frame. "I am so tired," she said.

"Do come in then and sit down for a moment and have a cup of tea," suggested Sister Alphonsa. But the woman stood by the door and made no move to come farther in. She shook her head sadly.

"They won't — no one will let me come near them any more. I have grown used to keeping my distance. You can perhaps see that I am cancerous ; in fact, I am one of the cancerous poor that I am told you are helping, and it was suggested I come to you. I hated to come," she added impulsively, taking a step or two into the room, as though not noticing she was doing it. "I suppose I was proud, but I waited until I saw how obnoxious I was to everyone about me."

Sister Alphonsa's eyes were full of tears. This was not the usual type of patient who came to them, this well-bred, quiet-spoken woman. Sister Alphonsa was wishing wildly that they weren't so very poor, otherwise she could have rented a room somewhere near at hand for her, and taken care of her in that way. She was counting up the scarcity of ways and the smallness of means, when suddenly their visitor spoke again.

"I know that of course you can't take me. I did not know you were so very poor too. You are crowded here now. You can't take me, can you ?" The eyes turned on the two women were so eagerly hoping for the answer she did not really expect to hear.

193

Sister Alphonsa hesitated. "Well, our beds are all filled."

The woman turned to the door again. "Then there is nothing left for me but suicide."

Sister Alphonsa rose hastily and ran over to her to put her arms around their visitor. "Oh, then you are not a Catholic, are you ? If you were, you could not say such a thing."

"No, I am not. Do I have to be to come in here ?"

"Oh, no, no, that wouldn't matter at all. It is just that we are so crowded here."

The woman began to cry. "They are going to turn me out of my room. All the house is so afraid of me that they move away if I come near them. I had some money saved but it is gone now, all but a tiny sum. And I had thought that you would help me at the very last. I have been counting on it and waiting for it."

"Sit down here for a moment, will you please, until I come back ?" asked Sister Alphonsa, and she beckoned Sister Rose into the other room. Once in the kitchen with the door closed, she said distractedly, "We can't let her go. I know I promised, but how can I keep it now ?" She looked at Sister Rose's face and added, "And you won't let her go nor will I. It was just for such people that we came into this work, anyway."

So they went back to tell the poor woman that she might stay with them. Her face lighted up. "Thank God," she said.

"Now we must manage a bed for you," said Sister Rose.

But their caller shook her head. "Oh, not yet. I can manage for myself for a few weeks more. It was only that I wanted to have a place to die in where there was kindness around me. As soon as my money is all used up, I'll come back. Thank you for your great kindness." They both knew she ought to stay for the cancer was far advanced, but in the face of such courage, they could say nothing. So she went away.

During the next days they thought of her often, standing there so proudly, so unwilling to be a burden until she could come to them honestly and with nothing of her own to keep her. But

194

they were sure they would never see her again, and they kept her faithfully in their prayers.

But three weeks later, at twilight, she came back. She was in a terrible condition now, bent with pain, and haggard. They put her in the cot they had set up for her, back of screens for privacy. Her condition was such that Sister Alphonsa felt she must handle it herself. First they found they would have to cut her clothing from her. She tried her best to help take it off, and Sister Alphonsa patiently gave her pride every chance until at last the woman saw she was not a help but a hindrance.

Even that first case in the Hospital had not been so dreadful as this one, and when at last the patient was in a satisfactory state of cleanliness, both nurse and patient were thoroughly exhausted. As Sister Alphonsa bent over the cot, the woman looked up at her. "I am comfortable for the first time in a year," she whispered. "Thank you." And she fell asleep.

The doctor who came in the morning said she would hardly live another day, the cancer was so deep and so close to the heart. He promised to come back later to see her. In the morning the patient told Sister Rose what she wanted done for her. She would like her Bible brought from the little hand trunk she had brought with her. She was by religion a Baptist and, at the urging of Sister Alphonsa, she agreed to see her minister and gave his name and that of the church. When he came the next day she was already in her coffin, and he did the best he could for her : prayed beside her. "I think I have seen her in my church," he said, "but I am not absolutely sure."

They found her Bible well worn and marked ; especially the Psalms were much underscored. She had whispered to Sister Alphonsa just before she died that there was money in the trunk to bury her, and this had been thought mere raving on her part, but they found a little roll of bills tucked in the flap of the trunk, and with this they paid for her funeral.

The Community was living more and more according to the religious Rule of Dominican tertiaries. They named the house in Cherry Street St. Rose's Home, after the great Dominican tertiary of South America. They said the offices now. When they left Water Street, they were wearing the semi-religious garb, permission for which the pleas of Sister Alphonsa had at last gained from the Archbishop.

They had a tiny chapel now where Mass was said one day in the week. On the other days they went to the earliest Mass down the street at St. Rose of Lima Church. The chapel was a room on the second floor, and on the left and right of it were two larger rooms, most of the light for which came from the doors leading into the chapel. In addition to giving the patients light, it gave them a chance to hear Mass, and Sister Alphonsa saw to it that the most bedridden cases were put in these two rooms.

To Anne MaGuire, who had been cook and housekeeper and friend to the Hawthornes years ago and who still lived in Concord, she wrote a letter that told about their life on Cherry Street :

Friday 5.

"Dearest Anne :

It is hard not to find it possible to get to Boston and Bedford and Concord, but all my hopes of this kind have been laid aside until we get more of us women together. We have thirteen patients under our care in this home and one across the street. We have been very busy and also have been sewing for our chapel and altar, as we hope 'for all things' in our religion. My two nieces come once a week to help me and are so interested in the linen and silk curtains we are making for the chapel, which is a small room between the bedrooms, for in the French charity which our work copies in many ways, the Mass is celebrated in the presence of the sick women, the doors being thrown open for this. But our house is so small that we cannot have a large chapel and large wards. I hope our dear Lord will come nevertheless for our constant adoration and comfort. When I have made my profession I must write you again, dear, and tell you about it. The Dominican Father comes to hear our profession, but we shall do all that is required in a simple humble way, for we are poor and deserve no fine display, only praying to be rich in sincere devotion, which cannot be seen by the eyes unless one is a saint indeed. Do pray for your old friend, that she may die a 'good and faithful servant,' for if I died today I should get no praise from our Lord's lips at all. For yourself, my darling Anne, my tender love and a prayer on the happy morning of December 8th when I shall indeed be a Dominican Sister. — 'Sister Mary Alphonsa.' "

196

On the one morning when Mass was celebrated, the altar candles would be lighted, illuminating the statue of Saint Rose of Lima, and the pictures painted by the talented fingers of Sister Rose. It lighted, too, the features, often with bandages over their disfigurement, of those patients who could sit up in wheel chairs or perhaps even kneel at a *prie-dieu*.

The priest began the Mass. When he came to *"Sursum corda,"* Sister Alphonsa's heart always answered. And, when he said, *"Gratias agamus Domino Deo nostro,"* she echoed it with all her soul. How blest they were, all together here, and knowing that soon their Lord would be with them too.

The call of the Preface to thanksgiving. "It is truly sublime," she thought, "uttered here in the house of surely approaching death."

"Vere dignum et justum est," said the priest. "It is making death a way to life," she thought triumphantly. The bell tinkled for the Sanctus. Then thrice for the coming of the Lord. The celebrant communicated, so did the Sisters, and then came the moment Sister Alphonsa had longed for for so many months. The priest went, ciborium in hand, to the patients in the chapel, to those in their chairs, on to the rooms at each side, and then to the floor above. Sister Rose carried a lighted taper ; the little server held the communion board. The Bread of Life was being given to her sick. Sister Alphonsa, on her knees in the little chapel, thanked God from a full heart.

In August of 1899 they had become tertiaries in Community by permission of the Archbishop, but not yet with the habit of the order. Father Thuente was their spiritual adviser and their confessor, and was a constant help.

Christmas of that year was blessed for many reasons, but especially so because the Archbishop promised them that when they were six in Community, they might have the Blessed Sacrament reserved in their chapel. Several women had been accepted as postulants, and in October of the following year, they were able to write that they now had the necessary six in their group, and

197

the longed-for permission was granted. There were those who were surprised that Archbishop Corrigan should give this permission not only for Mass but for reservation of the Blessed Sacrament as well, but, when it came to his ears he said only, "Let us help them to the best of our ability, for if this be work of men it will come to naught, but if it be of God you cannot destroy it."

Now in the plain little chapel on the plain little altar they might, as they came and went to their prayers, to their work, know their Lord enthroned among them. And in December came more happy news : the Archbishop had told Father Thuente to give the Dominican habit to the two women. On the Feast of the Immaculate Conception they received it and made their first vows and were called the Dominican Congregation of Saint Rose of Lima.

Father Thuente conducted the ceremonies. He preached a sermon to the two women and the few postulants who made up the entire congregation. It was a very short sermon, for he knew they must hurry back to their patients, from whom they could hardly spare even this little time.

There was deep peace now in the heart of Rose Lathrop. She had come, she felt very literally from the dark to the light. She had helpers now and she knew more would come. Enough money was coming in to keep the patients fed and warm, and to keep them all from being ever really hungry. She had authority behind her now, and could know herself part of a great group whose past and present was the doctrine of helpfulness to man and worship of God. And she had the happy knowledge that, when the world grew hard, when difficulties beset her path from misunderstanding friends or critics of her methods of care, she could go for a moment into the chapel and rest in the Lord. The little lamp's flicker showed her that He was at home in her Home.

Now that the Blessed Sacrament was permanently on the altar, Father Bandenelli, a Passionist, procured for them a relic of the True Cross and sent it from Rome to them by a young priest just ordained and on his way to be a curate in their own parish.

198

A relic of Saint Rose was obtained also, a fragment of the silk in which her body is wrapped. The Passionists sent them a relic of Saint Paul of the Cross, the founder of their Order.

During the first years of the work, the question at intervals had come up regarding the caring for men patients. The disease, Sister Alphonsa had learned, affects more women than it does men, but in women it is more often a surface disease and so more easily discovered than in men's cases which are usually deeper and not so easily located. She had therefore devoted herself to women's cases. Besides, the small space at their disposal gave them no chance for a men's ward, nor could they afford a man nurse. They did, of course, occasionally dress an outpatient's wounds, but that was all.

She had chafed for some time at this inability to take in all who came, but she had to be temporarily satisfied with the women. She kept hoping for better days which to her meant more beds, more rooms for her poor who were still to come, and more postulants.

They had, some months before, put one old man with a face cancer near them to board that he could be dressed each day and fed, but the wound grew so large that it was the same story over again which they had met with so often : the people in the tenement house grew alarmed, and he had to go back to his daughters who neglected him almost entirely. The Servants of Relief had not the means for even the smallest place for men or a male nurse to care for them.

Just as Sister Alphonsa was realizing something must be done about this problem, the president of a western railroad, who had heard of the cancer charity, wrote to ask if they could not take in one of his men. Sister Alphonsa wept to think she could not do it, and Sister Rose repeated the arguments they both knew so well. "We are too crowded now. Our patients and our nurses are all women. We can't do it unless we have more money."

Every word was true, of course, but this last case aroused Sister Alphonsa to a full determination to persevere until she was able not only to help destitute men sufferers, but, somewhere in the future, to a complete carrying out of caring for all and any of either sex, provided, only, they were incurable and destitute.

While the question was still being debated and mourned over, the door opened to a visitor from a charity organization, a woman who had brought them several of their women patients. "Will you take a male cancer case ?" she asked them abruptly.

Sister Alphonsa looked at the visitor reproachfully. "You know we can't."

She nodded. "Yes, I know and I wouldn't have come to you if the case were not so urgent." And they knew that must be true. "If such women and no other kind," commented Sister Alphonsa later, "stooped to the poor, a great sharp iceberg of a problem would melt into spring loveliness." So she prepared to hear the tale of this worthy case, trying to harden her heart even while she listened.

"Perhaps," hinted the visitor, instead of beginning her story, "if you came over with me to see him, you would feel the way I do about the old gentleman."

"But, my dear, it would be dishonest to go as if we were going to help him when we have no place or funds to do it." She saw the pleading look on the other's face, and impulsively said, "All right, I'll go over tomorrow to see him if you leave me the address."

The visitor seized her half victory. "Oh, he is very near here. And don't wait ; come now. Tomorrow would be too late, for all arrangements have been made to send him to the almshouse on the Island."

By that last remark she had won. The Servant for Incurable Cancer got up and made ready to go with her. The words of her helper rang in her ears as she went. "Remember we have no room or money for a room."

But the visitor gave her no chance to become hesitant now. She hurried her a few blocks to a room above a saloon where the patient lay on a dirty unmade bed. Evidently he had been waiting for some one to come to take him away, for he was dressed

200

in an old tweed suit. Sister Alphonsa saw he was almost blind, and soon learned that he was very deaf, too. His cancer was a bad facial one, and it bore every evidence of neglect. But everything about him bespoke the gentleman, and she saw why the crafty visitor had wanted her to come to see him.

It was clear, too, that everyone had been afraid to come near him : the tumbled bed, the dirty cups and spoons, the empty milk bottles on the table on which dust lay thick.

"I guess," said the saloon-keeper who had come up with them, "that I'm the only one who comes near him now. My mother had the cancer, and it don't scare me like it does some. He was a second lieutenant in some regiment is the story, and he gets a bit of a pension — eight dollars a months, and that ain't much for anybody that would take care of him."

"Could he stay here a little longer ?" coaxed Sister Alphonsa. The saloon-keeper shook his head. "They won't have him here no more. But the doctor can get him in Bellevue."

The visitor snorted in a ladylike way. She too knew the iron rule : inoperable cases were sent away as soon as discovered.

"He ought to be put out of his misery with an overdose of morphine," said the saloon-keeper, as if sure the old man was too deaf to hear him.

Sister Alphonsa knew that this was also the opinion of certain doctors in the city. She looked at him and said quietly, "But you are a Catholic. You must know that they usually feel respect for life and believe each moment is given by God to hold out to us another chance for reparation and the purifying of our souls."

The saloon-keeper, a kindly soul, looked aghast at this doctrinal outburst and hastily crossed himself. "It was spoke in kindness," he said apologetically. But what was really worrying Sister Alphonsa was a certainty that the old man had overheard him since he had not troubled to lower his voice. He was struggling to sit up, to find a bit of pencil on the table and a scrap of paper, on which he wrote waveringly, "Repeat to me all that you are saying or I shall imagine everything."

So she told him what he was to do. He would be taken to

201

Bellevue — perhaps he could stay there. But the visitor added quite loudly that that was by no means certain. He might have to go to the Island.

Again he wrote slowly and with great difficulty : "Please take me to your Home."

She patted his shoulder. "I will do my best," she promised, and saw by his eyes that he believed her. He got up and stood very straight, and the way he shook hands with her told her that he meant her to know that an old soldier was trusting her word.

Sister Rose, who had fully expected her to arrive with the old man in tow, looked relieved when she came in alone. But at Sister Alphonsa's story, the tears of sympathy stood in her eyes, too.

They decided first to send a note to the priest of the parish where the old soldier had lived, and answer came back that he might come to St. Vincent's Hospital where he would be made comfortable for the rest of his days. However this sounded too good to be true, and they felt dubious. And in the early morning came a hurried message from the charity visitor : the old man had been taken to Bellevue and would be on his way to the Island that very day unless Saint Rose's could somehow find a place for him.

Their supply of ready money was still very small, at times practically non-existent. But they rented a room across the way, put in a cot and a chair and hired a carriage to go up later for the old man. Sister Alphonsa meantime flew up to Bellevue and found him still safely there in one of the wards. She had time, too, to take a good look at the ward itself. It filled her with dismay. She had forgotten, living in that poorly-equipped but homelike little Home, what a ward in a hospital can be like. It was not that she did not realize that such places where a certain mechanical order must be preserved must look like that, but she hated it with all her heart, so cold and barren and cheerless it looked to her.

"It looks like a skeleton," she told them later at home, "with

202

a few white grave clothes clinging to it, a long drawn-out gray place. It made me glad to know that we can provide a home for the human element. We have what they haven't, for all their efficient aides — a triumphant supremacy over rooms and cots and silence. The silence, I think, was the worst of all," she added, listening to the patients' chatter in the next room.

The old man smiled when he saw her come in. He tried to say something to her, and she put her ear close to hear what he was mumbling. "I thought you would come."

"Of course I did. And at two o'clock a carriage will come to take you out of here," she promised, and all the way home she was warmed by the gratitude in his eyes.

"Oh, why don't we give You all we possess, Christ," she thought, "and at once instead of stopping to consider how much to give ? All this worry and fatigue of ours, and our being scorned and criticized don't matter at all when compared with one solid fact for God and our neighbor."

When she went over to attend to him in the afternoon, he was in his neat little room with their old errand man as nurse. As the days went by he grew quite handsome with good care. He ordered about the errand man as if he were his orderly. The doctors at the hospital had given him three days to live. He lived for almost three months. He went back, too, to the religious duties which he had evidently neglected for a long time, looking into his prayer book now and then, though that was difficult ; but the nurses found his beads always on his wrist, and he enjoyed looking at the little holy pictures they brought for him, and he liked to have the parish priest come to see him.

He never told them who he had been in the past, but it was obvious that he came of a good family. And they knew he had not become a dependent until illness made him one ; for as long as his employers would let him keep the job, he had run an elevator for his living.

His great pleasure was to be read to, but finding a reader was not always easy. The few nurses were far too busy. The errand man was willing enough, but his small schooling had given him little fluency with the printed page. Sometimes Sister Alphonsa could commandeer a visitor. There was a nephew who came down occasionally to see how Aunt Rose was making out, and who found himself, instead, reading the British news to the lone male patient. It was through one of the readers that they learned the old man had let fall the fact that his father had been an officer in the British Army.

Dr. Storer came in one day to ask how the work was progressing. He had heard rumors of the man patient, and wanted to see him. Sister Alphonsa was pleased. She had taken people to see the old soldier more than once and with malice aforethought, hoping that when the visitors say how inadequate it all was, they would be moved to help win more from the public for an extension of their work. At least she usually received in this way the rent for the room that kept the old man from the Island.

Dr. Storer's daughter was with him, and she lingered behind the other two to take a look at the medal the old man wore always on his chest. When she joined them she said, "He couldn't seem to tell me what the medal was given him for, but he did manage to tell me it was to go to you."

Sister Alphonsa turned back to his room again. "Oh, you must keep that — don't ever give it to anyone."

But he smiled at her and said, "I want to give you something too." When it was clear that his death was only a few hours away, he tried very hard to tell Sister Alphonsa something, but she had to listen intently and bend very close to him to catch the faint whisper. At last the words reached her : "You have been very good — you have been a great blessing to me."

After his death the saloon-keeper told them that the old man belonged to a lodge that would pay for his burial. The nurses put him in the uniform which he had tried always to keep clean and well brushed but into which moths had cut large holes. Over the biggest hole, Sister Alphonsa put the medal, and over it a wreath and a bit of palm leaf. He had been put in a shed next a saloon by the undertaker's men, and, as she went out, she had to move away hastily lest she be bumped by a lurching drunkard who had mistaken the shed door for that of the saloon and might take away, she was afraid, even the medal from the corpse. So she waited until the man had got safely into the door he was hunting for.

"The next world," she said sadly to Sister Rose, "surely will be safer and kinder than this one is."

That afternoon one of the patients called to her to come to the window. "They are bringing the funeral this way," she explained. Sister Alphonsa stood there as the bearers approached. Outside the noises were hushed with that strange respect that death can bring where life cannot, and everyone stood silent along the street. Over the coffin was draped a little flag, and at the top of the coffin lay her wreath and bit of palm.

"The only friend who never deserted him," she wrote in her diary that night, "the man who dealt liquors to the poor with questionable Christianity, rode beside the hearse, and lifted his hat to the Servants standing tearfully for a moment in the midst of their hurried labor. So, unresistingly and silently the old Second Lieutenant gave his last gracious mark of respect to fraternal help."

2

Friends of other days and relatives never ceased finding their way to the narrow street of the East Side where the Mrs. Lathrop they had known was now the smiling Sister Alphonsa, in a white habit, her lovely hair no longer visible. Sometimes curiosity brought them, but usually it was affection and a still lingering worry about their reckless friend and kinswoman.

Julian sat looking at her one day. "You're too thin, Rose. All those white folds can't conceal the fact from me. You'll kill yourself down here. You can't keep this up."

"No, Julian, you are mistaken," she said soberly. "It isn't the work that tires me. It is the thoughtlessness and the selfishness of a country that provides so poorly for its dependents. When they tell us that about one in ten has cancer, you would think there would be homes for the aged, or county farms, or whatever name brilliant imaginations in this century are inspired to call poor-houses, that would set aside a department for such sick people, rather than to go around screaming that they want to get rid of them. Oh, what I could tell you about the diabolic unpreparedness and cruel fight in this field of work, would not be pleasant for the country's vanity. They are a little more rational about consumption now, but the only care given cancerous poor has been in the interest of science. They want to experiment on

206

them because they are poor and have to let them. But they don't do it down here in our Home ! Think of it, Julian, they say they are incurable, and then they try their new ideas out on them."

"Well, of course there must be a certain regimentation of it all," protested Julian.

"It is heartless organized drilling, that is what it is," she retorted hotly. "They pin on a human being with a soul inside him a huge card when he comes into one of the country's several landing places instead of finding a more godly method. You should have heard the things Emma Lazarus told me about that. And *this* treatment of cancer is as bad. And you ought to see the letters I get asking help for people — asked by people who could so easily help remedy the situation if they tried. As it is, they agree the best place for the sick poor is a shanty or maybe an operating table. Not to cure them, you understand, my dear brother, but to get more information for science. That knowledge is much more important than caring for the poor things. The disease is a sorrow from God — but this other is something very different."

"But perhaps they are merely fighting for betterment of the disease in their own way."

"Well, their methods are odd and I don't like them. They seem to feel it is a disgraceful, humiliating thing to have to care for these poor souls. But on a battlefield, serving the hurt becomes the normal thing, and they serve the lowest as well as the highest victims of ghastly wounds. Why is this any different ?"

Miss Alice Wheeler, who had studied art years ago under the gentle tutelage of Mrs. Hawthorne, came from her quiet Concord home to see if she could be of some help with this idea of Rose's. She tried her best to help, but found she could not do it.

"You do understand, my dear," she besought Sister Alphonsa. "I want to, but I can't."

"My dear Alice," comforted Sister Alphonsa, "I had two trained nurses, religious at that, a while ago, and they stayed only a few days and then went back to their hospital uptown.

But you can't imagine how it warms my heart to know you came to help me."

"But it is wonderful of you, Rose, to do this for these poor things," added Miss Wheeler.

Only the day before Father Lavelle at the Cathedral had said something very like that to her. "Sister, I think it wonderful of you to give your life in this way to the suffering."

And she had whirled about as she stood in the doorway. "Oh, no, Father, it is not wonderful. Perhaps foundresses in Alaskan snows or African heat should have such praises paid them. But last week someone actually said to me, 'The Servants of Relief are martyrs.' Imagine that. It was a very hysterical opinion of commonplace beings, and it is too bad to let the idea spread, for it is catching like smallpox. I don't want women who might come to us to decide they haven't such great courage as all that. We are necessary but not wonderful, Father." And she was gone, leaving a chuckling cleric behind her.

But with Alice Wheeler she spoke very differently. "You are not a Catholic, Alice, or I could explain to you a little better."

But Miss Wheeler was waiting, so she went on. "It is charity, Alice, that is so wrong nowadays. Our little charity here has come to the surface like a crocus where there was an old garden that was cultivated when charity really was in flower. You know in those long ago days they called the sick poor 'Our Lords,' and cancer and leper cases were held in honor by holy men and women, because they saw in them a reflection of Our Lord's sufferings. And then, there is a rather fantastic conception abroad of the sacrifices that nurses of the cancerous poor must make. Of course there is an element of courage in befriending those about us, but then not any more courage than living any other vigorous rôle — unless one happens to be a lizard. We have to have the sacrifice of donations, too, you know, as well as the sacrifice of lives — I don't mean exactly sacrifice, but rather the service of daily routine just as it has to be lived in any world of business."

She was silent for a moment.   "These lines often come to me, Alice :

> " 'Seaward at morn my doves flew free ;
> At eve they circled back to me ;
> The first was Faith ; the second, Hope ;
> The third, the whitest, Charity.' "

"That is very true," said Alice Wheeler.   "Who wrote it ?"
"George wrote it years ago.   Yes, very true words."

Some of her nephews and nieces of the Hawthorne and Mann clan came down one day to see how Aunt Rose was getting along. They did think she was a good sport, they assured her, but they really wanted to know why did she ever do it.

"Do you really and truly like these people — honestly ?" asked one who had just taken a long look into one of the wards.

She looked at him quizzically.   "Well, I have tried to like them — the very poor.   And I think I have finally reached the point where I like them very much — if they are rather good. But you see, child, I have to do more than that : I want to love them.   And the way to do that is by doing everything I can to show them that I'm not merely greeting them in passing.   I want to have them know that I recognize their claim to be the same clay as the rest of mankind."

She showed them a *Harper's Bazaar* article which had just been called to her attention : the story of a woman arrested for stealing two loaves of bread for her children, and the editor spoke of the bitterness of having to beg even if by so doing she might have stayed within the law, and of the magistrate who, instead of sentencing her, got a charity organization to look after her.   "It is a shame that such things should be.   But I always have thought it a perfect shame for bakers to put their best things in the windows for the poor, who have never had any, to see, and only get hungrier as they look at the feast on the other side of the glass. It's enough to turn their heads."

At first the nephews and nieces had been awed by Aunt Rose's strange new garb. The bright hair was hidden, white draped about her ; on her head sat an odd white affair, an unwieldy headdress that made her look, to their unaccustomed eyes, like someone dressed for a costume party as an abbess of the Middle Ages. But the gray-blue eyes, the warm smile, the clasp of the hands were still Aunt Rose.

"And now you see," she went back to their original remark, "I am ready to cut out — really cut out — my own likes and dislikes too."

They marveled on the way home : was this the Aunt Rose who had given them such delightful visits in New London, in New York, who had loved music and having a good time ? She was very different, they all agreed, but she was very much the same, too. "In the ways that count," said Hildegarde wisely.

3

By 1901 the house that had seemed such a palace when they moved into it, by comparison with the miserable rooms from which they moved out, was proving much too small. It was growing harder and harder, too, to find rooms here and there in the neighborhood for the male patients who still insisted in coming, because so many people thought the disease a contagious one, and would not rent their rooms. And the Servants of Relief could not afford an apartment for them. Matters had reached a point where they must absolutely refuse to take one more patient.

Dr. Coyle stared in amazement one morning when he came in and saw the sixteenth bed set up in a tiny linen room. Its occupant was a woman who would have died in the street had they not taken her in, they told him, but he still looked horrified. Sister Alphonsa, looking in his face, feared science would win, and not compassion for once, and the woman be sent to the distant almshouse. He met her pleading look and exploded, "Don't keep that bed in that closet any longer than you must," and went on to the next patient.

"A dangerous collision," she called it later, for the pale famished woman would hardly have lived to make the long journey to the Island.

Then a great thing happened. The little Community decided in their dilemma to make a novena to the Sacred Heart for guidance. The day after the novena was over a visitor was announced, a priest, Father Coutheny, who wished to see the head of the Home. "We are French Dominicans," he told Sister Alphonsa, "and we have for some years had a house at Sherman Park in Westchester County. We were unwilling refugees from our native land and found that an excellent site for us. But we are selling now and very cheaply, and it occurred to someone who knows of you that it might be just the place for you, since you are wanting larger quarters. So we are offering it to you first."

To Sister Alphonsa this seemed the direct answer to prayer. Sister Rose thought so, too, but she wanted to see the place before they committed themselves. They went together by train to look it over.

Sister Alphonsa knew that if she showed one grain of prudence or asked the advice of any sensible person, she would have nothing more to do with this fascinating proposition, but would remain right in Cherry Street where they were crowded, but at least secure, financially. But it was May, a gentle month of hope and promise. And Sister Rose, who had been definitely against the idea, was sitting in the train beside her. She had come along mainly because it would be in the nature of a vacation to have three hours away from the Home after three uninterrupted years there of steady nursing. But even she, the eminently sensible, the "attendant pessimist," as her Superior called her, was so moved by the loveliness of spring that before the train journey was half over, she leaned toward Sister Alphonsa and exclaimed, "Perhaps we can manage it somehow."

Sister Alphonsa smiled at her. "Hope simply must have its way on a day as lovely as this. Life and mercy have gone a-Maying, you see."

At the Unionville station they were met by an aged black horse, an old carriage, and a very old Frenchman waiting to draw them up the heights before them, which to Sister Alphonsa looked exactly like Mount Blanc. The convent sat on top of it, like a yellow train of cars in its narrowness and with its dozens of windows. They leaned out to look at the anemones and ferns and violets along the road and listen to the unaccustomed birds. Sister Alphonsa, listening very carefully, insisted they were saying that Rosary Hill would be theirs, and that the blue sky and the brown road would help them get it.

They drove past the large stone grotto, shaped like a shell, and dedicated to Our Lady of Lourdes. They alighted at the convent chapel, welcomed and led in by one of the French Dominican Fathers who had lived there, and to whom the property belonged. Small and bare and very simple, with five altars in it, it housed statues of St. Dominic and St. Catherine, and was dedicated to Our Lady of the Rosary.

The Frenchman took them out to his orchard and his garden, smiling at their pleasure, but always with a little sigh in his smiles. He was to go to China, they learned, and it was obvious he preferred this to all the gardens of the Orient. He showed them the fruit trees he had planted ; he led them up to admire his grape arbor ; he showed them his bees and expatiated on the quality of their honey. The little greenhouse had budding plants, and the vegetable garden was a mass of delicate green.

The Father's sighs were met by their smiles as they murmured to each other that they must have this ; they *must*. It was close to New York, thought Sister Alphonsa ; there was space, and to spare, for her patients, she mused, as she looked about her, already envisaging sick folk settled here and there in the sunshine, in little summer houses, men patients by the dozen, a sun porch for old ladies, but, over and above all, a place from which she would never have to turn old men away any more. And somehow, as she watched the Father's tall white figure, so great a contrast to the drunken figures that lurched against them on the East Side's streets, there seemed here relief for the Servants, too. The little grove on the hill would be a pleasant consolation for her sick, and, when she looked up into the smiling skies flecked with soft clouds, and when she looked at the lavender and blue hills, she said to her associate, "This must be our second Home."

The attendant pessimist came out of her own happy daze long enough to moan, "How can we pay the bills ?"

"What a thing to say !" rebuked Sister Alphonsa, and though the retort was weak, the voice was strong.

They followed their guide into the house, a cold austere place that daunted Sister Alphonsa, who liked plenty of pictures and flowers and statues about. But in the kitchen they found a big box of white chicks, not much larger than the eggs they sprang from, petted like infants by the Father in charge there. And every window they passed framed beauty.

As they went on through the rooms Sister Rose whispered, "It is a pretty ramshackle house." And it certainly was, but of course they both realized it would be a wonderful place for a hospital, and it would be a shelter for the time being. But to Sister Alphonsa had come another thought, almost more discouraging, and, as they went through room after room, her heart sank : miles and miles of inches, she thought, and they a tired handful of women.

No, they must not attempt it. They must consider this merely a pleasant little trip for the two of them, look out once more at the peach blooms soft against a May sky, at the blue marching hills, and go back to New York and stay there, like sensible women.

A few moments later they had agreed to take the property for the very small down payment of one thousand dollars, and they went back to New York the almost owners of sixty rooms, and nine acres. They would buy, they decided in the train, the two cows, the bees, the chickens, the old horse.

"And perhaps the old French coachman too," said Sister Alphonsa.

Saint Rose's was now entirely out of debt. A legacy of ten thousand dollars had lately been left the Home. They needed only permission from the Archbishop, which was willingly granted, and the house and grounds were theirs. The thousand dollars which secured it was made up of many small donations, some of which were given by Houghton Mifflin, Henry Holt, Miss Josephine Lazarus, *Christian Herald* readers, and *"Heretic,"* who sent a hundred dollars.

In June Mother Alphonsa took two postulants and moved to Sherman Park, while Sister Rose, in Cherry Street, contemplated her empty chair with great loneliness.

Mother Alphonsa looked around her when they had been brought to the summit by the old Frenchman (who had insisted on staying) and the black horse. "It is as if we have been living in a mousetrap and now were domiciled in the Catacombs," she exclaimed. They were all, of course, accustomed to rushing to and fro for the sick and to answering innumerable bells of visitors in New York, but this was entirely different. They really needed, said Mother Alphonsa, a tram-car or an automobile to get from end to end of the place. One solution might be to have a great many members and divide them into squadrons at different points in the house, and there each group would stay doing its work, and meet with the rest only for prayers or Community reunions. But strength came with going, and after a while they grew used to the greater distances and their muscles ceased from aching. Before a week had passed a few of the patients had been transferred to the new home, and on *Corpus Christi* day the Home was formally opened. A Capuchin Father sang High Mass in the chapel.

The following week more patients were sent up from the city. But two came who were not city patients. She opened the door one morning to a sad-faced couple, an aged impresario from Chicago and his wife who had once been an actress. When it was learned that they had cancer, they were unceremoniously put off the train taking them from Chicago to New York. Utterly penniless, they asked for help in the village, and were told of this house on the hill that took in people with cancer. Much ashamed of their plight, they had decided to go there, and were soon made content and comfortable and told they were at home.

Some of their friends in town had thought the little group

might be lonely on that tall hill.   But Mother Alphonsa was able to assure such anxious souls that they could never be that — not while they had the wind, and they had that all the time. That year was windy everywhere in the country.   Great gales swept the Atlantic, and inland, too, it blew wildly.   On the very first week of their settling at Rosary Hill came a terrible storm with black clouds holding — and emptying — masses of rain and hail.   The windows banged.   The house beams groaned. The front door flew open, and pictures and vases fell to the floor. A picture of George Washington had its frame broken to bits. In the chapel which stood on the tip of the hill, it sounded like March at the North Pole.

They looked at each other in dismay.   This was July.   What, then, of the winter ?   They began to remember with chagrin those who had told them not to buy the place.   They ordered fifty tons of coal.   They put a new frame on George Washington, and hung him up again.   Had he not known reverses, too, Mother Alphonsa thought.   Consider his poor little army, and how he had defied England.   She was certainly no stronger than the gales that roared around their Home.   They detected a smile in his eyes as he looked out over Rosary Hill Home.   They decided they loved the whole place even more than when they first saw it on a mild spring day.

The storms subsided just as some one told them that the water they were drinking was dangerous and that typhoid lurked in every drop.   They held up the clear glassfuls to the light and doubted, yet felt afraid.   There did seem to be a queer taste of kerosene in it now and then.   But Mother Alphonsa had a cheering thought that perhaps they might be the possessor of a vein of natural oil that would make them very rich.   Alas, for such dreams ; it was found that defective machinery had caused the oily taste.

Fire, too, it was pointed out to them, could sweep the place in the matter of minutes.   On this point they had to be philosophic and hope for the best, for this danger they realized themselves.   But the gales had passed and the sun and the clouds and

216

the flowers and birds very obviously wanted them, the Servants, on their hill. They were there to stay.

The look in the eyes of the group of patients they brought up as soon as the place was at all ready for them, was the one thing that kept Mother Alphonsa sure she had done the right thing. They stared about them as if they were coming straight into fairyland. They sat on the old porches : they strayed about the grounds and picked wild flowers. One woman whom Mother Alphonsa felt apprehensive of permitting to come, and who was included in the group only because she begged to come because she loved the country and wanted to die there and not in a city, came in from a short walk and said that she was "strong again and so contented." And Mother Alphonsa, dressing her later — she had a terrible face cancer with one eye completely cut away — felt that that alone had made her project worth while.

Patients not well enough to take walks could go driving back of the black horse. Milk from their own Jersey cow, vegetables from their own garden brought better health to them all. Mother Alphonsa's happiest days were those when a carriage load of sick, white and wan from the city, came through the wide gate by the chapel, as if, she thought, Christ took them to His compassion before He gave them to her keeping.

But the courageous Sisters grew alarmed sometimes before the summer was over at thought of the bills. Mother Alphonsa had never wanted to incur any expense that could not be paid in a day or two. Now the little bills grew to large ones, and she was forced to make debts of a hundred dollars at a time. The promises of funds and the fulfilments seemed to have longer and longer intervals. But even when she felt most worried, she wondered if it was right to be a coward at such a time. Perhaps it was better to risk everything for a good idea. So they put their trust in Providence, their hope in windfalls, their prayers for large donations.

When they owed two thousand dollars to various firms and tradesmen and needed three more for the Home, they made a novena. They made a second one, and at the end of it there

217

came a letter telling them that a legacy of two thousand dollars which they had not thought would be paid them until a year later, would be sent them immediately. So the Sisters went to the petty creditors, who had even suggested they sell their old black horse to help pay the bills, a horse that never ran even when it saw the fastest train speed past, that willingly climbed the roughest hill road with its freight of ailing bodies. The creditors became more agreeable when they had given receipts in full, and the black horse went trotting past their establishments with not one covetous glance from them.

They realized during this interval that even though Sisters can get along without almost everything, they must have a bit of food and warmth if only to remain useful. And patients must have much more. And of course they had not counted on needing heat until fall, but the windswept hill and the cold patients demanded that some of the precious money go for fuel. The little white chickens which the two Sisters had admired on their first trip were now grown to husky fowl, and they proved very useful when funds for meat ran low.

Sister Rose had opened the door at St. Rose's one morning to find Mother Alphonsa on the door-step. "Have you any money at all, Sister? I have nothing left."

Sister Rose had a twenty dollar bill which she had changed and shared with her Superior, but during that very week a friend who had heard of the straits, paid their most pressing bills. And just when the mortgage interest fell due — a thing they had been dreading — another legacy came to them and paid not only the interest but the heating bills for the winter.

Spring brought more postulants and a letter from Archbishop Corrigan, enclosing a copy of the Dominican Rule, with instructions to follow it as much as they could without letting it interfere with their work. They were now seven in community at Hawthorne and eight at St. Rose's. Visitors came to see the new Home, leaving their contributions. The grounds were planted, and the orchard set out. There were a few old apple trees on the place that made Mother Alphonsa think of Bronson Alcott : they were so full of old branches that would have made excellent arbors for him.   They had put up double windows now, too, warned by the past winter's cold.

It was well that they did at least this much to combat the elements, for the next winter proved a very bad one, bitterly cold, with much snow and high winds.   Again money ran low ; even Mother Alphonsa's letters of appeal brought in few funds.   She shook her head over the strangeness of things when she came to town to consult with Sister Rose.

"Our appeal has met with so little response this time.   But the story of a scientist finding a dinosaur's egg !   That can easily enthrall the human mind, while a charity like this that is asking to be developed into huge proportions, has to play second fiddle to a monster's egg !   How can anything a million years old be of more importance than a cancer sufferer of today ?"

"Perhaps some day our attempt will be a fossil, due to cunning and prevention," ventured a listening Sister.

"Then all I can say is that that has the look of a dim futurity just now.   I shall never be able to see why students of prehistoric life should hold the stage so that living human beings cannot compete with those of mummies.   The living need us, while some of these old Pharaohs have indicated very distinctly that they need nothing more from any of us.   But it is such fun to discover the past and play with bones that have had their human day.   It is no fun at all to know what to do about people of our own era.   It troubled my father years ago, and he used to say that he thought the present was burdened too much with the past, and he felt we needed to watch our present life for which we have all too little time.   He said once that he felt aghast when he thought how future ages would have to stagger along under more and more of this dead weight as more and more was uncovered.   And now I see how there is even more interest in those dead old bones than in the living ones."

"It seems," sighed Sister Rose, "that it takes a war to wake people up to suffering."

"Oh, yes. Let a great crowd suffer and people's hearts beat warmly for it. For mercy's sakes, let us always have vivid respect for the few as well as the crowds, would be my plea, for our neighbors in the tiresome locality of here."

By evening, with characteristic impulsiveness, she regretted some of this speech. A pile of donations fluttered in and made her feel still sorrier, as if she had been inveighing against these kind friends, who even then were speeding to help her and some of whom might possibly have a very keen interest in archæology. Her fingers were chilly, but she picked up her pen and began to write, knowing she could use the article later in one of her annual reports, and thus apologize impersonally if she had spoken unfairly.

She did not have to consider her words. Words were always easy. It was time that was hard to come by.

"We know well enough that the trouble is the old one. The cruel eddy of superior circumstances swirls over the poor and they sink out of sight, and the hero of the newspaper and the cigarette, the opera and canvas-back duck, etc., make hash of our searches for the grief of others by absorbing all the time there is. And the great saints are as dead as Balder. But even a dead creature of grace can argue well to one's instincts, and the superlative saint characters, these unanswerable jurists for right principles, can still teach the wisdom of facing our racial brothers and sisters with an encouraging glance and hand, no matter what the strain upon us, and the worse the surprise or difficulty, the more cordiality and diligent aid there should be. Why wait until one is dying on the battlefield before handing the cup of water from our parched lips to the man who is gasping with thirst ? Certainly there is an element of courage in befriending those such as we befriend, in an effective way ; but not more than in living any vigorous rôle. It takes courage to live, unless one is a lizard. To the constant sacrifice of donations for financing, there must be added the sacrifice of lives ; that is, days spent in the service of these sick instead of in such service of daily routine as is usually acted in the world of society or business. It is best not to employ professional substitutes to carry on our compassion for us. There is, perhaps, only one in a thousand who would be a kind paid attendant of the poor in any disease and especially in cancer. It is disagreeable to think, for instance, what would have been the experience, if charity had called an ambulance, of the man who tried to

220

reach Jericho and fell into the hands of robbers, but also of the hands of a man according to God's own heart, who felt every considerateness to be a matter of honor. Making the the last years or days of destitute cancer cases (either good people or those who have not unclasped the grip of Satan) dignified and very comfortable, and a life of growing acquaintance with death that is more and more filled with spiritual zest, is as evidently a duty for some of us as any other occupation leading men and women who are self-respecting, into certain grooves of usefulness. Like tuberculosis, cancer may finally fade to pale outlines, and suddenly disappear as demons have done before sanctity."

She sat back and laid down her pen. She had explained fully to anyone she might have hurt by her earlier remarks, just what she meant and how she meant it. She went to bed with her conscience at rest.

Next morning she found a cheering letter from Mark Twain in answer to one of hers asking for an article for her little magazine, *"Christ's Poor,"* which was flourishing by this time. August of 1901 had seen the first number ; its subscription price was fifty cents a year, and she had asked for contributions to help pay for the printing. There was little money to spend for illustrations, but she ran as a frontispiece for many of the numbers a cut of Millet's *Man With the Hoe,* and under it various stanzas from Markham's poem of that name. The little books were filled with accounts of incidents in the Homes, histories of the renting and buying of the houses, while Mrs. Watson became a serial, and her story ran through four or five numbers. There was, too, a complete list of patrons of the charity each month, including such varied persons as "Concord, Mass., "Mrs. Samuel Clemens" and "Lady Calling Anonymously ($300)."

Some of the numbers carried a picture of Christ with a hungry group about Him and under it her favorite scriptural verse : "I have compassion on the multitude."

In his letter Mark Twain had said he had no time just then for an article, but he could help in other ways : by telling others the needs of the institution, and that the chief need was money ; he, himself, as the Sisters well knew, had more than once helped generously in this very way.

221

"I know some," he wrote, "who have it, and have not been reluctant to spend it in good causes, and certainly if there is an unassailably good cause in the world, it is this. I am glad in the prosperous issue of your work, glad to know it will continue to be permanent, for that endowment is banked where it cannot fail until pity fail in the hearts of men. And that will never be."

Expenses in the city Home ran much lighter than the country Home. The biggest outlay there was the Relief Room ; hungry or evicted people, and food and rent sometimes had to be provided, even though such help was strictly outside their work. But at Rosary Hill there were greater expenses, or should have been, had there been the money for them. That winter they could not afford to hire a man to work about the place but did everything themselves. On the Feast of the Immaculate Conception, when Mother Alphonsa came down from Hawthorne to renew her vows with Sister Rose, the latter noticed how rough and red her hands were from heavy work. She tried to make her stay a day or two ; but she refused to wait even an hour after the ceremony, and went straight back to Rosary Hill to help the Sisters there. When, cold and shivering, she reached it, she found the pipes all through the house had frozen, and the Sisters were bringing in great heaps of snow and melting them to use for cooking.

It was fortunate that they needed little paraphernalia such as most hospitals must have, since there was no need for operations ; and it saved buying costly instruments and antiseptics. Very little was needed for salaries. The food was simple though carefully prepared, and it had been noted by the Sisters that their patients did much better on such fare than those who lived on the richer food of expensive institutions.

Nineteen-three bade fair to prove much like the year before : very cold, little money, hard work, and the inevitable legacy that always came just in time to tide them over. That year, too, their old friend, Father Thuente, now Prior of St. Vincent Ferrer, came to visit them and was immensely gratified at the way his protégées were progressing. And Father Kent Stone came, now a very old man, which fact however did not prevent him from having opened that very month, a new foundation of his Order in Scranton.

Mother Alphonsa showed him her new domain, and displayed proudly her quantities of space for her patients within and without doors.

"It is what a hospital should be," said Father Stone approvingly.

Mother Alphonsa nodded. "That is just what we are trying to make it. Perhaps the hospitals of the future may be like ours. We have no stern rules as so many almshouses have, either, and the nurses' inconvenience is not nearly so important as the convenience of the patients. And our sick don't have to get up at five o'clock to make their own beds and then stay up all day. And they don't have to stay in bed all day, either, if they are well enough to get up."

"The sick poor," said Father Stone from the depths of his wide experience, "are even more sensitive than we think, to such indignities."

"Indeed they are. That is why we have no system of scalped economy so that the patients feel everywhere the shiver of a loveless touch, and greediness in everything but the size of salaries for those who care for them. We try to avoid meanness of régime, such as cheaper food, stale or of unpleasant quality. And," Mother Alphonsa could never resist voicing her hatred of experimentalism on the unfortunate, "we have no operations or experiments here. They would do no good to such advanced cases as ours anyway. Some of our poor people have been so treated with radium or the knife that they come to us with hardly a shred of existence left. I don't think such means ever help many, anyway. If a case is healed over in one place, it returns in another region."

"What means do you use to help them ?"

"Oh, we have washes and various salves. They always improve the patient's condition for a time — sometimes for years."

223

"And apparently your only pay is love. But the salary seems to agree with you all. You are a healthy looking lot."

She laughed. "Our Sisters have always improved in health after entering the Community tired and subject to the ailments that always attach to women who have injurious hours and food. There seems to be a romantic notion abroad that our members, certainly the young ones, are squeezed of every ounce of vitality and endurance. If people would look at our solid and comfortable maidens, it ought to clear up such an idea."

"Perhaps they feel that it is hard on the body when a woman is making up her mind to become a religious," suggested Father Stone.

"Oh, of course all religious must have had a bad quarter of an hour before the final oblation is made. But any important step in life is the same. I know the kind you mean, though : they go through a prolonged self-questioning under the belief that they are studying the will of God. But often these hair splitters make the healthiest of all."

"Do you find it takes them long to get used to the work, Mother ?"

"Oh, it takes a week or so, and during that time it is trying But I have just been reading about Madame Garnier and her work. She founded a semi-religious charity for cancer, and among the fashionable young women who worked with her she noticed always this victory over sensitiveness after a certain time. It was good to read of others interested in it. Do you know, Father, that when we began, not one hospital would take the cancerous poor, and no one was helping them at all. Now the Gray Sisters at East Cambridge and the House of Calvary in New York City are caring for them, too."

4

The Christian Brothers had bought a house for their Noviciate at Pocantico Hills, and Brother Julian, of the Order, was in charge of it. St. Joseph's College sat on a hill of its own across from their hill, a tall building which, Mother Alphonsa had told Brother Julian when he came over to meet his new neighbors, "very nearly interferes with the white clouds edging the blue."

The Sisters at Rosary Hill had good cause to be glad of St. Joseph's College and its noviciate master. When the days were black with cold or lack of funds, Brother Julian would be sure to select those days as the ones to come to see them, through the woods and up their hill. When he saw the many empty spaces in their house he said to them, "God is certainly blessing you. All of us at college are praying for you." Brother Cyprian often came over with him, and Mother Alphonsa loved to see him come, for she said that he had a smile that could cheer the frost out of a southern peach crop.

After especially fierce thunder storms, Brother Julian would go with some of his students at his heels to see if the little group at Rosary Hill were still safe and sound on their unsteady porch. And often, in those first hard years, he used to telephone the Sisters to come to some festivity — perhaps a *Corpus Christi* procession, occasions when the invited Sisters, the students, and the laity walked through the trees, long lines of them, saying the

Rosary in concert, as the priests and acolytes passed from shrine to shrine under the incense.

Sometimes when the telephone rang very early in the morning it would be Brother Julian : he had been reading the morning paper, and the Sisters had had a legacy left them.

He was a very busy man and Mother Alphonsa was a very busy woman, but they were kindred souls to whom a few words exchanged had the value of a long conversation. And if ever, in the face of adversity and the difficulties of responsibility, even her strong will faltered, it was heartening to know that tonight Brother Julian was praying earnestly for her success, and that to-morrow or the next day he would bring over some students to recite for the patients or sing to them, or perhaps send a special cake baked for them in the kitchens of the College.

Almost immediately with the establishment of the Home at Hawthorne had come the problem of a place to bury the patients who died. Down below near the river a large Catholic cemetery called the Gate of Heaven had been established for some years. In this the Community bought a plot for their own use. Later the daughter of Longfellow had placed here a granite cross in memory of her husband.

Mother Alphonsa pointed out to a visitor at the Home a clump of trees below to the left. "And down there is our cemetery."

The visitor shivered. "I should hate to be almost in sight of my grave like that," she said.

Mother Alphonsa smiled. "No, it is not a dreadful thing. It is the one thing, you see, that completes their home for our patients."

It still happened occasionally that a patient was brought to her attention too sick to be moved, as in the early days on Water Street, and then one of the Sisters went to dress the sick person. Of course there had been no thought of taking over also the expense of burying these out-patients. But one woman, as Mother Alphonsa was dressing her in the mean room her relative grudgingly granted her, said weakly, "You'll let my funeral be from your chapel, Sister, won't you please ?"

She promised it, not thinking that she might also be faced in that case with the duty of burying her. When this thought came to her suddenly as she was scurrying through the snow to the monastery of the Salesian Brothers to ask them to take the Blessed Sacrament for Viaticum to the sufferer, she stopped in the lane and thought it over.

"What does God wish for this poor woman ?" she questioned herself. "And why should the poor soul be denied the consolation of services in the House God gave us to put His poor in ? He meant it for life — and death, too."

Later, when the coffin stood in the chapel, with many of the patients at the funeral services, she was glad she had not decided against the woman's request. And it was from that moment that she had worked for money for a cemetery plot for them all, "a consecrated burying ground — a more Christian introduction to the life beyond this world."

There had been talk for some time among friends of the Community of starting an Auxiliary to give financial help in buying drugs and appliances, to get sufficient gauze and cotton for their always increasing needs, to supply the Homes with medicines and alcohol and sherry. Various means to help raise it had been suggested.

Dr. Walsh, who had never taken his eyes from the group since first he went to see them down on Water Street, offered to give a lecture to raise money. They decided to combine his lecture with the opening meeting of the Auxiliary. It hurt Mother Alphonsa that in that case her patients could not hear the lecture, too, but Dr. Walsh promised to come up some time later and give them one all their own.

It was a gay and festive gathering, and Mother Alphonsa had an opportunity to play a part she loved — that of hostess. The day was the Feast of the Apparition of Saint Michael, whose name, in addition to that of the Most Holy Rosary, was added to the dedicatory name of their chapel. It was a fine day in mid-May, and Dr. Walsh had chosen Saint Francis of Assisi for his subject. The lecture was in the open air and the guests sat in and about the newly built summer house, while Mother Alphonsa rose to welcome them. She waved her arm in all directions before she sat down. "And besides an Assisi lecturer, please note that we also command Assisi views."

Three hundred and fifty had been invited, and to judge from the throng, everyone had come. Father Wilson came to represent Saint Vincent Ferrer's Convent. Father Timothy Hickey introduced the speaker and did it admirably, since he was speaking to an audience many of whom were Protestants, neighbors of Rosary Hill and well-wishers. He told them of Saint Francis walking through the spaces of outdoors while he was meditating, of how most of Christ's discourses were carried on in the open.

Father Smythe, of Manhattan College, was there. Father Damien of Valhalla, and Father Costerot of Pleasantville, both helpers of the Sisters in times of need. And in addition, many of their charitable benefactors came : Mrs. Arnold, a convert who had been interested in Rose Lathrop's project since its inception ; Mr. Warren Greene, a Protestant who helped them greatly with much needed legal advice ; Mrs. Warren Mosher, who talked with Mother Alphonsa of the first days of the Summer School at New London, and dozens of others who had, in the past, given time and money to this charity, and were now gathered with the laudable ambition of furthering it still more.

Mother Alphonsa and her Sisters had planned to have luncheon served out under the trees, and benches had been set up here and there. But the sun departed from the hill, and so they were served instead in the summer-house and in the long corridors running the length of the house, and it became a meal of most delightful informality.

Afterwards Sister Amanda of Saint Hyacinth's School sent a group of small boys to sing at Benediction, a sedate little crowd, but the Sister in charge was in a constant state of alarm lest one of them would slide along the tempting terrace or chase one of the four sheep grazing contentedly near at hand.

At four o'clock the Very Reverend Father Mercier, Prior of Saint Michael's Monastery, gave Benediction of the Blessed Sacrament at an altar where sunlight and dogwood and the golden gleam of candles mingled in loveliness.

Mother Alphonsa had had a fine day. She had been the hostess of a very successful social affair. And the establishing of this Auxiliary would, she knew, mean the lifting of many difficulties for her in the future. Also she had been able to show her guests the new summer-house and the remodeled greenhouse.

Earlier in the spring Mother Alphonsa brought one day a letter to Sister Rose to read. It was from a woman who asked, "Could you use a small sum of money, only a thousand dollars, to bring a little brightness into the life of some one who suffers ?" The memorial was given, she added, in memory of her brother, and she hoped that if it were possible, it could be used for one purpose.

"Small sum." Mother Alphonsa's voice was full of awe though her eyes sparkled. "One thousand dollars a small sum !"

Despite debts that called loudly for that money to pay them, and the fact that one ceiling was waiting, as she said, for a mere whisper from gravity to fall, it was decided to use this gift for the male patients, as more fitting to honor the brother's memory, and that it should be a summer-house for them. There would be enough left to make the greenhouse a useful thing.

"What it is now," said Mother Alphonsa in disgust, "is a tantalizing foolery."

The women patients were willing, in fact, preferred to sit indoors much of the time, but the men loved to be outside under the trees or in Saint Dominic's little garden, taking their shawls and pillows with them. This was fine unless a shower came up and drenched them. Without a doubt a summer-house was the best answer for that "small sum." The greenhouse was really

229

mostly for the men, too. They liked to garden a little, and in the winter the plants would serve to amuse them, thought Mother Alphonsa, discussing the matter with her friend and adviser from the next hill.

"Those little glass panes in there now keep flinging themselves on the Sisters' heads. And the broken bricks let in even the very fattest of the neighborhood rabbits who appreciate greatly the seedlings and young sprouts."

"Can you heat it?" asked the practical Brother Julian.

"We cannot," said Mother Alphonsa as briefly. "But there are heating pipes. I admit at present they merely cool the greenhouse, but we can repair them and the plant, and then in the winter the sick folks can have little squads of flowerpots assigned to different members. All the poor old things want anyway is a warm spot in winter, and an airy one in summer, and this will give them both."

"Are you still letting them smoke?" asked Brother Julian in a voice that was meant to sound warning, but turned out to be merely sympathetic.

She did not answer directly. "I suppose," she said meditatively, "that the spirits of fire insurance companies would sink to hear it, but any evening you come around here you will notice a pungeant suggestion of Veterans' Tobacco on the air. But we do watch the threads of blue smoke — each Sister just about looks after one thread, and after it ceases, makes sure there is no fire left. But now we are going to have a summer-house for them. Do you know it is two whole years since the old one blew down? There is the old bench left that was too firm to blow away ; but now this grand gift will give us a chance to have a place for them to sit in again."

In the summer of 1904 a letter came to Rosary Hill from Concord. Mrs. Daniel Lothrop wrote that she was planning to celebrate the hundredth anniversary of Nathaniel Hawthorne's birth with talks and papers at the Wayside. Many people of literary importance had been invited to attend. Thomas Wentworth Higginson and Charles Copeland would speak, and Mrs. Julia Ward Howe had promised to say a few words. Mr. Sanborn would be there to tell what he remembered of her father. Julian Hawthorne had promised to come. Would his daughter also come and perhaps read a paper about her father on one of the two days of the celebration? Mrs. Lothrop would be very happy to give her her own old room at the Wayside while she was in Concord.

Mother Alphonsa laid the note aside with only a small tinge of regret. She had very little time even for regrets, she thought to herself. How would she ever find time for a paper? She wrote to Mrs. Lothrop, with a sudden recollection of her sitting in her little wicker chair by the fireplace, plotting out another Pepper story, and shielding herself from the direct blaze with a fire-screen which Rose Lathrop had painted for her. Time for painting ornamental fire-screens! She laughed at the absurd thought, as she drew toward her pen and paper to answer the invitation.

"My dear Mrs. Lothrop :

"Your most interesting letter and kind invitation reached me in our Country Home for the cancerous poor. I am so glad that you are all to gather to give my father so much honor. But I have no prospect whatever of being able to be present. I have tried very hard for a couple of years to leave my work among the poor to go to Concord, or its neighborhood, but have been prevented very imperatively. This is usually because, taking care of the dying, and few of our patients live beyond expectations for some months or years, we are constantly thrown into extremely arduous situations, when every one must join in watching, laying out the dead and seeing to the last rites ; and, too, new patients are to be received, which entails much preliminary work, until they are refreshed and settled. We do all our housework as well. When I have more members of our band of women for both Homes, I shall expect to get away occasionally for journeys in several directions. I am so glad that my brother will be present, and I wish with all my heart that I could be, and could add my words of interest to the commemoration. That however I could not do as I am not used to addresses such as will

231

be given. But I am I think a good listener, and grieve that I must lose the interesting experience.

"Gratefully and cordially your servant,
"M. Alphonsa Lathrop, O.S.D."

Perhaps she did not realize as she wrote the letter how some of its phrases would astonish the Concord audience. "Laying out the dead." "We do all our own work." Perhaps she did envisage it and smiled to herself to think how it would affect them. The letter had been addressed "Mrs. Rose Lathrop." Concord could not imagine her as Mother Alphonsa and did not try to, sending her letter by the name by which they had known her.

She was hailed on her way to Vespers, while thinking that perhaps her letter had been too short, and she ought to write more on the subject of her father, by old Mrs. Williams, who had been an out-patient in the Relief Room in town and was now a permanent guest at Rosary Hill. Mother Alphonsa sighed, for Mrs. Williams was given to gloomy musings of an unanswerable sort.

"Mother, why is it ye say prayers every little while all day in pieces like that? Why don't ye put them all in one place at once?"

Mother Alphonsa, her mind full of Concord and the past, felt this was hardly the time to come to the defense of the canonical hours of prayer, so she smiled vaguely, patted Mrs. Williams' shoulder and started on.

But she was not to escape so easily. "I think the Sister is using my money for the new dishes," she complained.

Mother Alphonsa laughed. "Oh, no. I gave her the money for them myself. Yours is in the little bundle you gave me, right in a safe place in my desk."

"Well, if ye say so," Mrs. Williams said, and allowed Mother to go on, but grudgingly.

The latter shook her head with a smile for the vagaries of the old lady who, when she came to them to stay, had handed her a small grimy bundle, announcing it was money for her funeral. Carefully counted in her presence, it was found to amount to exactly forty dollars and it was, as she had been assured, put care-

232

fully away. Rest and care had so improved the old lady's body and mind, that she began to develop worries of her own, first and foremost the fear that everything in the house was being bought with her money.

Only the week before Sister Mary Frances had come in to Mother, her shoulders shaking with laughter. She had seen Mrs. Williams give a good hard look at the new organ in the chapel, and after the services had heard her say in a fierce whisper to her neighbor, "When I came here they had nothing. Now they can buy pianneys."

But Mother Alphonsa, after reassuring Mrs. Williams, thought to herself that her letter had certainly been too brief. She would telegraph to Mrs. Lothrop that she would send a short article about her father which could be read during the Centenary.

She meant to write it the next morning, but Monsignor Flood, who had recently been appointed their spiritual adviser, came up to pay them a call. As she went to greet him she found herself feeling a bit ashamed of their shabby old home. She need not have worried.

He got out of the carriage, gave a long look about him and said, "I cannot have that at my home." She looked too, and saw his gaze was riveted on a great bank of pink rambler roses climbing up their gateway. It *was* lovely, and she forgot to regret the rickety house.

"Perhaps he merely meant to put me at my ease about the old place," she said to Sister Rose when Monsignor Flood had gone, "for he is a sculptor and a very successful one of the wishes of others."

They sat on a bench looking at the river while she told him some of the difficulties confronting her. Then, these out of the way, she began to smile.

"Monsignor, we have a great problem on our hands here. Perhaps you can solve this for us, too. I have just written a little article for my magazine and called it 'Tramps ; or, the First Blue-birds.' The worst of it is that when times are hard with us, they

233

are hard with tramps, and then we have more men than ever come to ask for a meal. We had nine for dinner yesterday."

"Perhaps," suggested Monsignor Flood with twinkling eyes, "if you just turned stern and sent them away — "

"Yes, if ; but the minute I ask a question — and I always do — I find out they are human beings. And they do work so nicely for fifty cents a day — some of them do, anyway. The Fathers who used to live here said to us, 'Be nice to them but not too nice,' before they went away. It is so hard to follow that advice."

"Do you think there are dangerous characters among them ?"

"Oh, no, it isn't that. But you see if a meal is good, it is telephoned about as if it were stocks, and the rise or fall of a pudding is of sensitive importance. No, I'm afraid our tramp table is a fixture. If I didn't feed them I would be unhappy. My father told Emerson once that he would rather give even to an impostor, for he said otherwise the lamentable figure he spurned would limp at the heels of his conscience all over the world."

"At least that is nearer right than wrong philosophy," agreed Monsignor Flood.

When evening came, and quiet, she sat down at her desk to write the article. What should she say about him — the father who still filled her life with his ideals, his love for the people of the world ? Julian, she knew, would handle the facts, and do them better than she could, but there must be a little laurel leaf from her. She dipped her pen in the ink and began to write. She had wondered what to say. Now the words wrote themselves, and she found it difficult to stop.

"My dear Mrs. Lothrop :

"The reason I have not sent a paper to be read about my father's life in Concord is that I am no longer free to use my time if the sick need it, as our patients have done for a number of years now. The Order to which I belong, which especially combines the active life with prayer, would sanction my going to Concord for so important an occasion ; but as yet the women tending the twenty-five cancer cases whom we harbor in the Country Home are too few to allow any of us to fall out of line for a day. Your last kind letter, however, gives me the opportunity to

234

express at least a few thoughts to be added to the bright and eloquent words aroused upon the hillside which possesses so many memories of great souls now unseen, whose very presence spoke, so that we hardly needed to hear words from their generous lips to know that they had blessed us in their thoughts.

"You believe that this Wayside echoed with unspoken words as it traversed the homes of Hawthorne, Alcott, Emerson, Canning, Hoar and others. However noble and brilliant their speech, their vigor and frankness of insight called forth the uninterrupted response of those who dwelt near them!

"The presence of my father filled my heart ; he approached, and every nerve started to position. But he also, though silent, filled me with suggestions of exalted sentiment far more vividly than the printed pages of the princes of literature, ready for their mastery of the imagination in the library, or than the unerring lines and tones of superlative sculpture and painting, recalled in the decorations of our home.

"Since my hourly contact with the roughest side of the world, its anguish of pain and ugly disease, its base cruelties and frightful lapses into evil, I keenly recall the beauty of the rarefied dignity of thought and peacefulness of spirit which made the invisible home of my parents here, of which the outward reality was never permitted to be unworthy in its humble sweetness of aspect, enriched with every distinguished reminiscence and all faultless criterion only, as it stood for them beside the high road of common things. But though the atmosphere of our home was full of honor and art, and references were only beautiful and inspiring, and all disgust of every sort was eliminated from fancy and motive, yet my father's personality, containing as it did the analytical knowledge of the world's greatest monstrosities of evil, and wearing, in the later years, the never-relinquished black of one who had stood at the bier of human nature, yet this personality was the most tranquil that the Wayside held, the one who, in the end, gave greatest delight of geniality and highest counsel of demeanor. I do not understand whether it was by the magnetism of genius (that vividness of myriad faculties) or whether it was by the sense brought to me that my father had mastered a wondrous condensation of perception, but I seemed to have a delicious recognition of the results of art at its finest flowering, and the enchanting perfections of godlike character, when we met. There were no regrets ; all was joy and strength in these meetings, brief or extended, even after his great mind and heart appeared to have become, as I said, the unforgetting friend of the self-slain race.

" 'Bab,' as he called me, with a low, cheery note of the voice, breathed deep as he came near. His full, sensitive but nobly strong lips were nearer a smile than a sombre droop ; his eyes were chiefly radiance, though often, in those years, full of the long lights of revelation ; seldom sparkling with the lesser beauty of frivolous sympathy, as I had seen them shining in England. 'Bab' was silent as the toad under the silent flowers beside the terrace where we sometimes sat together, or as the pine needles on the hill which rustled, but only in a whisper, under his feet, as we walked there in brisker autumn. But his silence kept me busily occupied.

"Dear Mrs. Lothrop, the limit of time is reached for me, and I find I have said nothing definitely descriptive of my father's life at the Wayside. One thing I will add : the clearest picture in my mind, always, as I look back to that time between 1860 and 1864 is that of my father and mother stepping side by side about the grounds, looking at a branch here or a vine there. He talked then. Her head was almost always lifted ; she was looking straight forward or up at a height of summer loveliness. He was usually looking down, though not without a ready willingness to follow her command, and also look at some simple grace of the verdure or sublimity of the sky. But he did not forget the grass blade or the pebble of the mystery of our earthly sojourn.

"Very truly yours,
"M. Alphonsa Lathrop, O.S.D."

She looked at the clock. She had written longer than she meant to. But she sat very still for a moment in her chair. So vivid had she made it all to herself, so complete in each other had been those two at The Wayside, while a little girl had watched them there. Set deep in time was the picture, and so perhaps perishable, but also set deep in love and so everlasting. She folded the sheets and put them in the envelope, and was just writing the address when a knock came at the door.

"Old Mrs. Sims is very bad, Mother. You told me to let you know," whispered a low voice.

"Yes, Sister, I'll be there right away." She put the letter in a box with the rest for tomorrow's post and went back to her work.

In October of 1909 Mother Alphonsa saw that the time had come for another appeal to the public's generosity. They had so little money and so many patients that a plea for help must go forth. Her first letter went to the *Times*.

"It would seem," she wrote, "that the Servants for Relief of Incurable Cancer were never perfectly at home except in the field of mendicancy, because of their unerring success in rapidly using funds supplied to them for the needy of New York, and hastening back to the starting point.

"The city house, St. Rose's, is still crowded with twice the number of bedridden women that it should contain. The Sister presiding over the House would be glad to show it on Saturday and Sunday afternoons to anyone who cares about these prisoners of suffering, but the sight of the crowded space may show why we are pondering the question of enlarging the building. This Sister's great grandmother was first cousin to Commander Donough, and her mother was second cousin to Keenan of the glorious charge, so that the appearance of the sick rooms at St. Rose's does not parallel her great courage. She would like more such rooms rather than unhoused cancer cases. Yet first we must beg for immediate needs, or all the eighty-five souls of the charity will go hungry. We need clothing for the winter for men and women ; we need additional heating apparatus for the Country Home at Hawthorne. On account of the large number of deaths, we must pay a considerable sum for the funerals which we are bound to provide for those patients who are without other friends.

"We have but one hundred dollars in the world. Besides our sick, it is not hard to dare to be poor and to have so much faith in God and His people."

The *Times* published her letter. It always did, for they were very refreshing letters. In the same issue the *Times* carried the news of the death of Francis Lathrop at his home in New Jersey, where he had lived less than a year since moving from his old studio in Washington Square.

As the years went by, many of the financial difficulties were, to a great extent, ended. Various legacies enabled them to pay off their entire mortgage. Mr. George Schrader, of Hartsdale, close to Hawthorne, was so interested in the work that he paid for many of the improvements around Rosary Hill. He built a sun parlor where the women patients could sit during the day, for it was often too cold for women so far gone in illness to sit outdoors. He helped with landscaping the grounds, bought trees and plants to beautify it. And he built an amusement Hall, where the patients could come for musicales or plays or other entertainments put on for their benefit.

After the Hall had been blessed by Monsignor McGean, who came from New York for the ceremony, a troupe of colored minstrels, sent by the same Mr. Schrader, played and sang old plantation songs for the guests.

Archbishop Falconio, the Papal Delegate, came to visit the Home, gave a short talk to the Sisters, and spent some time visiting with the patients. When he was ready to go, Mother Alphonsa handed him a little bag, which clinked with its load of small coins.

"The patients have been saving these for you for weeks," she told him. "They are for Peter's Pence, and we have been waiting for Your Grace's arrival to give them to you."

Mother Alphonsa had received a gift herself a little while before the gift of the coins to the Archbishop. She loved giving presents, and she loved writing letters. And, lo, here were the two things in one, and for her. On the feast day of her patron saint in August, the men patients had written her a letter.

When they had asked time and again, these old men, "Is there no place for us ?" she had been obliged to shake her head, but she had not been content until she could take them in, to share, she said, the sunshine.

"That is something," she wrote in *Christ's Poor,* "that must not be denied to anyone, for it comes straight down from the king of planets, who has even seemed to weave the robe of light Christ wore when He revealed His divinity most evidently. We could not refuse sunshine when we really had it to give."

And here was her reward, in this ill-spelled letter from her old men.

"Mother Alphonsis," it began.
"Rev Mother
"We the male paitents of the Rosary Hill home this being the Feast day of vour patron Saint Takes opertunity of Congratualing you on the grand work you are doing for us poor men and women

238

that the great allmighty has seen fit to affect with a Teriable dissace but kind Mother and kind Sisters what would be the condition of these poor men and women only for the home like this with saintly Mother and sisters and the Consolation of our Holy Church at all times surrounding you now dear Mother in conclusion the following pateints Sends you their gratitude and congratulations and wishes the Sisters and yourself many years and that God may prosper your work and that when the great allmighty calls you home to that home beyond the Clouds he will have Bright Crowns of Gold waiting for you there where their is no more pain or trouble but all happiness for ever is the wish of Jas J Spearing and all the other patiants."

Mother Alphonsa sat back with the letter in her hand, and the tears welled into her eyes and fell on the note. She felt an extraordinary desire to show the letter to her father and her mother, so that its humor and pathos could be shared with them who would have understood it so well.

Had someone long ago called these people she worked among uninteresting? How blind they were who thought that, when business and art and fashion were all adopted by those consecrated to them, God should be without an army devoted to His commands in any field He pointed out! "And He asks us," she thought, "to be humble and meek, to remember we are dust, and, as we prostrate ourselves to offer Him all that we are, we find the sick poor at our side. They lie as low as we have bent before our Commander, upon the ground where we belong."

5

In 1909, Mother Alphonsa and Sister Rose made their final vows. It was on the Golden Jubilee of the Immaculate Conception, the same feast on which they had at last received the habit for which, as the Archbishop told them when he granted them permission to wear it, they had gone through a long and difficult noviciate.

Nine years ago on that same Feast day they had at last been granted permission to wear the religious habit, and had received the name of the Dominican Congregation of St. Rose of Lima. There were only a few postulants then to witness it. Now there were many more, Sisters, and novices, and postulants, about them for the ceremony.

In 1910, a letter came to Mother Alphonsa from Monsignor McGean of Saint Peter's Church in Barclay Street that caused her to rush down from Hawthorne to consult with Sister Rose. She waved it at her as she came into the hall. "A member of the parish wishes to donate fifty beds to St. Rose's Home. Fifty beds — oh, what *shall* we do now with a house that holds only sixteen beds ? We simply must enlarge the place right away."

But Sister Rose counseled caution, as always. Next day a letter was sent to Monsignor McGean, full of thanks, but containing also the statement that St. Rose's would hold only, at the most, sixteen patients. If there was no reading between the lines, there certainly were a few strong prayers there.

A few days later came an answer : The family in question would give twenty-five thousand dollars for a large new building if a like amount were donated or raised by others. This was the signal for another letter writing appeal. She wrote to the newspapers, to friends. But donations came in slowly, and funds were very low. The outlook for immediately securing the fifty beds seemed dim.

During that hot summer, when people slept on sidewalks, and even St. Rose's with its river breezes felt the heat terribly, Mother Alphonsa came in quite frequently from Hawthorne to look over possible sites for the day when the twenty-five thousand would be forthcoming. She walked through the neighborhood, not noticing the heat at all in her eagerness, and the place to which she went oftenest was one at the corner of Front and Jackson Streets. It was a place she had always coveted. "Think of the sun porches we could have, and what windows facing the river. And Corlears Park across the way. It is the location we must have." Sister Rose, too, found it excellent, but what she wanted most to see was the twenty-five thousand dollars that would buy it. And that had not yet come in.

At last Mother Alphonsa decided they would make a novena to St. Joseph for the necessary funds. The other donor — the one of whom they were sure — had put no time limit on his own donation, but things were moving too slowly for Mother Alphonsa. It was time for a novena to accomplish something.

The novena was begun and finished. Small welcome amounts came in, but no large sum. Another novena was begun and finished. St. Joseph appeared to be merely pondering their needs. But Mother Alphonsa stood up among her Community with a militant lift of her head. "We shall go on making novenas until we have raised the twenty-five thousand," she said simply but definitely.

So the Sisters set to work to pray with hope of greater success. And this time St. Joseph heeded the storming of Heaven. Mr.

241

Cornelius Cronin called on Mother Alphonsa with the welcome news that he would give the other twenty-five thousand. Permission to buy and build was obtained from the Archbishop, and they made ready to buy a plot. When it was found difficult to buy the property Mother Alphonsa had set her heart on, her advisers suggested some places in the neighborhood. But she had looked upon that corner too often to be lured away from it so easily.

"Mr. Dominick Lynch selected it for his home a hundred years ago, and very well did he choose," she told them. "He was the man who brought Italian opera to this country and maintained it until it could support itself. We didn't know all this when we began, against all reason, to pray for a new home. But we had seen this location. It was near the river and the park. It was on a corner. We have prayed for it for years. And now we must have it."

Her advisers approved highly of her choice when they found that Mr. Dominick Lynch had picked a high spot of ground. His cellar, they were told, was always dry although his neighbors might have water in theirs.

"Besides," added Mother Alphonsa, to clinch all arguments, "you can see the Navy Yard right opposite. Our patients can get spectacular and resounding entertainment there — and free."

In 1911 the place had been secured. Best of all it was paid for with solid cash — thirty-seven thousand dollars. In the fall, as soon as all the leases were ended, the tenants moved out and the rickety buildings were pulled down and the cornerstone laid.

There were new neighbors now at Hawthorne, Mother Alphonsa told Sister Rose, three women from Boston who had come to help the Maryknoll Fathers in their work. They were handling all the secretarial duties, which would mean a considerable saving for the Fathers.

"They are living in that little house between us and the Maryknoll group," she said. "When we heard the house was rented, we asked in the village who was living there, and they said it was 'a band of pious women.' "

This name stuck to the little group, and the three apparently did not at all mind being called that. The Sisters at Rosary Hill were much interested in them and, since they had no chapel of their own to attend, invited them to make use of their chapel for Mass. The Pious Women, in thanks for this, left one morning a big basket at the chapel door, full of fruit and vegetables from their own yard. When they came out after Mass, they found the basket had been emptied, and in place of their offering were eggs from Rosary Hill's hens. During the late summer and early fall, this pleasant interchange of products went on.

Evidently Mother Alphonsa had spoken to some of her patients about this group of women who had given up their lives in the world to work voluntarily and with no salary for those who needed their help, for one morning an amusing incident occurred. As the three were going up to the altar to take their Communion with the patients who were well enough to do so, a small woman with a very large bandage around her head stepped forward suddenly, waved back the other patients with a majestic sweeping gesture of her arm, and with a more gracious gesture of the other arm waved the dazed three forward alone. They obeyed her and, as they came down from the altar rail, they received another deep bow from the mistress of ceremonies, who then allowed her co-patients to move toward the altar.

At the end of the year the Brothers bought a great tract of land at Ossining, and the Pious Women moved to that town and lived in a house on the grounds. They intended, they told Mother Alphonsa, to call themselves the Teresians of Maryknoll, and they showed her the gray habit they had devised to wear. She smiled, remembering her own early efforts with the garb that the Daughters of the Puritans wore down on Water Street.

By March of the next year the building in New York City, simple in architecture, Spanish in its outlines, bore a roof. Mother

243

Alphonsa stood in Corlears Park looking proudly across at her building. She looked out at the harbor — their house would have an uninterrupted view of it. Liberty in the distance seemed waving her torch, or perhaps she was lifting it to the success of the new Home. The Brooklyn Navy Yard was opposite, and the busy ships rushing up and down were no busier than the men hammering away to finish the new St. Rose's.

It was in this same little park she had stood, so many years ago, trying to get courage for the days ahead by watching these boats, this sky of sun and tumbling cloud. It was to the park she had sometimes come at night, weary and spent, her heart aching because of the poverty and pain of the world, to get courage for the next day, to pray as she stood there, not for such a tall building as she saw now rising before her, but for just enough money each day to buy food and warmth for her poor old women on Water Street. She had prayed for a few more rooms for her poor, and God had given her two whole houses. Surely His blessing must be on her work. Surely St. Joseph's, too, he who knew that the first requisite of human beings is a home.

In the middle of December, the Home was formally opened to the public. Cardinal Farley came to bless it. The streets were packed and the park was jammed with the crowd, the sympathetic, the merely curious. But the former predominated, for many of them knew this figure in white. They had known her when she slipped among them in blue suit and hat. Some of them, now grown, were the children she had often talked to as she went about her errands. They had known her when she went up and down in the gray costume with white bonnet which, just because it looked official, had given her a certain authority among them. And now they watched her in her white habit, serene and smiling. They had all watched the building of this Home, this trim red building among the rickety tenements. It belonged to them, too.

Mother Alphonsa passed among her guests, happy as a child, and, as Sister Rose put it later in her diary, she was "extremely active." She was pleased with the curtains and furnishings of the

Home, all of which she had entrusted to Sister Rose to select, just as she had announced that Sister Rose was to have this house in her charge. This caused some surprise, for everyone thought that, of course, Mother Alphonsa intended to make her headquarters in the fine new building. But, whatever were her reasons, she stayed at Hawthorne while Sister Rose was in complete charge of the New York house.

For one thing she probably knew her Sister Rose, and knew that she could be trusted to make the money go a long distance — better than she, herself, could. She had taken the full measure of her worth that long ago day when she had begged her with her eyes not to leave her, and Alice Huber had responded not with a few additional hours, but with a lifetime of work.

She waited only until the new Home had its patients, three of them transferred from Cherry Street. Many who had hoped to come had died before the completion of the Home. Many prayers had been uttered by earlier patients for a permanent Home. But even now those who knew they would die before the removal took place, had rejoiced with the rest. "Now I can die content," one old woman had said when she heard of the gift for a new home, "you've got your house. My prayers did help." It was a delight to see the patients' eyes widen at this magnificent newness, wide halls and shining floors, windows that looked out on the river.

But it was an even greater delight to superintend the bringing in of some who could not be accommodated before. Mother Alphonsa stopped for a long look at the empty beds. Empty beds ! More beds than she needed ! Of course she knew that it would not be long before each held its tenant, and that made her feel rich, too, since she counted her wealth in the number of poor sick she was sheltering, as some count theirs in gems or works of art. But just now, just for a few minutes, she must stand and drink in the wealth of those empty beds, clean and waiting.

She went back to Hawthorne, serenely unaware. or at least acting as if she were unaware, that she left in New York a Sister Rose with her hands full. There was a men's ward there now. The new patients who were waiting to be brought in were an unusually sick group. So much money had been spent for furnishings and other necessary things that money was very low. And there would be no time to go to Hawthorne to consult with her Superior. Satan would have been dumbfounded had he tried to find mischief to do for even one moment of Sister Rose's days and nights.

Mother Alphonsa was helping with the new Home, though not by her presence. She knew there was additional and immediate need of funds to keep the new house going. Very lately her friend, Dr. Walsh, had suggested a series of lectures for them which had cleared about three thousand dollars, a sum she still held intact. She decided to send a letter to the *New York World,* and tell her good friends, the public, of their needs.

"To the Editor of the *World,*" she wrote.

"It may be that the readers of the *World* will listen indulgently to the stated fact that $3,000 has been obtained by the Servants of Relief for Incurable Cancer, through the gift of Dr. James J. Walsh, of a series of Lenten lectures ; for the readers of your magnanimous paper last spring contributed $25,000 (or more) to the charity of these Sisters, which aids the destitute suffering from cancer, both men and women, when a large new city hospital home was to be built for such afflicted citizens.

"Dr. Walsh's gift is the first nugget in a huge supplementary sum now needed for the new Saint Rose's Home on Corlear's Park, East Side, which will cost fully $100,000, all equipment included, not any of which has been thought unnecessary by the wisest Knickerbocker of them all. It is a completely fireproof building, upon which the Building Department has commanded a capacious fire-escape, probably from a keen American sense of humor. The view of the East River from the windows and roof garden of Saint Rose's, is exhilarating. If anyone can gaze upon the blue waves and gliding schooners peppered with an intermixture of hastening tugs, and not feel glad at heart, he must have been born under a delinquent star. It is for this noble but strictly practical Home that the Servants of Relief are to brace themselves for a second pecuniary begging endeavor, with Dr. Walsh's $3,000 as a cheering send-off.

"Very gratefully yours,
"Mother M. Alphonsa Lathrop, O.S.D."

246

New York, they say, has a generous heart for misfortune if once it is called to its attention. New York also takes delight in being asked for help in some form outside the ordinary begging way. Mother Alphonsa's pathetically dramatic cause, and her charmingly expressed letters no doubt shared equally in responsibility for the large response that followed.

At Rosary Hill there had been much difficulty at first in the men's ward in trying to find the right kind of man to act as nurse. The hired nurses had proved far from ideal, and for a time the patients who were well enough to do it, took care of those who were beyond caring for themselves.

During this time there came back to Mother Alphonsa's mind the recollections of letters received during the years from Brother Joseph Dutton, who long ago had cast his lot in life with Father Damian on far away Molokai. Perhaps he would come to help her. Her imagination soared as she pictured an Order which would care for male cancer sufferers as lovingly as the women were cared for by her Sisters. Perhaps his leper colony, the trust left him by Father Damien, was on so sound a basis now, that he could be persuaded to leave it. She picked up her pen.

"Dear Brother Dutton," she began.

"Many years ago I began to wish to write to you, in answer to your charitable and noble-hearted sympathy for not only our sick poor, but the women who had dared to enter upon establishing a work for such a class as had inspired our compassion. Perhaps you have never known what it is to be assailed by many adverse conditions ; perhaps your sorrows have sprung more from isolation and the extreme of misery for your patients. But one thing I am sure you have suffered in common with us, and that is the unending strain of fatigue and piled-up chores of attendance upon terrible sickness, which with me and my companion in founding, on starting our work, seemed to change our mental perceptions and abilities ; so that while we were keen about anything for the benefit of our dear ones, we lost the capacity for talking with any elaboration, for spelling the simplest words, now and then, and for taking into consideration the events in the life-progress of our friends ; while the time for letters was usually towards midnight, so that I, myself, have ceased all this time to talk to my friends with the pen, except when charity demanded.

"But in spite of all this tangle of tales, I intended to give myself the joy of writing to you. It seemed as if in all the world there could not be anyone who would know so absolutely what we are trying to do, and why, as yourself; and so, with your blessed kind words, I felt that you were our Brother indeed. When I finally set about writing, what do you suppose it was that kept me silent as time went on ? I knew that if I wrote to you, I should ask you to come and help us. I felt that you would inevitably hold us in contempt if I did so, for at that time you were an absolute necessity to your poor lepers, who now perhaps have been 'launched' by your system of work taught to others, upon a long future (as a people) of adequate care. Never for a moment have I ceased to lean upon you, as a model, and as one whose heart is open to our sufferers ; and you know how often I have heard of you, and sometimes from you, in some way ; and in the crushing, but gloriously false news that you had left this world for your reward.

"For the last year the determination has seemed to fill me with hope and joy, now to ask you to come and establish in New York a work for cancerous men among the destitute (sometimes of the types which are refined and have seen better days) gathering around you men who did not feel called to the priesthood, but are willing to give their time to God in tending the sick. These cancer cases need you, as the Lepers did, whom you have now established in perfect safety, as a class, for devotion from their fellow beings. We have long nursed an average of fifteen men at a time, with the assistance of a paid orderly. You can imagine what that means. The doctors all tell us that no paid orderly is temperate, and few of them kind. It does not satisfy me. I want for the men, who always have a department in our Homes, the same honorable devotion of attendance that we give our women. My intention has always been to have a home adjacent to any house we have, exclusively for the use of our male cases. We have a fine large Home newly built in New York, and the first floor is given to the men, so that with those here, we now tend about thirty-five, or more, men at a time. Next to our new Home, which is in a really superb location near the East River, there is a huge high tenement, reaching to the next corner. I want it for space for a house for cancerous men ; and I want you to come and found a charity for them, in connection with our charity for the women. All has been done for your Lepers, speaking broadly. I know that you wish to remain with them always, and that the day is not long enough for the kind acts which you wish to do for them, and for individuals

248

among them. But I beg you to remember that God has given you the capacity and the exalted reputation which will enable you to do for these others, despised, avoided, loathed, but tender of feelings, and deeply humiliated, and frequently unconverted souls, the supreme act of causing to exist a charity for them which can never die. Our work for women has been, and is full of weakness and stupidity, but you are — Brother Dutton. All would rise up and help you, and there is no question of the means for it all.

"I know of at least one very great priest who thinks it is a splendid possible outlook for cancerous men who are destitute. I shall at once do all in my power to cause the tenement property to be purchased, and to raise money for the building of the houses needed ; but if you would take my words to heart, I believe nothing would lag or fail in a great popular interest and help. Think long, dear friend, before you draw away from our poor in this field, the hand that can help them, secure for them tender love instead of cruel service, and from souls who would serve God in this new way (new to these latter days) the opportunity to group themselves under you. With love and reverence,
"Your Sister, M. Alphonsa Lathrop, O.S.D."

That year one of the men told Mother Alphonsa late on Christmas Day that he intended to receive Baptism on New Year's Day. He received the rite with many of the patients grouped about him in the chapel. The baptismal font stood very close to the little Crib, decked with its Holy Family and shepherds and sheep.

"It is a real New Year's gift to the Infant Jesus," declared Mother Alphonsa with deep satisfaction.

The patients who came to them who were Catholic had often been careless about their religious duties for years. To have such a one return to his Faith, or to have some one who had had nothing to do with religion express a wish to share in its consolations, these were among the Sisters' deep joys in caring for their patients. They had banded together to care for the sick bodies, and that they could do without co-operation, but to care for the sick souls, that request must come directly from the patient. When it did, the Sisters rejoiced with the rejoicings of the angels from Heaven over the soul that knew life in a body that was soon to know death.

To her novices at their conference that Christmas Day she said, "Don't forget that the simplest reiterated command of Christ is al-

249

ways to serve the poor.   Christ may have placed it first in the series of His commands because we immediately understand it, and because it abases pride at a stroke, if we serve the poor as Christ and His Saints did.   All else in the spiritual life develops from this art, or it never really develops at all.   Piety without humble works is that monstrosity — self-righteousness.   And we can no longer believe that our Divine example is too great to imitate, for we are told precisely how to do it in definite records of living widely diffused."

6

On a sunny morning in 1914 Mother Alphonsa gave herself the gift of a rare and precious half hour, to be spent in simply walking about the grounds of Rosary Hill. Everything she looked on was peaceful. In the blue distance Saint Joseph's cross gleamed in the sun. The Hudson rippled with little dancing waves. The trees swayed in the light wind. In Saint Dominic's garden she heard the voices of patients saying the Rosary together. From the windows of the women's summer-house she saw faces looking out, enjoying the loveliness of God spread before their eyes.

Everywhere about her peace, even though it was peace in the midst of pain. But in the world outside there was no peace, for the nations were at war. She fell to thinking of the Civil War of her youth, those bitter days of a conflict which, his friends always insisted, shortened the days of her father's life. She had a vivid recollection of the marching boys on the Lexington highway, standing at rest while Mrs. Alcott and Louisa fed them lemonade and cookies. She felt the pain that made Louisa faint that day, for she knew now what suffering meant, just as Louisa had seen it at first hand in the military hospital. Louisa had seen the torn bodies, the broken limbs, and had comforted the dying. Rose Hawthorne the child had wondered at her grief, but Mother Alphonsa knew now what Louisa must have gone through in that brief hospital experience.

But in the cases about her here it was a caring for necessary wounds ; those others had been unnecessary wounds — the wounds of hate. She sent a prayer to Heaven for a quick ending to this horror.

She thought of the quotation from Bishop Potter which she had read to the novices at yesterday's conference ; the war had brought it to her mind :

"Many people think that harmony would be brought about through the passing of laws to compel people to do this or that and to prevent their doing certain other things. That is not the way in which the Republic was founded, nor in which present evils can be righted. The Republic was founded through personal sacrifice upon the basis of human brotherhood. The need today is that men shall rise above mere selfishness."

As she walked along she tried to think of something other than war. There was the first meeting of the Drug Auxiliary under the able charge of Mr. Henry Reel, who had come to her some years before, announcing that since he had retired as a druggist, he would like to be of some help to her in the department which he understood. She had welcomed his assistance. He was now their right-hand man in the work. She thought of the recent Board Meeting of the Trustees, among whom were the Reverend James McEntyre and two of their oldest benefactors, Mr. Cronin and Mr. Warren Greene. She thought of the letter Brother Joseph Dutton had written her last week. She had pen and paper in her pocket : she would send him an answer now while she had the time. He had not been able to join her in the enterprise in which she had hoped he would be able to embark, but his encouragement and his prayers meant much to her.

"Beloved Brother," she wrote.

"I wanted to write you instantly your letter reached me, but I was called away from my momentary solitude, and then the fulness of administration struck me dumb, as the great sunsets from little Concord's hills grew more and more magnificent to my sight years ago, and one lived only to look at the anthem of color. But how I love the thought of you ; indeed, I always have. You have been always surrounded by love and veneration, and surely it must have seemed to you to make a palatial home about you. As for me, I have suffered great loss in not writing to you often, and receiving your generous gifts of reply. But I am a coward in many ways, and since I have undergone severe trials and one tragedy since getting into the field of work, my nerve has often relaxed, and where I loved most, I have shrunk from my own voice. All my dearest friends wonder why I cannot write to them, but more easily to strangers. And so in these many years I have been dead to your kindness, your superb sympathy and brotherliness, and I have even been so rude to you. Can you not imagine, nevertheless, how I welcomed and kissed your gifts to our poor ? I am sure you have seen suffering enough in others to know how agony makes the soul creep away from the pitying hand, if, alas, the soul is not brave as a soldier. Dear great life, you dared to become an Apostle, and they always come too close to Jesus to escape His consummation, His courage, His glorious wounds. May God be with you. "Your loving servant, M. Alphonsa Lathrop, O.S.D."

She was just preparing to go back to work when she heard the sound of steps on the gravel path. A man was shuffling toward her, cap in hand.

"If you could take me in, lady. They said you take in poor people that are sick. And I'm sick — real sick."

He was, indeed ; a casual glance at his face showed that, but when she asked for details of his illness, she found she could not take him.

"You see we take only cancerous cases here. For your sickness there are hospitals, and I shall give you the address of one that will surely take you."

He eased himself against a tree while she wrote down the address and went to get him money for the fare to the hospital. He thanked her and began to move away. But when she saw how ill he really was, how weak, she could not let him go like that even though he was not of her elect.

"Wait a moment. Don't go yet. I'll give you a bed for the night and in the morning you will feel more rested to take the trip."

253

His gratitude was childlike and simple, as it often is, she had found, with old sick folk who have become accustomed to neglect. One of the Sisters showed him a couch in a small empty room, and he dropped gratefully into it, after being fed.

Next morning Mother Alphonsa woke very early — before four o'clock, with the feeling that there was something on her mind, some reason for waking so early. Suddenly she knew : the old man whom they had taken in for the night. She rose and dressed hurriedly and went to his room softly. She opened the door. He was awake, too, sitting on the edge of the bed. When he saw her he got up, took a few steps toward her and fell, a sudden gush of blood from his mouth reddening the floor. When she stooped to him, she saw that he was dead.

Brother Julian, paying an early morning call, looked in surprise at Mother Alphonsa, usually the most immaculate of religious. "What are those stains on your habit, Mother ?"

She glanced down and saw the disfiguring brown spots.

"We had a guest for the night," she said gently, "and early this morning he started on his journey again, but to fairer mansions than this old wooden affair."

Some weeks later there was more sad news. Pope Pius was dead.

"He loved the poor," wrote Mother Alphonsa to Sister Rose ; "he understood them from having sprung from them, and he loved the truth and lived the teachings of Christ. To restore all things in Christ was his chosen mission, and he accomplished it when he prayed for enemies that it seemed hard to echo his prayer. He is gone — the dove that was suddenly imprisoned from his Venice ; this great heart that was so full of artistic fire. It is terrible to lose his human hand out of the world."

During these next years, when the War raged, Mother Alphonsa lost by death some of her greatest aides. Mr. Cronin died, and Mr. Edward Smith — the two men who had made possible the new Saint Rose's — and Mr. Greene who had been their legal adviser since the charity's earliest days. Mother Alphonsa herself fell very ill with grippe, and Sister Rose came hurrying up from New York to help her. She found her in a stupor, too weak and ill even to greet her. But in a few days, with her customary vitality, she pulled herself out of danger and began to convalesce. She came back to health to find the worst news of all : the United States had entered the War.

It was quiet enough on Rosary Hill. The river was too far away for the people up on the hill to see anything out of the ordinary, except that perhaps there were more craft there than usual. But down at Saint Rose's it was different. There transports filled with soldiers went up and down the river. Along the shore people waved and cheered madly and ran along the bank waving goodbye to the boatloads of boys.

Mother Alphonsa was watching them on a day in late summer from the windows of the sun room. Sister Rose had been delighted to see her, for she came down very seldom nowadays. She shook her head when she saw the cheering people edging the water.

"Pope Benedict has sent out a strong appeal for peace ; but will they accept it — do they even want it ? It is so lovely at Hawthorne now. The hills are all scarlet and gold, and the wild asters are a gorgeous purple. War seems so far away — so incredible. But it isn't far away — not while it is in our hearts." Her eyes were gray and clouded with sorrow.

As she went through the wards greeting old friends, she came to the bedside of six-year-old Sammy, one of her favorites. His dark little Hebrew face smiled when he saw her, and he clutched her habit happily. From the depths of it she drew out a little American flag. "I've been saving this for you ever since the Fourth, Sammy."

But the hand that had been outstretched for the gift suddenly drew back. He shook his head. Mother Alphonsa was amazed. "Don't you want it, Sammy ? You make me feel very badly."

To make his idol feel badly was more than he could bear. He reached his hand out for the flag and clutched it. He looked at

255

her a bit fearfully. "Can I have it," he whispered to her, "when I'm a Jew ?"

She reassured him and told him it was his flag, too, and she wished for Emma Lazarus to join her in her anger at the persons who had made a little child feel thus in the country of his birth.

Julian Hawthorne came to see his sister before he went abroad. She insisted on showing him her new ward. "Come along and see my guests," she invited.

She showed him a wizened little Italian woman who had been with them for seven years.

"Years ? I thought they die quite quickly after they get the disease."

"They mostly do nowadays," said Mother Alphonsa bitterly. "She came to us before she was experimented on. They die now of too many opiates and too much cutting. Lots of our cases are mainly surgical."

In the men's ward they passed the bed of a young man — not thirty. "But he is so young," Julian was aghast as they went through the ward. "I thought it was a disease of middle age and old age."

"Oh, not always." She took him into a room where a boy of twelve lay in bed, chalky white, emaciated, listless. "He is too sick even to notice we are looking at him. He has cancer. One of my first cases down on Water Street was a two-year-old child, and recently at Saint Rose's one little girl was brought in of less than two years with a pitiful cancer in defiance of infancy."

She showed him all her guests, though Julian would have been willing to leave some of them unseen, but he could not disappoint this sister of his, so anxious to show him the guests in her Home.

A bell rang softly from inside the house, and Julian rose to go. "My dear, I may not see you again for a while, but you know I shall be thinking of you wherever I am."

"And I of you, Julian. I shall keep you in my prayers."

Julian thought of the quiet of her face as he was driven to the station. He remembered the little girl whose temper could be so easily lost, who was very insistent on getting what she wanted. He remembered the woman who had learned, and resented learning, how temperament can interfere with the smooth ways of marriage. She had conquered much since those days, lost something, and won a great deal. "She said she has found beauty," he mused, "and perhaps it is the only beauty that is really worth while."

In the spring of 1922 a letter came from New London to Rosary Hill. It contained an invitation. When Cousin Emilie Learned had gone to pay a visit to Cousin Rose at Hawthorne, she reported back to Church Street that Rose looked very tired, so she and Mrs. Bunner were inviting her to stay with them for as long as she could be spared from her duties. Would she write and tell them that she would come, and when ?

She read the note through twice. It warmed her and made her happy even though it brought the tears to her eyes. This letter she must answer right away.

"Dearest of Millys :" The pen flew along.

"If I waited a thousand years of delighted pondering, I could not give myself the pleasure of that visit you offer me, which is so unexpected a vision and would be so full of happiness. Yes, in spite of the sorrows of life, to go back to the past as your guest would be to think only of the happiness you and yours gave me, and would always provide for me, as for others, my very dear and rare friend. If you were with me for a little while in our Home, you would be, yourself, quick to see why I have never left them for a visit to any of my friends, who have generously asked me to be with them for a rest, or gone off on one of those ideal trips to Bermuda or elsewhere which doctors prescribe for humdrum prisoners of duty, as if they were to be had at the drug store. If I had you at the head of one of our Homes, it would be easier to amuse myself, but my absence would be used, when it occurred, to open a third and a fourth Home, and so on. We have been starving in the need of able women in rôles of responsibility. They will, no doubt, come finally, but our work is the least attractive in the world. I am now in the deeps of writing thanks to several hundred benefactors who have not heard from me since my illness at our city Home where I was kept fourteen weeks. I must see to our Noviciate which is here, and supply some articles to several magazines, besides sending out about two thousand of our last report — a job interrupted through my illness. This is the sort of life that goes on and on and needs you so badly, even aside from attending to the forty or more patients here, and everything.

"And now I am planning a Country Home, to be typical of what we want for them all in future. It is fortunate that we are a simple little crowd, in a very simple field of labor, or of course we would not be able to manage at all. I will not tell you the fact that your invitation, so kindly and nobly given, in a charm of circumstances offered and loving words, has been of the greatest refreshment to mind and heart and will help me all spring and summer just as you wished the visit would do for a little space. I shall think of it, knowing so much what would happen, as if it had come to delight me. I shall picture to myself you and Mrs. Bunner in your dear home ; and dear unique New London, with its trees and walks and seashore, so that a great deal of the strength and zest you so kindly wish for me will really be mine because of your letter. You and your sister are so kind and good to think of having a creature in a habit with you and a weary hermitress in your care. But really I am not such a person after all. God reward you, dear friend.

"Lovingly yours,"

She started to sign her name as usual, M. Alphonsa Lathrop. But she made only the first stroke of the M. Then she wrote it over with another letter and signed it Rose.

Deep within her she knew she would have greatly enjoyed that rest, though she would not admit it openly. She wrote her frame of mind into a letter to Brother Julian, in answer to some pictures he had sent them for their walls.

"Thank you for the cards and so on to a poor old crippled dame like me. I got too tired and nearly died. I am greatly ashamed of my shattered state. But I am getting well. Thanks for all your prayers. Do not pray for me any more, for my health will be fine when a beautiful day lets me get out for a ride. Sister Rose wants the choristers again. She is very musical, but during the last year or so, her voice cannot be depended on, as she works too hard and gets too tired, so we would like the choristers or that bevy of reverend brothers who came last fall to sing and play. I wish they would come often. I had a wonderfully good time, myself."

But Brother Julian shook his head and went right on praying for his neighbor's better health.

258

The War had ended, but its results were noticed for a long time afterwards by the Servants of Relief. There were fewer contributions. It was very hard to get coal, and the price of foodstuffs soared and soared. For institutions which live by the money that comes in from day to day, such times are difficult indeed.

But they managed to survive — Sisters and patients, too. The ceremonies of reception and clothing in the Dominican Order, came around at their regular times. The little Community was growing to very respectable proportions. Mother Alphonsa sat among her Sisters, and thanked God for the girls and women who were with her, and whom she could leave behind her, to keep the work going. She knew, though she would not admit it, that her last illness had greatly impaired her powers. Even working too long in her garden wearied her, and that was her very lightest task.

An idea which she had put at the back of her mind during the hard years of the War and those that followed it, now kept coming forward more and more insistently. Ever since they had moved to Rosary Hill, she had hated the fire-trap they lived in. It covered them, of course ; it kept off the rain, most of it, anyway, and the wind and snow, but continually in her heart was the fear of a fire. It would be almost impossible to save the place if a fire ever started. As for the patients, she hardly dared think what might happen to them.

Now, in 1922, the world seemed better financially. She decided to send out appeals for a new fireproof building for Hawthorne. When she wrote to Archbishop Hayes for permission to begin asking for funds for the new buildings, he wrote back his warm approval :

"I hasten to advise you that you have my fullest approval of your plan to raise funds for a new building at Hawthorne for the proper sheltering of those afflicted with incurable cancer. I am sure there is scarcely anyone who will turn a deaf ear to your plea in behalf of those commended to your care. Your work is well known, and people of every race and creed are deeply appreciative of what you are doing."

The first set of appeals brought in an unusually small response. She sat down to compose another lot, and these brought in a splendid answer. From all over the country contributions arrived. Quite obviously these donations were due to two factors. First, the interest in the form of charity. Second, and fully as important, the delightful letters whereby Mother Alphonsa lifted her begging to heights of charm, and made the giving a pleasure. With her letters to the newspapers, she was always unusually happy. Receiving as they did, so many boring letters, those from Rosary Hill were hailed with pleasure and always saw the printed page.

She sent out postcards to her friends, too, with a picture of the Home at Hawthorne, and above it she wrote in her firm slanting hand, "A view of our present unsafe Home," which phrase of indignation, fact and pleading mingled, helped to make the fund flourish.

Cousin Milly Learned was among those who sent a check, and Mother Alphonsa wrote back her thanks. She was very scrupulous about answering the gifts herself, perhaps knowing that this was her *métier* rather than Sister Rose's, who did better among the columns of figures that kept the Homes' accounts balanced.

"How lovely of you," she wrote, "to put your hand to our new Home and hasten its rising from risky ground. Thank you warmly for your gift which I shall remember when I see the simple dear walls standing forth, D.V. This dry summer has been a blessing to me, and to the first portion of our fireproof Home, and I have been out so much that I am growing much stronger. Please pardon me if I send you word when twenty-five of our sickest men and woman are transferred from this wooden Home, and any good news I can report of us. In two days three rich old ladies sent me nine thousand dollars for the building, which has made me hope for good fortune till enough money is collected. I hope you are all very well and greatly blessed. With grateful love and thoughts of you, and Adelaide and Alfred alive in Heaven, and the young Alfred and Horace and Mrs. Bunner,
"Your devotedly interested
"M. Alphonsa, O.S.D."

Some years before Columbus College had burned to the ground. It was just such a wooden structure as their own, and its burning had done nothing to reassure Mother Alphonsa about their own Home.   Fortunately there had been no loss of life, but all property was lost in the blaze that burned the dry boards so swiftly.   She had seen a priest wrapped in blankets and with hair burning, fling himself out of the burning building, in one hand the statue of Our Lady, in the other, the Blessed Sacrament. That burning building was ever in her mind's eye, and this incident kept her hoping above all others to make her dream a reality, and quickly.   She redoubled her writing.   Since she insisted on answering personally each donation, this writing was far more than a pleasure or a pastime.   It was difficult work, and the result was that several times she had a return of her old malady, the grippe, and some heart attacks that alarmed the whole Community.   But she always emerged from them and was soon out of bed again, pen in hand, covering page after page with her flowing lilting phrases.

7

There were many ways in which God sent people to help Mother Alphonsa other than the direct method of the check-book. There were Dr. Walsh's lectures, always profitable because always interesting. There were the matinée benefits which George Cohan staged for her. There was the interview, too, or rather the article which Maurice Egan wrote for the Book Section of the *Sunday Times*.

It was, in a way, the work of her pen, too, for Mr. Egan reviewed several of the Reports of the Homes in which lay embedded little literary gems fashioned by Mother Alphonsa herself.

"These reports," he wrote, "are a flaming exception to the usual dull ones. They are the kind Saint Francis of Assisi might have made."

Skilfully, like a good propagandist, he transited from the Reports to the Homes themselves. He described Sisters there as "voluntary ministers of the involuntary poor"; he told them how Jews, Christians and infidels alike were treated here with care and courtesy, for all religious beliefs were always admitted without question, as is invariable in Catholic work : Syrian, Italian, Jewish, Icelander and Chinese, the humblest in origin and those once well set up in the world, peacefully fraternizing. Then he let Mother Alphonsa speak for herself after his glowing introduction, and she, characteristically, spoke at first in a satiric vein of those

262

who knew a great surprise when they noted her "joyful selection of cancer cases rather than the blind."

"There is nothing morbid about it," she declared, when Mr. Egan came up to discuss the article with her ; "people are simply using the word in a wrong sense. There was nothing morbid about my father's thinking, for instance. Extraordinary sinners came to him (he hated it, too) because his writing showed him full of compassion, and they knew he could console them. But it is the sinner who is morbid, not the man who pities him and who devotes his ability to helping him to sin no more. And that," she added with emphasis, "holds true even if the sinner is beyond reclaim. My father hated to have people come to him for help in that way, but they did it in dozens because of the matters he discussed in his books."

She wrote it down for Mr. Egan so that he could put her own words into the article.

"My first influence was my father's attitude toward moral and physical deformity and corruption. He consoled those who came to him in so far as this life holds consolation for enormous wrongs. My father's instructions harmonized with the melodious verities of God."

She wanted no direct publicity for herself. Her Homes, yes, there she was willing for any amount of publicity. But Mr. Egan won her over. "I like your human warmth and your righteous indignation," she told him.

"And I," answered Mr. Egan, "like the vitality of your love for those whom even love often flees. I salute you as the Servant of the Poorest of the Poor. And I like the card of admittance to your hospitality : Poverty and hopeless illness."

"You do put it well — and truthfully, too," she said warmly. "But the one important thing is that it was my father who made me see its inner beauty. It took a hold on me the first time I read it in his books ; and in long spaces of loneliness, the firm touch was often chilling. I thought about it for years and then, when reasons small and large alike had removed heaped-up impediments from my way, and when, in addition to my father's works, I read

263

through Joshua Davidson's noble work, then I wanted to do just one thing : give myself to those who needed friends, and cut off my personalities and worldly gains. After that, it was simple."

The article came out the following week, front page, with a large picture of Nathaniel Hawthorne in the centre of the page. It would have been useless to try to put a picture of Mother Alphonsa there, for she resolutely refused to have any picture of herself taken. Brother Julian had made more than one attempt and vowed that some day he would be successful, though up to date he had not found the proper means for doing so.

When Father Thuente came up to pay one of his infrequent visits, they told him what excellent propaganda Mr. Egan's article had proved to be ; and he told them what a fine bit of literary workmanship he had thought it. It had brought in a flood of checks and an interest in the Homes in the way of visitors.

"But all the writing in the world or the application of the Gospels, either, can't make some people understand," Mother Alphonsa shook her head at human nature in general.

He looked at the shadows under her eyes. "You don't look well," he charged her. "Can't you get more rest ?"

"Oh, rest." She waved away the suggestion. "It isn't that. It is that grippe of last year that left me with less strength than I am used to having. And, if you will not tell anyone, I will tell you a secret. I get so tired sometimes that I am afraid some day I shall be cross to one of the patients."

"I shall never reveal your fearful secret," Father Thuente promised her when he went away.

She insisted she was well enough, though the Sisters privately decided she was not, to attend the Annual Meeting of the Board of Trustees when they met at Rosary Hill. How could she not be present when at that meeting they were going to pick out the site for the first of the fire-proof buildings ? For it had been decided not to wait for all the money to be collected that was needed, but to begin putting up one building at a time as soon as enough had been collected for it.

The Trustees received much news at this meeting. The

264

Community had an electric well now, large enough to supply the great future Home which Mother Alphonsa was constantly envisaging. They had a passageway two hundred and fifty feet long from the old house, built wide and with many windows in it so that it might be screened in summer. Legacies had made these possible, giving them a chance to set aside the other money for the new building.

From 1896 to 1924 the books showed that the work had received about six hundred thousand dollars, none of which had been used for investments or permanent laying up, but only for the immediate benefit of the afflicted.

The running expenses of the two Homes now totaled about $70,000 a year. With $40,000 on hand, they were beginning the building. "It will," read Mother Alphonsa's account of that year, "be used at once to begin excavating an extensive new cellar on our hill composed of rock. The constructive work will proceed as far as permitted, by a total as yet unknown."

Also listed among the expenditures of the year, in her report, was one for $123 for "piano repair and violin lessons for young patient with talent, likely to live long."

She mentioned with pleasure one special gift, that of Mr. Cuddihy, who for a week had been carrying around with him a considerable sum gained from his friends and himself, for the Building Fund. He would show its pleasant bulk to the people he met, tell them what it was for, and thus attract more funds to his pile, eventually bestowing on Mother Alphonsa this rolling stone that had acquired a goodly amount of valuable moss.

"But now," said Sister Mary Frances, after the meeting was over and the markers for the site of the new Home were in place, "now you should really go to bed, Mother."

But no one could persuade her to go to bed immediately after so great a decision had been made. Instead she began that evening, in her mind's eye and on paper, to house every patient and every Sister in a new building where fire could never penetrate. This new house they had planned for today was merely a beginning — nothing more.

265

The Sisters were out watching the excavating beginning when one of them reported a strange little car coming up the road, and showed it to Mother.

"It looks like an auto-gig," said she, studying its advance, "and whoever, except a new patient or Brother Julian, can be coming so early in the morning?"

It was only nine, too early for visitors, and they gazed in wonder at the tall military looking person who was disentangling his long legs from the odd vehicle.

"Oh, it is Father Talbot Smith," cried Mother. "And we have not seen him for so long! What a pleasure this is," she called, going toward the visitor with outstretched hands; "it has been such ages since last you came to us."

He greeted them all gaily. In the difficult early days up here he had been a great help, having a habit of unerringly choosing the bleakest day, the one when money was scarcest and confidence lowest, to put in an appearance. His gay, vibrant personality, his strength of mind and body alike, had always been a refreshing thing for the tired anxious Sisters, inspiring them to better efforts after he left them. He explained that he had been obliged to curtail some of his visiting because of his health. That was why they had not seen him for so long.

Mother Alphonsa took him through her wards and showed him her patients. She even gave him a chat with the men's nurse, a strong husky who had been a cavalryman in the War and still had a military bearing.

"The men don't bear with the disease as patiently as the women, do they?" Father Smith asked him.

"Well, Father, it's this way. For a while they are worse but you'd be surprised the fun some of them has. They don't feel the pain all the time, you see, only off and on. The rest of the time they sets or walks or just looks, or maybe helps to entertain."

"Dying patients entertaining dying patients? Mother," he turned to her, "I've heard much of how you bring cheerfulness and happiness here, but I have always thought of it as the consolations of religion mainly — a happy death — "

266

She laughed. "But there are by-products of religion. You should see some of ours. He ought to have seen Sam," she said to the ex-cavalryman. "He was very tall, Father, and very black, and he said he was a 'professional music maker.' He said all the things he could do came to him as an 'inspiration from de Lawd.' The Lord certainly made him versatile. He could play a guitar and an harmonica and jingle bells on his feet, 'all to oncet' and he always gave credit to the Lord before he gave a performance. Oh, Father, I wish you could have seen him on a holiday, all dressed up in a terribly high collar and stiff white cuffs, simply strutting. He was so full of activity that it seems strange he is so quiet down there," and she looked down toward the trees that hid the Longfellow cross in Gate of Heaven Cemetery.

They were back now in chairs looking out over the blue Hudson. The other Sisters had scattered to their work. Mother Alphonsa began to notice something different about Father Smith — a curious remoteness, a sort of uneasiness.

"Do you try out any of these new ideas in curing that one reads about nowadays ?" he asked.

"I am afraid I have little patience with them. Of course part of the trouble is that the sick have been made so terribly depressed by their condition before they come here. We give them a new outlook, maybe, just by keeping them clean so that they know they are not an offense to the people about them. Of course, just that feeling of trying something new, something that may cure them, puts hope in their hearts and makes them, perhaps, even feel better for a little while, but underneath the physical degenerative processes have gone right on. In a way, we do the same thing, but we help and give them another sort of hope, making them feel they are really wanted instead of an offense to eyes and nostrils. But we don't pretend. They know when they come here that we know they won't recover. We play fair."

"You don't think this disease of cancer can ever be cured, Mother ?" he asked suddenly and yet slowly, still looking out at the autumn bright hills, the distant cemetery with only a tip of stone visible here and there through the leaves.

Somehow the silence after his question gave to her the effect of a cannon shot. She looked more closely at him than she had before, and in his eyes read the reason for his remoteness, his interest in possible cures.

She waited a moment before she found courage to answer him. "Never, Father," she told him.

When he said goodbye, it seemed to her he had said it without words. But once back in the funny little car, his long legs securely folded in, his old smile flashed out to her in farewell.

By April the new building was ready. Monsignor McEntyre came up to bless it. The Sisters held a reception for their friends. It was a radiant smiling spring day, and Mother was as active as the day, moving about among her guests.

When the guests had gone, everyone was tired out, and all the Sisters who were not actively busy sat together for a brief recreation period, relaxing and feeling proud indeed of the accomplishments of the last few months. In the minds of all was also the thought that now they could stop for a little while, and that Mother could rest now and get back her strength.

In the midst of these serene thoughts came the brisk voice of Mother Alphonsa. "Now we must begin to work hard — very hard, for the big building. This of course is only a beginning."

As Sister Rose had said on one occasion, she was still "amazingly active."

To Brother Julian — she could always confide in him — she sent a hint now and then of her realization of her weakening condition. She had asked him for a small picture of himself for her office, and sent him a note in thanks.

"Your picture is perfectly beautiful, just as if you were appearing in person. I have that dreadful dead feeling and could not write sooner. It would take a person as strong as yourself to get through the frequent business interruptions of my little days when things are humming. Soon all the matters of our new house will be finished, and then I hope to come over and thank Our Lady for her answer to my prayer before the children's statue. God bless you all — it is unnecessary to ask this, but there cannot be too much blessing."

268

And in a later note :

"I am weary of all these ill turns and disappointments. I have been like one struck down in this dear battle of ours of many tribulations and perplexities and only at times able to mingle with the happy greetings around me. However I may grow better even at seventy-four, and see the beautiful pictures you have painted both inside and outside your great dwelling. Meantime greet Our Lady's statue for me, and remember I am sorry to be dumb as a fish, or a poor dead Sister."

Of course she did get better. She always did. In a few months she was writing solicitously to Brother Julian :

"Please take some of this sherry, sent me by a rich friend. I can take only weakened claret. I also send a bottle of medicine called Brown's Mixture which our friend, Mr. Henry Reel, makes up for us. It is wonderful for a cold, and makes all the Sisters feel well. Two tablespoons three times a day, and lie down if possible. But that isn't imperative. Saint Patrick bless you."

8

In August Father Thuente came up to see Mother with a suggestion. "Mother, you know this is your Jubilee — your Silver Jubilee. Twenty-five years ago I received you two as tertiaries down on Cherry Street. You surely will want to make an occasion of it."

She nodded in remembrance of that long ago day when Father Thuente had come all the way down to the East Side to find out who was this person who was so deftly caring for old Mrs. Daly.

"What a dear old thing Mrs. Daly was. And what a wonderful wake Tim had for her. I sent them down two dozen pipes and enough tobacco to last the night — remember ?"

But he brought her back to the subject he had come to discuss. "As I was saying, you must make an occasion of your Jubilee. Don't you want me to come up and preach the sermon for you ?"

She leaned forward, her eyes twinkling. "Yes, I know what you priests do when you get up in the pulpit for occasions like that. You tell such lies, such great lies. Besides, we can't really spare the time."

But she had to have her Jubilee — there was too much insistence on it.

The fifteenth of August was a bright day with a smooth blue Hudson and the first purple asters of autumn to greet their guests. A great crowd came, many more than the little chapel could hold easily. But walls had a way of expanding for Mother Alphonsa : there was always room for a few more where she was concerned.

She met Father Thuente with deep regret in her face. "The Smiths can't come, not either one of them. They have written me a nice note, though, to tell me how sorry they are. Wait a moment — I want you to read it."

She drew it from her pocket, and he read the short note and handed it back to her. "Very nice indeed."

Mother Alphonsa put it carefully back in its envelope. But it stuck, and for all her pushing would not go in. She drew out the letter and shook the envelope and a folded slip of blue fell out. She picked it up and looked at it, and handed it silently to Father Thuente.

In addition to the nice little note, the Smiths had sent her a check for fifty thousand dollars. Her eyes were shining. "Now," she said, "we have a solid foundation for our building, *Deo gratias.*"

Monsignor McEntyre officiated and Father Thuente preached the sermon, as he had invited himself to do, putting in all the lies Mother Alphonsa had accused him of wishing to tell. But he told facts too.

It was a very happy day for Mother Alphonsa. She circulated among her friends, calling their attention to this and that improvement at Rosary Hill. And, to round out the day, a cablegram was received from Rome bringing her the blessing of the Holy Father.

Brother Julian, who with some of his students and associates, was one of the guests, had been evolving a little plot meanwhile : this was the day when he meant to get a picture of Mother Alphonsa, who had steadfastly refused to allow any one to take any, even after Brother Julian had pointed out the unfairness of asking for one of his and refusing hers.

She was adamant, so he and Brother Amedy devised a way. The latter had brought his little camera along and was holding it carefully out of sight of Mother. When the band in the stand was resting for a moment, Brother Julian went up to ask the band-

271

master to play, at a special signal from him, the Blue Danube. Long ago he had discovered that this was her favorite melody.

He and Brother Amedy went up to Mother, the latter with his little camera all cocked for ready use, but held back of him. Brother Julian raised his hand. The band swept into the Blue Danube, and, as he had hoped, Mother Alphonsa turned toward the players, a smile on her face. But the smile faded when she heard a little click and saw Brother Amedy quietly and unostentatiously closing his kodak.

She was angry then, and still annoyed the next day, but on the third, when the picture had been developed, she laughed gaily at Brother Julian's discomfiture. Brother Amedy had snapped a little too soon or a bit too late. The snapshot showed only the back of a Dominican habit — no glimpse at all of a face.

She had seemed her strong untiring self all that day. And Sister Rose, watching her in animated conversation with her guests, said, "I think she will live to be a very old woman, don't you, Father Thuente ?"

In 1926 Mother Alphonsa celebrated her seventy-fifth birthday. The previous summer Bowdoin College, during the centenaries of Hawthorne and Longfellow, conferred on Mother Alfonsa the degree of M.A. in honor of her father and the work she was doing. The month before that she had received the medal given each year by the Rotary Club for an outstanding accomplishment, this time for faithful service to the poor, "in recognition," it was engraved, "of her Mercy and Valor and the free gift of a life of service to hopeless destitute sufferers." The members came up to Rosary Hill with their wives and, wonder of wonders, Mother allowed her picture to be taken, Mr. Pirie McDonald, the President of the Club standing beside her as the camera men snapped them both. Where Brother Julian had lost, the *Times* had won.

She had come through the winter very well. There had been lots of snow and that always invigorated her. Those winters at

272

Concord about which she had wailed to Hannah in Redcar were in her blood, and in snowy weather she bloomed.

She was feeling her best when the medal was bestowed on her, and she wrote Sister Rose that it was a "distinguished and noble meeting." A light luncheon was served under a big tent set up in front of the new building.

Her health continued good ; in fact, it was Sister Rose who had fallen ill. When Mother Alphonsa heard the news, she hurried down from the country, her arms loaded with blooms for the altar, wine for the invalid, little gifts for the patients. She sat down by Sister Rose's bed. "You have been doing too much," she scolded. "Now you must rest as long as you need it."

Sister Rose smiled. "Just as you are always resting."

She accepted the thrust. "But just as soon as I have collected enough for the new Home, I am really going to stop. I am so tired of writing. The minute the new Home is up, I am going to give all my time to the Sisters and the work."

Sister Rose agreed that that would be a fine thing. But when Mother was ready to go back to Hawthorne, she spoke the sentence with which most of their visits ended, "Please don't overdo."

"Certainly I won't," promised Mother, and departed. "And I'll come soon again."

But the next months were very stormy and in the spring she was too busy to get away, and it was Mother's birthday before they met again. This time Sister Rose, who had spent the day at Hawthorne, returned to New York more at ease about her Superior's health.

"Last time she was here she said she was going to stop writing. Has she ?" asked a Sister.

Sister Rose laughed. "She has a brilliant mind and a ready pen. I doubt if she can ever stop putting pen to paper. It was really a delight to see her today as bright as the garden, and that was lovely."

Before the beginning of Lent, Dr. Walsh had come up to Rosary Hill to discuss the Lenten lectures he was going to give for the benefit of the Homes.   This work of love he had been doing during various years, and Mother Alphonsa's gratitude was deep as it had been when she first wrote the *Times* the note about his having provided the "nucleus" for their Home.

He found her in her chair busily writing.   "Is it a book this time, or an article, or a letter ?" he asked.

"Do you know — a book might be a good thing.   I've been thinking this morning what a lot of valuable information we have collected during all these years of work.   How best to relieve pain for the hopelessly sick ; how to help do away with the odor of cancer.   You see the patients feel terribly about that, and it upsets their nerves and so makes their physical condition worse.   And I'd like to tell them how some dressings and some treatments are literally worse than none, for they aggravate the condition instead of helping it.   And I'd tell them how cheerfulness toward these patients is almost the best treatment of all."

Dr. Walsh agreed. "An excellent idea !   I have always been amazed as I go through the wards to see the wonderful effect such kindness has had in overcoming many disturbing physical symptoms.   Only rarely does one note among cancer patients treated in their own homes such good effects.   You relieve the pain of mind and that can sometimes cause even more discomfort than the pain of body."

She thanked him with a smile, and went on : "What I was really doing just when you came in was dreaming my favorite dream.   You know hundreds of years ago ladies used to visit the sick as part of their duty as Christians, and this personal contact was excellent for both sides.   I wish we could tie up better that old personal charity with the social service work of the present day.   I should like to see organizations of women to help in this personal way with incurable cancer cases, and of course with all other incurable diseases, too.   So much God has brought me that I wished and worked for, that perhaps I shall have that, too."

She thought about her idea for a while after Dr. Walsh had gone, but then so many things came up that she put it away for an easier time.   For one thing, Aunt Kate was giving away her

274

bonnet again, which meant that the best tact of all had to be brought out to cope with the situation, and the best tact was Mother's, so she went up to see about it.

Aunt Kate had been with them for some time. Terribly ill when she came, good care and pleasant surroundings had made her much better ; in fact, she grew so plump that Mother said "her outline formed a faultless circle." At least it made them all happy to know she was slipping out of life much more easily than when she came to them. She had few possessions, but one of them was a dainty bonnet made of ribbons and laces which she took carefully out of its tissue paper each time she went into the chapel, and which she put carefully around it when she came out and her devotions were over. Occasionally she felt her end was near, and then she would hasten to think of some one really worthy of it on whom she might bestow the precious bonnet. But so far it had actually been given to no one, since Aunt Kate always began to feel better before it had left her possession.

Now, Mother had been reliably informed, she had done so. She had selected a young woman who had recently come to the Home, who was still shy and ill at ease among them. Mother arrived on the scene just as the actual bestowal was in progress. The dismayed recipient was looking at the black object rather fearfully, but accepting it politely, to Mother's extreme relief.

By evening Aunt Kate felt much improved and knew she would need her bonnet to say her prayers. She discussed the burning question with Mother : would Alice give it back to her ?

Mother volunteered to see if she could persuade her, and did so, relieving the embarrassed Alice of the black bit of millinery. Aunt Kate held her chiefest treasure close for a moment before she put it on her head and started for the chapel.

Mother Alphonsa watched her go in the door, dipping her fingers carefully in the little holy water stoup as she went in.

On the fourteenth of June Mother Alphonsa stood on the grounds of Rosary Hill and watched her greatest dream take visible form : her new fire-proof building that would hold one hundred beds, each of which in the mind's eye of Mother Alphonsa was already nicely blanketed and sheeted, and holding an occupant.

It had been decided to build the whole group in the Spanish style, hollow tile and concrete and tiles, and for the past year she had been working over the plans and had made her own decisions on even small details. She had worked with the architects, and remodeled many of their ideas closer to her own desires. The work had been so well planned that the date of the consecration was already decided on.

Then, during the next few weeks she seemed to lose interest. Her enthusiasm was ebbing now that accomplishment lay so near. But though to those about her she seemed well and active as usual, perhaps her real condition was more nearly as she had described it in a letter to a priest she knew, Father Kelly, to whom, thanking him for a contribution, she said : "I am not rude. I am silly with old age and overwork, and my letters toddle along very slowly to my dear friends."

When Sister Rose came up to Hawthorne for a week-end, Mother Alphonsa asked her to have Monsignor McEntyre come up to talk with her if he had the time. They had a long talk, a very long one, and then Sister Rose joined them and they walked about the new building, talking over changes in plans, all of which Mother Alphonsa discussed with her usual vigor. But when she was called to the telephone, he said to Sister Rose, "Mother does not look well. I think this is the first time since I have known her that I have seen her look badly."

She thought him mistaken, though she too had noticed that of late Mother did not move about as much as she usually did. She was content to sit for long stretches in the new and very comfortable chair which Sister Rose had ordered for her birthday, content to let the flowers grow without her helping hand, to let the Sisters handle the minutiæ of the patients' lives.

Early in June Sister Rose brought to Hawthorne a girl who wished to enter the noviciate. She was pleased to see this time a color in her cheeks, a real gaiety in her voice.

She had come to the door herself to greet them. "Mother, why did you come down here? We could have come to you," protested Sister Rose.

Mother Alphonsa looked at the girl, shyly waiting. "I wanted to welcome this child myself," and she turned her radiant smile at the newcomer.

The girl stepped a little way off. "I wore my graduation dress to show you," she said.

Mother looked at it carefully, the little ruffles, the lace at the throat. "My dear, how lovely it is. Oh, I feel the Lord has indeed blessed our work when He inspires little girls like you to work for His poor."

A cloud of pigeons swept past as they spoke. "We really should chase those birds away," said a Sister passing by. "They do a lot of damage."

"I know, I know," agreed Mother Alphonsa, "but I love to see them. When I first came up here and things were so very hard, I was often very lonely and they were such a consolation to me."

Sister Rose spent the night. It seemed to her that evening and the next morning that Mother looked at her occasionally with the air of one who wanted to say something, but could not make up her mind to do so. Whatever it was it went unsaid, and she bade her a cheerful goodbye and sent her love, as she always did, to Saint Rose's.

When she got back to New York she felt worried. On impulse she called Hawthorne to ask how Mother was. "Just fine," said the answering Sister. "She has been out at the new foundation to watch the men mixing and pouring concrete, and now she has just come in from working with her flowers. I heard her say as she went upstairs that she hasn't felt so well in a long time."

So, Sister Rose, assured, went about her work.

Next morning the telephone rang very early. There was nothing alarming about that since it rang at odd hours because of extremely sick patients who needed immediate attention. The

Sister who answered it came to Sister Rose with the message. She seemed to find it hard to speak. "That was Hawthorne calling. Mother is very ill."

"They must be mistaken," said Sister Rose. "Yesterday they told me she was feeling fine."

Sister looked at her again. There was silence for a tragic moment. "Mother died in her sleep last night."

"No, no !" cried Sister Rose, "it can't be true. Mother can't be dead."

But it was true. She had felt so well that afternoon that despite her avowed intention to write no more for a while, she had started out on one last set. She wanted to establish a Community Building for her Sisters. For that, not enough had been collected. So once more the speeding pen had been at work — that afternoon and evening.

It was after ten when Sister Mary Frances met her in the hall. "Oh, Mother, you look so tired. Why don't you go straight to bed ?"

Mother Alphonsa knew she was tired. Something was drawing at her strength and making her think longingly of bed and sleep. She held up a sheaf of letters ready to mail. "I'm going right away, but first I want to go into the chapel and leave these begging letters with Saint Joseph for the night. Then I promise I'll go."

When one of the Sisters went to call her in the morning, there was no answer. She had died during the night in her sleep.

There were many, many who grieved at her passing. There was Julian, her brother, who only a little while before had spent an afternoon with her and gone away rejoicing at her evident good health. There were those who had befriended her in the early days of her work — Father Thuente and Brother Julian and Dr. Walsh, and many others, clergymen, and doctors and laity. There was Cardinal Hayes who had so greatly appreciated her work and who had said, "When on the Saw Mill River Road I always look toward Rosary Hill Home ; it is always an inspira-

278

tion." There were the many who had helped her in her later years. There were her poor, those still living for whom she was making this world a better place. There were her Sisters and novices and postulants, a sturdy band now.

Deep was the grief of Sister Rose, who had been with her for twenty-six years, worked with her, shared her joys and sorrows. She had a sorrow now that could not be shared with the one person who was no longer there to share griefs.

Excepting for the letters that Saint Joseph guarded for her while she went to a peaceful rest, Brother Julian was the last person who had a note from her. He had gone over to Rosary Hill to see how she was a few days before. Sister Rose had told him that she was too tired to have guests that evening. Next day a little letter came :

"My seeming rudeness at not being able to see you was a deprivation which I had plenty of solitude and leisure to ponder over. It is so great a privilege to see even your house in the morning sunshine — or at any other time. And you too. May God keep you."

Among the many comments on her death in the newspapers and magazines, none expressed her passing better than the *Literary Digest* which said that she had "embarked upon the most beautiful adventure of all for which she had prepared so many."

In the presence of the Archbishop, many monsignori, priests who had known her and worked with her, with her own Sisters about her, and the laity who had helped her with her appeals so often, the Very Reverend James J. Walsh preached her funeral sermon. None could know better than he the hard road she had traveled. He, too, had formed a religious community for a special purpose. He spoke as he would of a comrade on the Way whose aims were also his aims, who had won through obstacles and difficulties.

He announced his text : "Thou shalt love the Lord God with thy whole heart, with thy whole mind, with all thy soul and with all thy strength. And thou shalt love thy neighbor as thyself."

279

He spoke of those who work for God in different ways, of their courage, their faith in ultimate good. Then he spoke of her.

"Through twenty-five years and more she has labored, offering her soul's love to her God, and she has given that body — not a strong one — to the work of God while it was day. She gave all that she had to the service of her Master. She loved Him with her whole soul as she loved Him with her whole mind and with all her strength, and she loved her neighbor as herself."

"When one works to save somebody, to help those who are blind or deaf, or who cannot walk, this task we can understand more easily, and we can realize that even people without faith would be attracted to such work as that. With the incurable it is different. One watches the ebbing of life day after day ; there is no turn of the tide ; there are no visible results. Not from any natural motive did Mother Alphonsa do this work ; but from the one motive of pleasing her God and serving Him."

What, perhaps, not many of those present knew was who stood at the beginning of the Way : Sophia Hawthorne, her heart alight with love of God, with the beauty of holiness, who taught it to her small daughter, by precept and example, by taking her through the ancient churches among the treasures of paint and stone that were colored and carved for the love of God ; who showed her God in the sunrise and the sunset and in the small ways of the family.

And Nathaniel Hawthorne, who loved his fellow men so much that he felt the greatest sin was theirs who neglected their condition, who turned away unhelping from the disease and ugliness that poverty brings.

Into her hands they had put that love of God and love of man, and she had welded it and put it to use in service, in very truth, to Christ's poor.

Long years before, to Emma Lazarus, she had read a paragraph from Frederick Ozanam, telling her of the difficulties and trials he went through to accomplish his purpose, even yet, she felt, only partially understood and only partially acted on. It was the

280

INDEX

Agassiz, **Louis, 80.**
Alcott, Abigail, 66, **67.**
Alcott, Bronson, 9, 63, **64, 65, 73-4,**
109, 124, 219.
Alcott, Louisa, 67-8, 73-4, 109, 251-2.
Alphonsa, Sister M. *See* Lathrop, Rose
Hawthorne.
Amedy, Brother, 271, **272.**
American Copyright League, **114.**
Assisi, 40.
Atlantic Monthly, 71, 72, 86, **101, 114,**
118.

Bacon, Delia, 20.
Bandenelli, Father, **198.**
Bartlett, Dr., 64.
Benedict XV, Pope, **255.**
Bennoch, Francis, 18.
Blithesdale Romance, **by Nathaniel**
Hawthorne, 8.
Blodgett, Mrs., 15.
Bolsena, Italy, 54.
Boston Courier, **105.**
Boston, England, 26-7.
Bowdoin College, 13.
Bridge, Horatio, 85, **87.**
Bright, Henry, 17-18, **59-60.**
Brown, Mrs. Walter, 109.
Browning, Elizabeth Barrett, 38, **44-6,**
55, 56, 67.
Browning, Robert, 38, 44, 46, **55, 94.**
Brownson, Orestes, 128-9.
Buchanan, James, 18.
Bull, Ephraim, 9, 11, 64, **75, 107.**
Bunner, Mr. and Mrs. H. C., **119, 123,**
124, 257.

Casa Bello, 43-8.
Channing, Ellery, 8, 63, **80.**
Cherry St., cancer home on, **192** *et seq.*

Christian Brothers, **225.**
Christian Herald, **176.**
Christ's Poor, 189-91, **221.**
Chappells, Mr. and Mrs. Alfred, **119-**
20, 122, 123, 128, 129, 130.
Cohan, George, 262.
Concord, Mass., 8, 9, 28, 62 *et seq.,* **107,**
135, 138.
Conway, Moncure, 60.
Corrigan, Archbishop Michael, 183, **184,**
196, 197, 198, 218.
Costerot, Father, 228.
Coutheny, Father, 212.
Coyle, Dr., 153, 211.
Cronin, Cornelius, 242, 252, **254.**
Cuddihy, H. Lester, 265.
Cushman, Charlotte, 18.

Daly, Mrs. T., 181-3.
Damrosch, Walter, 132, **146.**
Dolliver Romance, by Nathaniel **Haw-**
thorne, 72.
Dresden, 91 *et seq.*
Drug Auxiliary, 252.
Dutton, Brother Joseph, 247, **252-3.**

Edward VII, 39.
Edwards, Henry, 126.
Egan, Maurice Francis, 262-3.
Emerson, Mrs. Ralph Waldo, 75, **143.**
Emerson, Ralph Waldo, 4, 8, 10, 70, **71,**
80, 117, 123.
England, Hawthornes in, 14 *et seq.*

Falconio, Archbishop, 238.
Fall River, Mass., Rose Hawthorne La-
throp Free Home in, 281.
Farley, Cardinal, 244.
Fenwick, Father, 136.
Field, Mr. and Mrs. James, 66-7, **118.**

285